SELECTED PROSE

MacDiarmid 2000:
the Collected Works
from Carcanet

Selected Poetry
edited by Michael Grieve & Alan Riach
Selected Prose
edited by Alan Riach

Hugh MacDiarmid

SELECTED PROSE

Edited by Alan Riach

CARCANET

This selection first published by
Carcanet Press Limited
208–212 Corn Exchange Buildings
Manchester M4 3BQ

Copyright © 1992 Michael Grieve
Introduction and editorial matter copyright © 1992 Alan Riach
All rights reserved

A CIP catalogue record for this book is
available from the British Library.
ISBN 0 85635 987 4

The publisher acknowledges financial assistance
from the Arts Council of Great Britain

Set in 11/13pt Bembo by The Comp-Room, Aylesbury
Printed and bound in England by SRP Ltd, Exeter

Contents

Acknowledgements   vii
Introduction   ix

Part One: 1920–1945

1. A New Movement in Scottish Literature (1922) — 3
2. Introducing 'Hugh M'Diarmid' (1922) — 9
3. On Scottish Drama (1922) — 13
4. A Theory of Scots Letters (1923) — 16
5. Programme for a Scottish Fascism (1923) — 34
6. Art and the Unknown (1926) — 39
7. The Waterside (1927) — 44
8. Scottish Gaelic Policy (1927) — 49
9. Clan Albainn (1930–31) — 54
10. English Ascendency in British Literature (1931) — 61
11. The Scab (1932) — 81
12. Life in the Shetland Islands (1934) — 85
13. The Last Great Burns Discovery (1934) — 98
14. The Burns Cult (1934) — 103
15. A Plan for the Unemployed (1934) — 106
16. Five Bits of Miller (1934) — 111
17. Major C. H. Douglas (1934) — 115
18. Charles Doughty and the Need for Heroic Poetry (1936) — 125
19. The Great McGonagall (1936) — 137
20. Scottish Arts and Letters: the Present Position and Post-War Prospects (1942) — 151

Part Two: 1945–1978

21	On Modern Scottish Drama (1948)	173
22	Knoydart Land Seizures (1948)	179
23	The Coronation Stone (1950)	184
24	The Key to World Literature (1952)	187
25	The Dour Drinkers of Glasgow (1952)	191
26	The Politics and Poetry of Hugh MacDiarmid (1952)	201
27	In Memoriam James Joyce (1955–1956)	220
28	My Election Contest with Sir Alec Douglas-Home (1964–1966)	239
29	Ezra Pound: 'The Return of the Long Poem' (1965)	254
30	Growing Up in Langholm (1970)	268
31	Metaphysics and Poetry: an interview with Walter Perrie (1974)	274
32	The Poetry of Bertolt Brecht (1976)	286
33	Previews (1976–78)	289
	Index of Names	293

Acknowledgements

The provenance of individual items is indicated in the introductory note to each one, but I would like to acknowledge the editors of previous collections of MacDiarmid's prose works: Kenneth Buthlay, editor of *The Uncanny Scot: A Selection of Prose* (London: Macgibbon & Kee, 1968); Duncan Glen, who edited the *Selected Essays* (London: Jonathan Cape, 1969); and Alan Bold, editor of *The Thistle Rises: An Anthology of Poetry and Prose* (London: Hamish Hamilton, 1984).

Hitherto uncollected items have been included from various newspapers and journals, which are discussed in the introduction. There are also items taken from MacDiarmid's prose or poetry and prose collections, *At the Sign of the Thistle: A Collection of Essays* (London: Stanley Nott, 1934); *Scottish Scene: or The Intelligent Man's Guide to Albyn* (London: Jarrolds, 1934); *Scottish Eccentrics* (London: Routledge, 1936); and *The Company I've Kept* (London: Hutchinson, 1966).

I would also like to acknowledge the late Martin Spencer, formerly of Edinburgh University Press, who encouraged me to undertake the editing of this book in the first place, and beside him the conviction and support of my present publisher, Michael Schmidt and the professionalism of Carcanet's Scottish editor Robyn Marsack. Walter Perrie kindly granted me permission to include his interview with MacDiarmid. I would like to thank MacDiarmid's bibliographer, W. R. Aitken, and his 1964 election agent, Alex Clark, for their helpful interest. The staff of the Mitchell Library (Glasgow), the National Library of Scotland (Edinburgh), Edinburgh University Library, the library of the University of Waikato (Hamilton, New Zealand) and the British Library (London) have all be exemplary in patience, courteousness and helpfulness. Especial thanks go to my uncle, Mr Macarthur Cunningham and my parents, Captain J. A. Riach and Mrs J. G. Riach, who have helped me access some very obscure items. Finally, my thanks are due to Michael and Deirdre Grieve, for both their generosity and their trust.

Introduction

Hugh MacDiarmid once described his role as that of the catfish in the aquarium, stirring up the torpor of the more docile denizens. His writing career, he said, was a volcanic activity: massive eruptions of soot and dross, but torrents of hot lava also, scorching all before it.

It began early, with contributions to the school magazine and local newspapers. But by 1908, aged sixteen, he was reading A. R. Orage's London-based *New Age*, the most highly-charged intellectual journal of its day, and in 1911 contributed his first essay to it: a densely written piece entitled 'The Young Astrology', which argued the thesis that if nations, cultures and geographies exert their influence on individuals, it is surely consequent that the vaster, universal context will pull the destiny of individuals and of mankind into unknowable futures. A weird blend of pre-destination and élitism fuelled the argument, and the tone of the prophet was struck. The First World War was only three years away. As a significant example of MacDiarmid's – or rather, C. M. Grieve's – early writing, the straightfaced sobriety of this article is a nice contrast to another pre-World War I item from a local Scottish paper, the *People's Journal* of 1912, the parodic 'All Night in a British Opium "Joint": Confessions of a Scotch Opium Smoker', by 'Our Special Commissioner'.

A third aspect of Grieve's early writing is the journalism he contributed to the *Monmouthshire Labour News* in 1911. He had gone to Wales to work on the newspaper's editorial committee and as a reporter, living in Ebbw Vale after sixteen years in the Scottish borders and three years in Edinburgh. He was immediately caught up in battles between striking coalminers and the police. Cavalry had been ordered into action by Winston Churchill, then Home Secretary, and fixed bayonets were used by the infantry. In August, numerous riots took place throughout South Wales, and Grieve spent as many sleepless nights reporting on them for his newspaper. To his early mentor, George Ogilvie, he wrote, 'It's like living on the top of a volcano down here'. But the strikes were put down, the riots ceased, and by the end of the year the paper Grieve was working for had closed down.

The intellectual élitism evident in the *New Age* essay, the intense involvement in political struggle which was the fuel of his experience in Wales, the irreverent humour of the de Quincey pastiche in the *People's Journal*: these were the principal components of the writer C. M. Grieve was to become. Although for reasons of space none of his pre-World War I writing has been republished here, it is worth noting.

'Hugh MacDiarmid' had not yet been invented. These early pieces were published anonymously or under Grieve's patronymic. Later, a whole regiment of invented writers signed their names under essays, articles or reviews. For convenience, and to maintain the function of the author's name, we shall refer to 'Hugh MacDiarmid'. But much of the journalism was signed by C. M. Grieve, and any researchers who come upon the names of Arthur Leslie, A. K. Laidlaw or A. K. L., Isobel Guthrie, James Maclaren, Stentor, or Gillechriosd Moraidh Mac a' Ghreidhir (and there are others) will recognize a familiar style. The first items in the present volume were acknowledged by C. M. Grieve. 'M'Diarmid' (as it was then) appeared in 1922, and reappeared as 'McDiarmid', 'Macdiarmid', and 'MacDiarmid'. The last spelling stuck.

He served an apprenticeship in discipline in the First World War, both in dealing with the shock of the experience, and snatching time from midnights to write his poems, stories, sketches in prose and his letters home. And the universal conflict he foresaw in 'The Young Astrology' left him after its engagement with a zealous temper, a mass of knowledge of human behaviour, a packed imagination, a political courage and – miraculously – a vivid and infectious sense of humour.

On his return to Scotland, he pitched a new camp and set out to work. He was joined by others: between 1920 and 1934, major publications had appeared by Neil Gunn, George Blake, Eric Linklater, Fionn Mac Colla, Naomi Mitchison, Nan Shepherd, Marion Angus, Catherine Carswell, Edwin Muir, William Soutar, James Bridie, Lewis Grassic Gibbon, and others. He was therefore not alone in his efforts to reconsider the culture and history of Scotland from the position *of* Scotland, rather than from a position which subscribed to the Anglocentric hegemony of economic and cultural power. But certainly in the 1920s, enough of the old guard remained in positions of established authority to make his efforts seem unlikely. Creating a small army of pseudonyms was the one way to swell the ranks. Profligate publishing was a means of spreading the word. He set up, edited and ran his own journals. He published articles in the press, the literary magazines and the political periodicals (such as they were).

A bibliographical list of MacDiarmid's contributions to ephemeral publications would fill a volume in itself. A select list of the journals and papers is staggering enough. He edited *The Scottish Chapbook* (monthly, 1922–23), *The Scottish Nation* (weekly, 1923), *The Northern Review* (monthly, 1924), *The Voice of Scotland* (an irregular quarterly devoted to Scottish republicanism, 1938–39, 1945–49, 1955–58), *Poetry Scotland* (no. 4, 1949), and *Scottish Art and Letters* (no. 5, 1950), and he was acting editor for Compton Mackenzie's short-lived London-based radio magazine *Vox* (1929–30). In the 1920s, he contributed literary items to local Scottish newspapers such as *The Dunfermline Press*, and he was the chief reporter for the weekly paper *The Montrose Review*. He contributed literary and political articles throughout the 1920s and into the 1930s to *The New Age*, which brought him into print in the company of Ezra Pound and the influential economic theorist of 'Social Credit', C. H. Douglas, as well as the austere Parsee composer K. S. Sorabji (who for decades refused to allow his enormous piano compositions to be performed as he believed no performer capable of playing them), and the French philosopher and critic Denis Saurat. MacDiarmid knew Saurat, Douglas and Sorabji personally, and corresponded with Pound, meeting him finally in 1970.

For Orage and the *New Age*, MacDiarmid's contributions included major reviews of Wallace Stevens, D. H. Lawrence, Rimbaud, Valéry, T. S. Eliot and Gertrude Stein, as well as speculative essays on 'Scotland and the Banking System' or 'Psychoanalysis and Aesthetics'. Space has not permitted the inclusion of these articles in the present book, but they will be collected at a later date. It is worth mentioning MacDiarmid's preferences for the complex metaphors of Wallace Stevens, the acid-tests performed on language by Gertrude Stein, the overt intellectualism in the work of Paul Valéry and, by contrast, his critique of Lawrence's *Lady Chatterley's Lover*. MacDiarmid reviewed the book in 1928, pointing out that Lawrence had compromised his novel by giving Lady Chatterley a reliable private income. While agreeing with Lawrence that female sexuality was a force that modern literature had not fully encountered, MacDiarmid questioned whether Lawrence had been adequate to his task in the novel. 'The number of people who can copulate properly may be few', MacDiarmid wrote; 'the number who can write well are infinitely fewer.'

Meanwhile, he had been commissioned to write a series of 'Contemporary Scottish Studies' for *The Scottish Educational Journal* and initiated an attack upon almost every respected member of the literary and educational establishment, deploring the conservatism of the reactionary novelists and educationalists, and welcoming the promise of modernist techniques in the early work of Neil Gunn, or in the lean and stylish prose of Cunninghame Graham. At the same time, he was contributing a mass of anonymous or pseudonymous syndicated journalism to dozens of local Scottish newspapers each week.

He described his activity both as a poet and prose writer and polemicist retrospectively in his 1943 autobiography, *Lucky Poet*, thus:

> The poetry I want turns its back contemptuously on all the cowardly and brainless staples of Anglo-Scottish literature – the whole base business of people who do not act but are merely acted upon – people whose 'unexamined lives' are indeed 'not worth having', though they include every irresponsible who occupies a 'responsible position' in Scotland today, practically all our Professors, all our M.P.s, and certainly all our 'Divines', all our peers and great landlords and big business men, the teaching profession almost without exception, almost all our writers – 'half glow-worms and half newts'.
>
> My work represents a complete break with all these people – with all they have and are and believe and desire. My aim all along has been (in Ezra Pound's term) the most drastic *desuetization* of Scottish life and letters, and, in particular, the de-Tibetanization of the Highlands and Islands, and getting rid of the whole gang of high mucky-mucks, famous fatheads, old wives of both sexes, stuffed shirts, hollow men with

headpieces stuffed with straw, bird-wits, lookers-under-beds, trained seals, creeping Jesuses, Scots Wha Ha'evers, village idiots, policemen, leaders of white-mouse factions and noted connoisseurs of bread and butter, glorified gangsters, and what 'Billy' Phelps calls Medlar Novelists (the medlar being a fruit that becomes rotten before it is ripe), Commercial Calvinists, makers of 'noises like a turnip', and all the touts and toadies and lickspittles of the English Ascendancy, and their infernal women-folk, and all their skunkoil skulduggery.

By the 1930s, MacDiarmid was becoming increasingly unpopular and his writing was less frequently published by the more respectable institutions. He contributed more often to little magazines and newspapers committed to the struggle for a new Scotland. These included the *Scots Observer* (1928–34), edited by William Power, *The Modern Scot* (1930–34), edited by James H. Whyte and *The Free Man*, edited by Robin McKelvie Black. On another front, T. S. Eliot published two literary reviews (one on Scottish theatre apropos a book about Sir David Lyndsay) and the major essay 'English Ascendancy in British Literature' in *The Criterion*.

In the 1940s and 1950s, MacDiarmid published regularly in *The National Weekly*(1948–53), and also in colourful but short-lived publications, such as *Scottish Art and Letters* (1944–50), and the *Scottish Journal* edited by William MacLellan (1952–54). He also contributed to *Enquiry, Lines Review, Agenda, Forward Scotland, The New Alliance and Scots Review, Scots Independent, Jabberwock, Akros*, and other magazines and periodicals. After international recognition came with the publication (in America, first) of his *Collected Poems* in 1962, and of critical and introductory books on his work by Kenneth Buthlay and Duncan Glen in 1964, his provocative volatility seemed quaint enough for him to be accorded the status of an esteemed man of letters, an elder statesman of modern literature.

When he was in his eighties, from 1976 to 1978, the *Radio Times* commissioned a series of columns 'previewing' BBC radio and television programmes. His flair was still intact and he took the opportunity to offer wicked comments on programmes he had no wish to see foisted on the viewing public. When the *Guardian* commissioned him to review Brecht's *Poems* in 1976 he wrote a brief essay in which he claimed, with mischievous deliberation, that Brecht, Karl Kraus, Vladimir Mayakovsky and Mao Tse-Tung were the four most important poets of the twentieth century.

MacDiarmid's prose, like his poetry, can be seen as part of a life's work, and it is most rewarding to read the prose alongside the poetry and with an understanding of the shape of his intellectual development. His work goes through both the course of modern Scotland and the course of modern poetry, throwing new light on the essential questions, offering hopeful answers to erstwhile intractable problems.

The arguments which develop, dip, and resurface in MacDiarmid's career are as apt to appear in a poem as in a newspaper article or a literary review. He contributed freely a series of prefaces, forewords and introductions to books by friends or books he had edited. Some of these introductory items contain his essential arguments worked out much more extensively than is warranted by the material they ostensibly introduce.

At the heart of the debate in Scottish intellectual life in the period between the wars are questions of identity defined by language, nation and class. These questions had developed from the 1920s. They had at least two crucial points of introduction. The first was the series of three causeries (or editorials) which Grieve had written for *The Scottish Chapbook* in 1923, collected under the title 'A Theory of Scots Letters'. Together, these form an essay which presents MacDiarmid's case for the importance of the Scots language in poetry, but which also opens out the language question to considerations of the relation between language and psychology (what can be expressed and what can be thought or felt or sensed but remain beyond expression), and language and politics. Scots, like Scottish Gaelic, had been brutally discouraged since the eighteenth century, although it had never been outlawed. Whereas the Gaelic language had been legally suppressed, Vernacular Scots was simply made the butt of comic contempt and caricature. The second point at which these critical questions of language, class and nationality were introduced to Scottish letters, was the series of articles for the *Scottish Educational Journal* collected in 1926 as

Contemporary Scottish Studies. Here, established novelists, poets and dramatists of 1920s Scotland were subjected to MacDiarmid's closest interrogation, and compared to younger and less widely accepted authors whose work MacDiarmid judged more fit.

The movement known as the Scottish Renaissance developed through a consideration of these questions in the 1920s and 1930s, in poetry, prose and drama, as well as in literary essays, scholarly study and debate, and the rediscovery and eventual republication and reconsideration of older Scottish poets such as Dunbar, Henryson, Douglas, Sir David Lyndsay, Robert Fergusson, and even Burns and Scott. It has taken until the 1980s for the nineteenth century to be revaluated in William Donaldson's work on popular literature in Victorian Scotland. But the process of critical revaluation which began in the 1920s continues.

Conspicuous by its absence from the questions of language, nationality and class is the question of sexual identity. Sexual repression in Scotland has surely always been as fraught as linguistic repression. As early as the 1920s, MacDiarmid recognized the need for the development by women of adequate literary means of expression, means by which women could express in literary forms their own experience. Such experience, MacDiarmid suggested, was not only beyond the reach of the male imagination but could conceivably alter for good the shape of imaginative literature, and indeed what literature could be. MacDiarmid is at least proto-feminist in these remarks, and his political consciousness certainly grappled with feminist ideas. His poetry returns at key points to questions of sexual identity, in the famous lyric 'O wha's the bride' from *A Drunk Man Looks at the Thistle*, for example:

O lass, wha see'est me
As I daur hardly see,
I marvel that your bonny een
Are as they hadna seen.

Through a' my self-respect
They see the truth abject
    – Gin you could pierce their blindin' licht
    You'd see a fouler sicht! . . .

It would be very misguided to stigmatize MacDiarmid (even at his most polemical) as a mere chauvinist, although this has sometimes been done. He was continuously engaged in a political struggle for various kinds of independence, and the extremes he went to are often better thought of as strategic necessities than as irresponsible excesses. This concurs with the number of pseudonyms he used and the sheer quantity of essays and articles he produced. MacDiarmid was continually engaged in a multi-faceted series of explorations into different fields of discourse, often leading him towards different destinations at the same time. His imagination conducted a dialogue with itself, and he pursued its movements self-consciously, recognizing its multi-faceted nature as an active principle, offering himself as a token of coherence in the constant proliferation of meanings. In a letter to the sculptor and poet Pittendrigh Macgillivray dated 1 November 1926, he wrote this:

> In scores of directions I find two very different impulses animating me – 1/ to avoid coming to any conclusions on certain fundamental matters: i.e. moral and ethical problems; and 2/ to experiment with the artistic expression of every different attitude to them I can conceive, i.e. to make every different attitude as wholly mine at a given time as I possibly can and find to what extent I can make a 'convincing' poem of it.

As Peter McCarey has said, MacDiarmid did explore and take up positions which were mutually contradictory and he did express mutually exclusive ideas, but he did so not in a spirit of irresponsible eclecticism but rather in the poetic exploration of his world, his politics and his metaphysics. 'He was not "hopelessly contradictory" in the positions he took up: he was full of hope.'

It was this sense of hope which shifted his attitude towards Edwin Muir, in the famous conflict which began in the 1930s and continued in the 1940s and later. MacDiarmid had considered Muir one of the most penetrating critics and foremost poets of the 1920s, particularly in his reassessment of aspects of Scottish literature such as the ballads. When MacDiarmid and Lewis Grassic Gibbon were co-editing a series of books for the London publisher Routledge, they invited Muir to write on

Sir Walter Scott. Each book in the series was intended to address a particular aspect of Scottish culture in terms of a modern sensibility. Thus Compton Mackenzie wrote on 'What Catholicism has meant for Scotland', William Power wrote on 'What Literature has meant for Scotland', Willa Muir was to write on sexuality in Scotland and A. S. Neill was to write on education in Scotland. MacDiarmid's contribution was to have been called 'Red Scotland: or, What Lenin has meant to Scotland'. Routledge refused to publish it. But in 1936, Edwin Muir's contribution, *Scott and Scotland: The Predicament of the Scottish Writer*, was published. Muir argued (or rather asserted) the case for the Anglocentric cultural hegemony and stated his doubts about the possibility of achieving a full and coherent, cultured identity through Scottish traditions. Sir Walter Scott's ambivalent position, that of a high Tory romantic whose vision of Scotland was doomed to nostalgia, Muir took to be the paradigm of the Scottish writer. The only solution for the literary artist in Scotland, according to Muir, was to abandon Scots as a serious literary medium (and consequently abandon the political and psychological faculties of the language) and enter an Anglocentric world.

The heart of the argument between Muir and MacDiarmid is a contradiction impossible to resolve. Muir's experience of Scotland was a more or less linear journey, from a very actual Eden lived in through his Orkney childhood, towards the hellish adult world of industrial Glasgow, from which the lucidity of intellect and letters was a massive relief. His poetry is elegiac, historical and pastoral. He writes of the pre-industrial world as the Eden which, for him, it literally was. His sharpest beams are thrown back, into Scottish history or the mythic figures of his own imagination.

By contrast, at exactly this time, in the mid-1930s, MacDiarmid was becoming increasingly committed to a philosophy, politics and poetry whose direction would be futuristic. He affirms human potential, sees the possibilities for saving human labour in a properly administered industrial society, commits himself to communism and welcomes the increasing diversity of electronic media. Superficially, the conflict is between a reactionary and a radical. But it is deeper than that. MacDiarmid's thinking had developed considerably from the 1920s, when he had aligned himself with Muir and others in a revitalized Scottish Renaissance movement. By the mid-1930s, he had reconsidered the national question in the light of communist philosophy. The question which drives him in the 1930s, fuelling his passion, is, in the words of George Davie, 'How is it that poverty and ignorance still persist on an enormous scale in a world where science has given us sufficient know-how to be able to end them?' What Davie describes as the backward-looking element in the MacDiarmid of *A Drunk Man* (and MacDiarmid described the poem himself as 'in one sense a reaction from the "Kailyaird" ' which he hoped to transcend) had been replaced by a more determinedly progressive dynamic in the MacDiarmid of *Lucky Poet*. There is a neo-Romantic strain in *A Drunk Man* which MacDiarmid develops away from in his later work, extending his horizons of enquiry as he moves self-consciously from a European context to a global one. The progressive dynamic informing this development had been rejected by Edwin Muir, and this was the deepest insult and hurt that might have been inflicted on MacDiarmid.

The progressive, poetic autodidact and self-elected educationalist responded to Muir's book by editing, with ironic echoes of Palgrave, *The Golden Treasury of Scottish Poetry*, which first appeared in 1940, four years after *Scott and Scotland*. MacDiarmid collected the poetry of 'more than half a millennium', including hitherto rarely translated work by poets writing in Latin or Gaelic, and supplying editorial notes to individual poems, arranging the poems in an idiosyncratic sequence so that the book could be read from cover to cover like a novel, and opening up with a thirty-page introduction whose main thrust is a lacerating critique of Muir's thesis. MacDiarmid backed this up with reference to Count Alfred Korzybski's *Science and Sanity: An Introduction to Non-Aristotelian Systems and General Semantics* (an 800-page blockbuster and a seminal book of the 1930s), which allowed him to reaffirm the psychological importance of the full range of Scottish expression and the inimical nature of English or Anglocentric political supremacy. His regret that he could not, for reasons of space, include such works as *Pearl* and *Gawain and the Green Knight* (which are traditionally accorded a place in English poetry) was matched by his regret that he could not, for legal reasons, include a fair representation of bawdry, with all its virility 'scandalously intact'. The Latin poems he translated with the help of George Davie, and he worked on the Gaelic poems with Sorley MacLean. His friendship with MacLean, who is now recognized as the major Gaelic poet of the century, coincided with his recognition of important new work being produced by young Gaelic poets in the 1940s, including George Campbell Hay. This also fuelled his anger at Muir's defeatism.

MacDiarmid continued the argument of his introduction in the 1942 essay on 'Scottish Art and Letters: the Present Position and Post-War Prospects'. His purpose was to link the kaleidoscopic vision of *The Golden Treasury* with the contemporary scene in such a way as to affirm the multi-faceted nature of Scotland's cultural achievement. To consider that achievement as Edwin Muir did, as a single and linear historical entity, seemed to MacDiarmid a hopeless approach. The best way 'to encourage more fruitful modes of procedure' (as he claimed he wished to do) was neither to think of Scottish literature as a minor tributary of English literature nor to isolate it as a minor and unimportant national tradition on the verge of total extinction. As Cairns Craig has said, both of these views are deeply at odds with the reality of its development.

The development of twentieth-century Scottish literature is synchronized not to the progress of literature in England but to international changes, particularly to the patterns of developing cultural independence among peoples who in the history of colonialism have had English introduced or imposed as their official language. Like modern writers from former colonial states, MacDiarmid wanted to get through to people deprived of the voice of their own experience. This involved an extensive reconsideration of national history, and a vigorous updating of popular sensibilities. To quote George Davie again, he was 'concerned with the necessity of finding educational techniques for communicating, so to speak, to the masses due respect for, and a certain amount of understanding of, the higher standards of intellectual rigour demanded by the revolution in the sciences'. In this his desire for progressive modernist literature was co-aligned with his concern for raising political consciousness. Just as the scientist J. B. S. Haldane wrote hundreds of articles for the Communist Party newspaper, the *Daily Worker*, in an attempt to get scientific ideas across to people who had no training in the sciences, MacDiarmid wrote about James Joyce for the same paper, addressing the same readers, in the same hope of bridging the gulf between specialist and non-specialist.

This attempt to educate the non-specialist was more than merely following the party line. The totalizing imaginations of the great Victorian teachers and moralists such as Carlyle, Ruskin and Arnold were an important precedent for MacDiarmid's activity. More immediately relevant, however, was the history of Scottish educational institutions. In the nineteenth century, the Scottish university degree was based on a fundamental grounding in mathematics, the humanities and philosophy. This led, albeit at an elementary level, to a more unified view of culture and society. Successful attempts were finally made to replace this 'general degree' with more specialist honours schools. George Davie (who was one of MacDiarmid's oldest friends and knew him in the 1930s) has discussed the implications of this in his 1961 volume, *The Democratic Intellect: Scotland and her Universities in the Nineteenth Century* (Edinburgh University Press) and its sequel, *The Crisis of the Democratic Intellect: The Problem of Generalism and Specialisation in Twentieth-Century Scotland* (Edinburgh: Polygon, 1986). Essentially, MacDiarmid's educational and philosophical background might be described by the title of Davie's books. His intellectual élitism and high regard for specialist and abstruse knowledge in all fields of activity was always connected to a sense of value in daily reality. This is stated clearly in *The Kind of Poetry I Want*:

> Poetry of such an integration as cannot be effected
> Until a new and conscious organisation of society
> Generates a new view
> Of the world as a whole
> As the integration of all the rich parts
> Uncovered by the separate disciplines.
> That is the poetry that I want.

The quasi-mystical hope which is sometimes felt in MacDiarmid's poetry, what Harvey Oxenhorn has called MacDiarmid's 'manger faith', is never entirely cut off from the mundane world of day-to-day politics. And the option of hardline prescriptive philistinism, the anti-experimental culture approved by Stalin's artistic director, the notorious Zhdanov, MacDiarmid always refused.

As a boy, Chris Grieve was extremely well read. Langholm Library, founded in 1800, was left a legacy by the engineer Thomas Telford, and MacDiarmid claimed that it held 'upwards of twelve thousand books' when he was living with his parents in the library building. That library, he wrote, 'was the great determining factor.' He had constant access to it, and 'used to fill a big washing-basket with books and bring it downstairs' as often as he wanted.

As an adult, MacDiarmid was involved in almost every sphere of literature and the arts. He had been taught English at school by Scotland's foremost modern composer of songs, Francis George Scott, and they were later reunited when Scott began setting MacDiarmid's lyrics to piano accompaniments. The subtlety of Scott's interpretations was not lost on MacDiarmid, and through conversations with Scott, and the composer Sorabji (whose most monumental work for piano, the *Opus Clavicembalisticum*, is dedicated to him), MacDiarmid acquired at an early stage in the 1920s a comprehensive knowledge of the most important developments in modern music. MacDiarmid's friends and acquaintances included the Scottish composer Ronald Stevenson and the pianist John Ogdon, and when Stevenson presented the great Russian composer Dimitri Shostakovich with a copy of his 'Passacaglia on DSCH for piano' in 1962, MacDiarmid presided over the ceremony.

If MacDiarmid's knowledge of music was theoretical rather than practical, he nevertheless put it to the most effective use, introducing anecdotes and illustrations to his prose and poetry drawn from musical lore and referring to a variety of works from the history of music. Allusions to the vocal techniques of Paul Robeson, Maurice Chevalier and Chaliapin can be encountered beside references to Villa-Lobos, Stravinsky, Schoenberg, Janáček, Bethoven, Mozart and Mahler. In a well-known argument in the 1960s, MacDiarmid clearly stated his preference for 'highbrow' classical music over the popular songs being produced in the folk-music revival. But he had grown up with the ballads and he understood something of the nature of

Scotland's distinctive contribution to musical culture. Classical bagpipe music – the art of pibroch – he considered to be one of Scotland's most important contributions to the arts, and he wrote eloquently on the Bach-like mathematical precision involved in playing such music. Of course, he was not a trained musician and he could make awful mistakes. He also referred in a poem to pibroch players conceiving and improvising 'new and ever louder diversions'. This is as far removed from what such pipers do as it is possible to be.

Similarly, in the fields of sculpture and painting, MacDiarmid was friendly with the major Scottish artists of the century. He knew F. G. Scott's cousin William Johnstone and collaborated with him on a book of poems and lithographs. In the 1920s, MacDiarmid, Scott and Johnstone considered themselves to be, potentially, a triumvirate of artists working in language, music, colour and form, whose visions might revitalize a grey, recumbent Scotland. But such unified effort did not occur. Each followed his own career. MacDiarmid was active in promoting Johnstone's work, however, and that of other modern Scottish artists, such as William McCance, and his friends included John Tonge, author of a notable 1938 volume entitled *The Arts of Scotland*, and the great painter J. D. Fergusson, whom MacDiarmid had praised in the 1920s. They met in the 1940s. Fergusson produced a series of illustrations to accompany MacDiarmid's 1955 volume *In Memoriam James Joyce* and MacDiarmid wrote a 'Foreword' to Margaret Morris's 1974 biography of Fergusson. MacDiarmid had, in fact, written his own analysis of modern art in 1950 and revised it in 1952 and 1965. Entitled *Aesthetics in Scotland*, this was edited by Alan Bold and finally published in 1984. MacDiarmid had been one of twenty-two people who applied for a position as Director of the Glasgow Art Galleries and Museums in 1939 and in some ways *Aesthetics in Scotland* consolidates his thoughts on what he might have done with such a post. T. J. Honeyman, who became the Galleries Director, remarked that if MacDiarmid had got the job, poetry in Scotland may have suffered, but his dynamic personality might well have 'stirred things up' in the art world.

MacDiarmid's interest in music and art continued to develop and his role as an activist and catalyst in the literary world touched the worlds of music and art at a number of points. His reading continued to be voracious throughout his life, but at various times he asserted an indifference to the novel as a literary form. He was, by his own admission, 'very far from being a movie fan.' Nor was he a regular playgoer, although he recognized the need for a Scottish national theatre in the 1920s and was supportive of the Theatre Workshop movement developed in the 1940s. He lacked in himself the ability any competent novelist and every dramatist must have: the ability to create others. Perhaps consequently, there is little *narrative* poetry in the corpus. There is a remarkable body of short stories and sketches, however, in which landscapes, characters and occasions are deftly caught, and MacDiarmid planned to collect these in book-form, and even projected more extended prose fictions. Richard Price has drawn attention to the fact that in 1926, MacDiarmid proposed to Neil Gunn that both of them should collaborate on a novel 'involving all Scots types' and 'ditto with settings in different parts of Scotland'. MacDiarmid went on to suggest that such a novel might adopt different techniques for representing different characters' occupations, utilize a range of linguistic registers and record a variety of dialects. But this vast proposition, which would have collected and surveyed Scotland's geographies, languages and class structure, and which MacDiarmid clearly thought might involve formal experimentation of a distinctly Joycean kind, came to nothing. Six years later, he was writing again to Neil Gunn that 'no fiction whatever matters a damn in relation to Scotland while any poem whatever above a very low plane matters a great deal.' Be that as it may, MacDiarmid certainly read, with pleasure and appreciaiton, not only Gunn himself but also Eric Linklater, Fionn Mac Colla and, above all, Lewis Grassic Gibbon (whose trilogy *A Scots Quair* comes close to being the kind of book MacDiarmid had envisioned). He continued to write short stories and sketches himself. A number of these are included here, but none of MacDiarmid's theatrical sketches or miniature plays; nor is there anything from C. M. Grieve's first book, a collection of prose 'studies' entitled *Annals of the Five Senses* (1923). Nor have I included any material from *Contemporary Scottish Studies* (1926; reprinted 1976) or *Lucky Poet* (1943; reprinted 1973). These will be reprinted in their entirety at a later date.

In this book, I have selected the most crucial essays from MacDiarmid's career and alongside these I have assembled a range of material from different sources. The provenance of each item is given in the relevant note in the body of the book. My intention was to present as much as I could of the diversity of MacDiarmid's prose, including fiction and interviews, while keeping true to the shape of his writing career. Thus his early attempts to fan the sparks of a literary movement into a flame are evident in his 1920s writing on the predicament of Scottish literature, especially in terms of poetry, language and drama, politics and theory, Scottish Gaelic policies and Major Douglas's Social Credit plans. The second section of the book includes samples of his journalism (reporting on forgotten moments in a history that requires revision: the 'asportation' of the Stone of Destiny and the Knoydart land seizures, for example). Comic writing is frequently in evidence: 'The Waterside' or 'The Last Great Burns Discovery' and 'The Dour Drinkers of Glasgow' operate on various levels of irony and humour simultaneously. Seminal documents for an understanding of MacDiarmid's poetry have also been included. 'A Theory of Scots Letters' runs into *A Drunk Man*; 'Scottish Gaelic Policy' runs into *Cencrastus*; 'Life in the Shetland Islands' is best read alongside the Shetland poems of this period; MacDiarmid's ideas about the long poem are given in the items relating to Charles Doughty, *In Memoriam James Joyce* and Ezra Pound. His political activities have been foregrounded, first in his early (1923) 'Programme for a Scottish Fascism' and his 1934 'Plan for the Unemployed', then later in his actual participation as a Communist Party candidate in the 1964 general election, when he stood against the then Prime Minister, Sir Alec Douglas-Home, and followed his election defeat with a memorable court case, defending the right of minority political parties to have access to media representation. Fond memories of his native place are recorded in 'Growing Up in Langholm' but his scurrilous, vitriolic pen is still handy for the last pieces of journalism.

Stylistically, MacDiarmid's prose is remarkable. It resembles his descriptions of a type of wayward Scot: versatile, erudite, filled with wanderlust spiritual and physical, indifferent to or incapable of mere worldly prudence. It is full of acknowledged and unacknowledged quotations yet it is unmistakably his own.

Much of it is characterized by the speed of its production, copy turned out for deadlines that must not be missed. Yet his literary essays are as frequently thoughtful and deliberated as they are provocative. MacDiarmid varied his style to suit the kind of journals he was writing for. Thus he produced the most vicious polemic in his self-published republican quarterly *The Voice of Scotland* but maintained a more lofty eloquence when writing for T. S. Eliot and *The Criterion*.

What is most characteristic of his prose is its lavish generosity. It overflows. Sentences extend themselves almost to breaking point, adding clause to qualifying clause, multiplying instances, digressing in parentheses, returning to primary objectives with a rhetorical flourish and coming to a firm halt at the ultimate appropriate moment. It is sometimes as if MacDiarmid is testing the syntax of the language itself, to see how much meaning it can accommodate, to give and get away with as much as he can. Only rarely does the syntax actually break down. Edwin Morgan has described MacDiarmid's autobiography in terms which serve to summarise his prose style generally: 'unique, chaotic, repetitive, careless in every kind of detail, yet bursting with suggestive ideas, curious facts, instant flytings, brilliant analogies, and pages of *vers libre* looming like extracts from that huge Shelleyan poem "which all poets, like the co-operating thoughts of one great mind, have built up since the beginning of the world".'

'I am a violent man,' MacDiarmid once wrote – 'I fight when I am attacked.' His critical and considered prose, his vitriolic journalism, his visions of a new society, his fictions, his self-depictions, all his work is engaged in a struggle whose end we do not yet know. In a famous comment in the 'Theses on the Philosophy of History', Walter Benjamin wrote: 'Only that historian will have the gift of fanning the spark of hope in the past who is firmly convinced that *even the dead* will not be safe from the enemy if he wins. This enemy has not ceased to be victorious.' Hugh MacDiarmid possessed such conviction. The present collection is both the evidence, and the pleasure, of that.

Alan Riach

Part One: 1920–1945

1 A New Movement in Scottish Literature

> This is the first editorial of the first edition of *The Scottish Chapbook* (vol. 1, no. 1, August 1922). The journal was edited by C. M. Grieve, and each editorial was entitled 'Causerie' – which suggests the manifesto. This one notes 'a distinct change in the air'. This number of the *Chapbook* also carried a dramatic sketch in English prose entitled 'Nisbet: An Interlude in Post-War Glasgow'. It was attributed to 'Hugh M'Diarmid', and marked his first appearance in print.

THE following remark introduced a special article in a Dundee paper the other week. (I will not say which. They are both equally bad. An Irishman might even say that each is infinitely worse than the other.) 'When the late Sir James Sieveright of Tulliallan died there passed away a Scot distinguished in many ways, and one whose knowledge of his Bible and the works of Burns made his a charmingly typical Scottish personality.' 'Literary criticism in England!' says Norman Douglas. 'Snakes in Ireland!' Exactly! But it is, as the above example shows, something very much worse than a mere absence of literary criticism that troubles us in Scotland.

Scottish literature, like all other literatures, has been *written* almost exclusively by blasphemers, immoralists, dipsomaniacs, and madmen, but, unlike most other literatures, has been *written about* almost exclusively by ministers, with, on the whole, an effect similar to that produced by the statement (of the worthy Dr John MacIntosh) that 'as a novelist, Robert Louis Stevenson had the art of rendering his writings interesting', and 'his faculty of description was fairly good.' 'To Scotland,' said Andrew Lang, 'the new learning came not as a key to the gardens of the muses, not as "a magic casement opening on the foam of perilous seas," haunted by Circe and the Sirens, but merely as a light on the Bible and on the disputes of theologians.' To reminders of this kind, Scotland, in the persons of its 'interpreting class', still replies as did Dr Hay Fleming, with humourless irony: 'In Mr Lang's opinion, "a key to the gardens of the Muses" may be of more account than "a light on the Bible"!' It is, however, rising in a great many more minds than R. B. Cunninghame Graham's in Scotland today: 'What profits it although a man, in the attempt to regain his soul, should be successful and should lose the world, if the same soul when gained should prove to be so shrivelled and so hide-bound that it were better to have lost it gallantly and kept humanity intact?' Which of us would rather be a Sir William Robertson Nicoll than a John Davidson, or a Dr Hay Fleming than a Lord Alfred Douglas?

A literary psychoanalyst, happy in his escape from the jargon of his tribe, would have expressed the true inwardness of the matter if he had scribbled on the fly-leaf of any volume dealing with Scottish life and letters published prior to 1914 the following quotation from that epigrammatic metaphysician, Leo Shestov:

> Nobody has ever doubted that it was a vice to be unstable in one's opinions. Three-fourths of our education goes to teaching us most carefully to conceal within ourselves the changeableness of our moods and judgements. A man who cannot keep his word is the last of men, never to be trusted. Morality, here as always making towards utilitarian ends, issues the 'eternal' principle; thou shalt remain true to thy convictions. . . . Men are terrified even to appear inconstant in their own eyes. They are petrified in their convictions and no greater shame can happen to them than that they should be forced to admit that they have altered in their convictions. . . . One need neither see nor hear or understand what is taking place around one: once your mind is made up, you have lost your right to grow; you must remain a stock, a statue, the qualities and defects of which are known to everybody.

He would have further demonstrated his acuity if he had proceeded to scrawl in the margin against any reference such a book might have contained to modern movements, or 'les jeunes', this excellent aphorism, 'Egoism in a man strikes us unpleasantly because it betrays our poverty.'

In my opinion, then, for several generations Scottish literature has neither seen nor heard nor understood what was taking place around it. For that reason it remains a dwarf among giants. Scottish writers have been terrified even to appear inconstant to established conventions. (Good wine would have needed no 'Bonnie Brier Bush'.) They have stood still and consequently been left behind in technique and ideation. Meanwhile the Scottish nation has been radically transformed in temperament and tendency; Scottish life has been given a drastic reorientation, with the result that Scottish literature today is in no sense representative or adequate. My opinions may not be readily shared perhaps. I comfort myself with the reflection that Napoleon is reputed to have had a profound insight into the human soul; Shakespeare also; and that their vision had nothing in common.

It was more obvious in Scotland, prior to the war, than Professor Santayana found it in America, that 'the tendency to gather and to breed philosophers in universities does not belong to the ages of free and human reflection', while, in an adaptation of his words, it was certainly strikingly true of what was accepted as the best in contemporary Scottish literature, that there was a cause rather than a reason for its nature, and that it had become prophetic in a fitful way to a whole class of earnest, troubled people, who, having discarded doctrinal religion, wished to think that their life was worth living, when, to look at what it contained, it did not appear so; it reassured them by teaching that a strained and joyless existence was not their unlucky lot, or a consequence of their solemn follies, but was the necessary fate of all good men and angels. It reflected obscurely a groping, burdened, mediocre life, living in a fog and worshipping a sun it had never seen.

It was little wonder that one welcomed the comic relief so abundantly supplied by such a man as Stopford Brooke, who, amongst other priceless declarations, averred that 'Scottish Poetry is poetry written in the English tongue by men living in Scotland. These men, though calling themselves Scotsmen, are of good English blood. But the blood, as I think, was mixed with an infusion of Celtic blood.' Not quite so mixed as these worthy opinions, perhaps! But let that pass. Sadly the preface to *Lyra Celtica* was recalled. Therein William Sharp declared, 'All Ireland is aflame with Song. . . . Scotland is again becoming the land of Old Romance.' He wrote with a passionate prematurity. Only those who kept their eyes on Paisley were rewarded – although, as one critic remarked, 'no attempt at renascence has ever been better equipped than that undertaken in the Lawnmarket of Edinburgh by Patrick Geddes and Colleagues', and another said of the forgotten *Evergreen*, that, while the organ of a band of social reformers in one of the poorest quarters of Edinburgh, it also touched an international note, and kept up the spirit of the best ideals in literature and art. Naturally, this being so, it speedily became defunct, and the movement of which it was the organ scarcely outlasted it. 'It is no exaggeration to say,' Sharp also wrote no longer ago than 1896, 'that at this moment there are more than a hundred Gaelic singers in Western Scotland whose poetry is as fresh and winsome, and, in point of form as well as substance, as beautiful as any that is being produced throughout the rest of the realm.' He must have imagined that miraculous band in some inconceivable moment of transition between himself and 'Fiona Macleod'. They were never heard of before, nor afterwards. No examples of their work were included even in *Lyra Celtica* itself. The Scottish literary revival proved to be a promise that could not be kept.

Today there is a distinct change in the air, however. An access of curiosity and imprudence may work wonders,

> Since prudence, prudence is the deadly sin
> And one that groweth deep into a life,
> With hardening roots that clutch about the breast.
> For this refuses faith in the unknown powers
> Within man's nature; shrewdly bringeth all
> Their inspiration of strange eagerness
> To a judgement bought of safe experience;
> Narrows desire into the scope of thought.
> But it is written in the heart of man
> Thou shalt no larger be than thy desire.
> Thou must not therefore stoop thy spirit's sight
> To pore only within the candle-gleam
> Of conscious wit and reasonable brain,
> But search into the sacred darkness lying
> Outside thy knowledge of thyself, the vast
> Measureless fate, full of the power of stars.

It is paradoxically true that where an excessive desire really exists for the creation of poetry and prose, which shall be thoroughly and progressively national, contemporary foreign literature will be nowhere else received with more attention. In short, even such a multiplication of Scottish books as has characterized the last two publishing seasons will not give a student of literature 'furiously to hope' so long as he knows that in this apparently eruptive Scotland quite important French books have not been heard of even by a chosen few twelve months after their publication in Paris, and that even English poets cannot acquire readers or a reputation in Glasgow or Aberdeen, let alone Edinburgh, until the commotion in London after their rapid appreciation in Chicago has had ample time to subside. I readily excuse any Sassenach who admits that he regards it as hopeless to expect anything good out of Scotland. An Isolated Great Man, perhaps – but no general 'hosting' of poets and artists, as in Ireland; no Georgianism even, as in England; no dramatic scintillations of national vitality behind the thick hedges of *mesquinerie*. I can readily excuse the ironical unbelief of such a Doubting Thomas confronted with improbable tidings of the appearance in Scotland of phenomena recognizable as a propaganda of ideas. None of those significant little periodicals – crude, absurd, enthusiastic, vital – have yet appeared in Auchtermuchty or Ardnamurchan. No new publishing houses have sprung up, mushroom-like. . . . It is discouraging to reflect that this is not the way the Dadaists go about the business!

Nevertheless, nothing would appear more impossible to a keen student of history or literature, than to find the revival of national feeling which has characterized post-war politics in Scotland unaccompanied, within a reasonable time, by literary manifestations of commensurate importance. A young Edinburgh artist interested me greatly not long ago by asking me to 'visualize a typical Scotsman'. When I assured him that I had this mythical personage clearly established in my mind's eye, he turned to a blackboard and rapidly sketched a Glasgow 'keelie', a Polish pitman from Lanarkshire, a Dundee Irishman, an anarchist orator of a kind frequently seen at the Mound in Edinburgh on Sunday nights, a Perthshire farmer, a Hebridean islander, and a Berwickshire bondager. I had to admit that in my wanderings I had met people precisely similar. 'These,' the artist remarked, 'are only a first selection of the varieties of the *genus homo* in contemporary Scotland. They serve, however, to show that the Window in Thrums gives an obsolete outlook on Scottish life.' The artist proceeded to make subtle strokes here and there. The result was that each of these acutely differentiated faces acquired a peculiar unplaceable resemblance – an elusive likeness that had in each case a faintly ennobling air. A like task confronts Scottish writers today. I believe that forces are now discernible in Scottish life and literature which will have a similar unifying and uplifting effect.

2 Introducing 'Hugh M'Diarmid'

'Hugh M'Diarmid' had appeared in the first issue of *The Scottish Chapbook*. In the *Dunfermline Press* of 30 September 1922, C. M. Grieve presented 'The Watergaw' and attributed it to an anonymous friend. It was in the third issue of *The Scottish Chapbook* that 'M'Diarmid' was named as the author of 'The Watergaw':

> Ae weet forenicht i' the yow-trummle
> I saw yon antrin thing,
> A watergaw wi' its chitterin' licht
> Ayont the on-ding;
> An' I thocht o' the last wild look ye gied
> Afore ye deed!
>
> There was nae reek i' the laverock's hoose
> That nicht – an' nane i' mine;
> But I hae thocht o' that foolish licht
> Ever sin' syne;
> And I think that mebbe at last I ken
> What your look meant then.

watergaw indistinct rainbow   *ae weet* one wet   *forenicht* early evening   *yow-trummle* cold weather at the end of July after sheep-shearing   *antrin* rare   *chitterin'* shivering   *onding* onset (of rain)   *reek* smoke   *laverock* lark (ll. 7–8: it was a wild and stormy night and it was wild and stormy in my heart then too)   *sin' syne* since then

It was thus in the *annus mirabilis* of modernism, the year which saw the publication of Joyce's *Ulysses*, Eliot's *The Waste Land* and Wittgenstein's *Tractatus Logico-Philosophicus*, that 'M'Diarmid' was born. It was also the year of Mussolini's march on Rome and the formation of the Italian Fascist government. This is the 'Causerie' or editorial from the number of the *Chapbook* (vol. 1, no. 3, October 1922) in which 'The Watergaw' appeared.

ONE of the objects of *The Scottish Chapbook* is to supplement the campaign of the Vernacular Circle of the London Burns Club for the revival of the Doric. This issue will, I hope, prove unusually interesting to every student of the Vernacular. The general aim of the Chapbook is, of course, to conduct experiments into the assimilability into literature of the whole range of Scottish life – including the total content of Scottish minds – to discover and counteract inhibiting agencies, and to compare the results with the most perfect assimilations into literary form of contemporary English life – or the life of other countries – with a view to determining the appropriate questions of technique and solving the appropriate problems of artistic economy. The literary cultivation of the Vernacular – as of the Gaelic – is merely one aspect of that; a problem within a problem; and I do not support the campaign for the revival of the Doric where the essential Scottish diversity-in-unity is forgotten, nor where the tendencies involved are anti-cultural.

The work of Mr Hugh M'Diarmid, who contributes a poem and a semi-dramatic study to this issue, is peculiarly interesting because he is, I think, the first Scottish writer who has addressed himself to the question of the extendability (without psychological violence) of the Vernacular to embrace the whole range of modern culture – or in other words, tried to make up the leeway of the language. It is an excessively difficult task, and I envy him his enthusiasm. What he has to do is to adapt an essentially rustic tongue to the very much more complex requirements of our urban civilization – to give it all the almost illimitable suggestionability it lacks (compared, say, with contemporary English or French), but *would have had if it had continued in general use in highly-cultured circles to the present day*. A modern consciousness cannot fully express itself in the Doric as it exists. Take a simple case. What is the Doric for motor-car? It is futile to say 'mottor caur'. The problem that faces a conscientious literary artist determined to express himself through the medium of the Doric is to determine what 'motor-car' would have been in the Doric had the Doric continued, or, rather, become an all-sufficient independent language. He must think himself back into the spirit of the Doric (that is to say, recover it in its entirety, with all the potentialities it once had, ridding it, for his purpose, of those innate disabilities and limitations which have brought it to its present pass) – and then, appropriately to the genius of the language, carry it forward with him, accumulating all the wealth of association and idiom which progressive desuetude has withheld from it until it is adequate to his present needs – the needs not of a ploughman but of a twentieth-century artist who is at once a Scotsman (as distinct from an Englishman or a Negro) and a 'good European' or 'Western World-Man'. . . . From this point of view the value of the Doric lies in the extent to which it contains lapsed or unrealized qualities which correspond to 'unconscious' elements of distinctively Scottish psychology. The recovery and application of these may make effectively communicable those unexpressed aspects of Scottish character the absence of which makes, say, 'Kailyaird' characters shallow, sentimental, humiliating travesties.

Doric economy of expressiveness is impressively illustrated in the first four lines of Mr M'Diarmid's poem. Translate them into English. That is the test. You will find that the shortest possible translation runs something like this: 'One wet afternoon (or early evening) in the cold weather in July after the sheep-shearing I saw that rare thing – an indistinct rainbow, with its shivering light, above the heavily-falling rain.' Not only so; but the temper of the poem is modern and the Doric is adequate to it. It is disfigured by none of the usual sentimentality. It has a distinctively Scottish *sinisterness* for which expression is too seldom found nowadays.

His Monologue is a deliberate attempt to thrust the Doric on to a plane corresponding to the plane of the most advanced school of modern English. Is it successful? It is, of course, a first attempt – a bit of studio-work. The *Chapbook* exists to print such. There is certainly no hope for the revival of the Doric as a literary medium if this monologue does not prove of absorbing interest to Vernacular enthusiasts. It will repay – it will not be intelligible without – careful study. It is a courageous beginning of an incalculable task. The whole trouble with the Doric as a literary language today is that the vast majority of its exponents are hopelessly limited culturally – and that the others (such as Mrs Violet Jacob, Mr Charles Murray, and Miss Mary Symon) only use it for limited purposes. Miss Symon, for example, champions the Vernacular in a brilliantly-written letter – in English. If she believes that the Doric can continue to live as a literary medium – I would prefer to say 'can be brought to life again', although according to Mr M'Diarmid it is not dead but sleepeth, is in a state of suspended animation, and has an unexhausted evolutionary momentum – let her endeavour to rewrite that letter, without the loss of a single implication, in the Doric. . . . Mr M'Diarmid has rendered an analogous service and has disclosed – shall I say? – a hope of resuscitation. He has done more. Stripping the unconscious form of the Vernacular of the grotesque clothes of the Canny-Sandy cum Kirriemuir Elder cum Harry Lauder cult, he has shown a well-knit muscular figure that has not been seen in Scottish Literature for many a long day. . . . It is an achievement which I hope Vernacular enthusiasts will not be the last to recognize.

3 On Scottish Drama

This is the editorial or 'Causerie', from the fourth issue of *The Scottish Chapbook* (vol. 1, no. 4, November 1922). MacDiarmid's sweeping polemic ('There has never been a Scottish drama') overlooks Sir David Lyndsey, George Buchanan and popular working-class theatre and music hall, but his commitment to dramatic and theatrical forms of literary expression was felt early and ran deep. He corrected himself in later years (see Item 21).

PROFESSOR Gregory Smith, in his delightful book *Scottish Literature* published a year or so ago, commented on the curious fact that there had never been any impulse towards the creation of drama in Scotland and, adequately to my thinking, disposed of the common assumption that this was entirely or even in the main due to repressive religiosity. Scottish Literature is unique in this respect. . . . I do not attach the slightest importance to the present Scottish Players' movement. Blake, Brandane, Neil Grant, J. J. Bell, Hugh Roberton, and others are writing plays superficially Scottish – or at any rate superficially subscribing to the stock-conception of what is Scottish – but, apart from the fact that these plays are in every respect inferior to English or Irish plays in their respective *genres*, and are entirely destitute of literary distinction or significance, it must be emphasized that in embodiment and effect they are not only not Scottish but anti-Scottish. The difference between the plays of these Scottish players and the plays of any English company is a distinction without a difference. The appetency for such entertainments exists in direct ratio to the denationalization of those who produce and patronize them; and – for example – is any Scot more denationalized, more incapable of reacting in a typically national way, than the Scot who imagines that extensions of village idiocy or calf-love akin to those with which the music hall genius of Harry Lauder has so long proliferated, or the exhibitionism due to inbreeding and sectarianism exemplified in Kailyard productions, or the cinema excesses of Celticism, are in the slightest degree

Scottish? These things bear the same relation to that which is essentially Scottish as the average best-seller bears to what is really literature. And just as the 'cautious Scot' myth is an English device, with which Scottish nationality has now been everywhere inspissated in the interests of Anglicization, so most of these debased 'Scottish' brands of letters and drama are made in England, or by Scots enslaved by the ubiquitous and incessant suggestioning of the Sassenach – now become in such a great proportion of cases auto-suggestion. (Do not Scots themselves enjoy jokes about Scottish meanness and religiosity as much as the English who inspired them?) ... and this explains why these so-called Scottish plays and stories are most popular in England. Scottish audiences have hissed Harry Lauder. No English audience will ever do so – until the Union is abrogated.

There has never been a Scottish drama. If there is ever to be one the psychological factors which prevented its developing naturally as in other countries must be overcome. I believe that the temperament and tendencies of the Scottish nation have so radically changed within recent years that the inhibiting agencies have been removed, and that the creation of a genuine Scottish drama is now feasible. But it will have to create its own forms and hypothetically, at any rate (for the actuality will remain commercially impossible for some years yet – the commercial success of the Scottish Players proves this) its own theatre. And the difference in form and production will be equivalent to the stupendous and tremendously underrated difference between Scottish and English psychology. The extension of the theatre into the midst of the audience, or the abolition of platform and scenic detachment altogether – the extensive readaptation of the method of progress by soliloquy along lines appropriate to Scottish self-disclosure – the deliberate extirpation of English influences and rejection of English expedients of all kinds and the search for effective Continental affiliations – all these must be considered.

It is futile to speak of a Scottish National Theatre until a start has been made to devise a national theatre-craft. At best the Scottish National Players will help indirectly by disseminating the idea that there is (or rather should be) a difference between Scottish and English drama, and intelligent people who witness these productions will see that nevertheless no such difference exists and ask why. Once a sufficient number of these intelligent people begin to ask why with sufficient urgency the problem of producing a really Scottish play in a manner which represents a definite effort to create a genuine Scottish national theatre, will cease to be insoluble.

In the meantime the healthiest phenomenon I have noted is the appearance of genuine dramatic criticism, based on some knowledge (sound if not over extensive) of contemporary European drama, in the columns of a Glasgow evening paper, over the initials 'W.J.' I know who 'W.J.' is. More power to his elbow! The interests affected do not like his methods, of course. They will probably take steps to have another member of the Staff sent to their plays – or, failing that, refuse tickets to the paper in question. In one way or another they will undoubtedly bring pressure to bear in the right quarters to muzzle 'W.J.' and I shall be surprised if they do not succeed. . . . I wonder if 'W.J.'s' notes are read by any considerable proportion of Glasgow playgoers. I hope so. They appear in the Glasgow *Evening Times*. If 'W.J.' gets free scope to criticize he will certainly do enough in six months to demonstrate the utter un-Scottishness of the plays Glasgow is permitted to see to create a very useful demand for Scottish drama amongst a public, who, by that time, will understand, without needing to be told, why the Scottish Players movement is not only not a movement – but the reverse of a Scottish movement!

4 A Theory of Scots Letters

This item runs together the editorials from three successive issues of *The Scottish Chapbook* (vol. 1, nos. 7, 8 and 9; February, March and April, 1923). The essay is a crucial document in MacDiarmid's career, collecting the seminal references from A. R. Orage (after Matthew Arnold, regarding the value of 'disinterestedness'), G. Gregory Smith, Thomas Hardy, Proust, Dostoevsky and Spengler, and associating Jamieson's Scots *Dictionary* with Joyce's *Ulysses* in a startling conjunction prompted by a 'moral resemblance' and a similar 'vis-comica'. These references and the ideas behind them are, of course, to be found in the poetry MacDiarmid was writing at this time, but they might also be considered in an international context of developing linguistic and literary theory, a counterpoint to the writings of Ferdinand de Saussure, on the one hand, and on the other, I. A. Richards.

I

WE are in a less happy position than was Thomas Boston, the author of the once-ubiquitous *Fourfold State* who put on record that 'on Wednesday, 4th August, about eleven o'clock in the forenoon was born to me a son whom. . . . I did, after no small struggle with myself, adventure to call Ebenezer.' We have been quite unable to find a more suitable title under which to gather the various lines of argument we propose to simultaneously develop in this paper. Noting our purpose to undertake 'a definite and systematic formulation of our Theory of Scots Letters', 'Man o' Moray' (who conducts what passes for a literary feature in the *Edinburgh Evening Dispatch* once a week) observes 'It would be much better not to do so. We have had quite enough of this high-sounding nonsense.' – If we had in view Scottish readers and writers of no higher calibre than 'Man o' Moray' we would be dissuaded by the obvious futility of our task. Doubtless a certain proportion of the readers of our *Chapbook* are still of that type. The majority, however, discovered early that 'it was not what they expected it to be' – which, of course, was precisely what we intended. But frankly, the circulation of the *Chapbook* is still too high to be above suspicion. 'If there must be theories of Scots Letters let them be temperately thought out and simply expressed,' continues 'Man o' Moray.' – 'He fails to remember that what is true of a man is true of a book, that the more apparent, obvious, and demonstrated the feelings, the more superficial, unreal and transient they probably are.' And in the sentences which follow that which we have just quoted, A. R. Orage, in his profound little essay on 'The Criteria of Culture', gives a clue to the spirit in which we are trying to conduct this *Chapbook* – and names the attitude of mind lacking which no reader will find this Theory intelligible, let alone illuminating.

> Culture I define as being, amongst other things, a capacity for subtle discrimination of words and ideas. Epictetus made the discrimination of words the foundation of moral training, and it is true enough that every stage of moral progress is indicated by the degree of our perception of the meaning of words. . . . One of the most subtle words, and one of the key-words of culture, is simplicity. Can you discriminate between natural simplicity and studied simplicity, between Nature and Art? In appearance they are indistinguishable, but in reality they are aeons apart: and whoever has learned to distinguish between them is entitled to regard himself as on the way to culture. Originality is another key-word, and its subtlety may be suggested by a paradox which was a commonplace among the Greeks; namely, that the most original minds strive to conceal their originality and that the master minds succeed. Contrast this counsel of perfect originality with the counsels given in our own day, in which the aim of originality is directed to appearing original – you will be brought, thereby, face to face with still another key-idea of Culture, the relation of Appearance to Reality. All these exercises in culture are elementary, however, in comparison with the master-problem of 'disinterestedness'. No word in the English language is more difficult to define or better worth attempting to define. Somewhere or other in its capacious folds it contains all the ideas of ethics, and even, I should say, of religion. The *Bhagavad Ghita* (to name only one classic) can be summed up in the word. Duty is only a pale equivalent to it. I venture to say that whoever has understood the meaning

of 'disinterestedness' is not far-off understanding the goal of human culture.

Nationalism in literature is the reaction of a distinctive essential of the spirit to the various time-influences to which it is subjected. And that which gives a recognizable if hardly definable unity to the work of all true Scottish writers, whether in English or the Vernacular, is a quality of 'disinterestedness' in the sense in which Orage uses it. This secret of the Scottish soul is laid bare (albeit in a false light of romanticism) by W. H. Hamilton when he sings:

> The lost cause calls me sooner than the true,
> Far sooner than the safe. Perchance I obey
> Some old religious rapture my forbears knew
> The problem unresolved save by this test –
> 'Whoever saves his life hath missed life's best.'
>
> To die for error. . . . rather than, being right,
> To rot or slumber or grow wise in my ease,
> – False doctrine, doubtless: be it so! . . .'

Consider in this connection what Professor Gregory Smith says in this passage from his most searching and stimulating book, *Scottish Literature*:

> There is more in the Scottish antithesis of the real and fantastic than is to be explained by the familiar rules of rhetoric . . . The one invades the other without warning. They are the 'polar twins' of the Scottish Muse. . . . The douce travesty which stands for the Scot with the general (the methodical, level-headed, self-conscious creature of popular tradition) never says as much as he thinks; he is as calm as a country Sabbath morn on the cantrips of his mind. But he is not the Scot who steps forth self-expressed in the Makars old and new despite the accidents or thwarts of history which stayed or appeared to stay the freer play of his fancy. . . . This mingling, even of the most eccentric kind, is an indication to us that the Scot, in that fashion which takes all things as granted, is at his ease in both rooms of life, and turns to fun and even profanity with no misgivings. We owe part of our strength to this freedom

in passing from one mood to another. It takes some people more time than they can spare to see the absolute propriety of a gargoyle's grinning at the elbow of a kneeling saint!

Is not that precisely why the most advanced literature today is unintelligible to many highly-educated people even? Professor Gregory Smith has in these words described the great vital characteristic of Scottish literature – a distinguishing faculty, which it can only shape forth poorly in English, but which is potentially expressible in the Vernacular to which it belongs. It is the predominant feature of Scots Literature old and new, and yet, do not the same phrases ('taking all things as granted', 'freedom in passing from one mood to another') sum up the essential tendencies of the most advanced schools of thought in every country in Europe today? We base our belief in the possibility of a great Scottish Literary Renaissance, deriving its strength from the resources that lie latent and almost unsuspected in the Vernacular, upon the fact that the genius of our Vernacular enables us to secure with comparative ease the very effects and swift transitions which other literatures are for the most part unsuccessfully endeavouring to cultivate in languages that have a very different and inferior bias. Whatever the potentialities of the Doric may be, however, there cannot be a revival in the real sense of the word – a revival of the spirit as distinct from a mere renewed vogue of the letter – unless these potentialities are in accord with the newest and truest tendencies of human thought. We confess to having been discouraged when thinking of the Vernacular Movement by the fact that the seal of its approval is so largely set upon the traditional and the conventional. The real enemy is he who cries: 'Hands off our fine old Scottish tongue.' If all that the Movement is to achieve is to preserve specimens of Braid Scots, archaic, imitative, belonging to a type of life that has passed and cannot return, in a sort of museum department of our consciousness – set apart from our vital preoccupations – it is a movement which not only cannot claim our support but compels our opposition. The rooms of thought are choc-a-bloc with far too much dingy old rubbish as it is. There are too many vital problems clamouring for attention. . . .

It is a different matter, however, if an effort is to be made to really revive the Vernacular – to encourage the experimental exploitation of the unexplored possibilities of Vernacular expression. 'The letter killeth but the spirit giveth life.' Only in so far as the Vernacular has unused resources corresponding better than English does to the progressive expression of the distinctive characteristics of Scottish life – however much these may have been submerged, subverted, or camouflaged, by present conditions (we shall deal later with the question of the relationship between literature and politics) – has it possibilities of literary value. If the cultural level of work in the Doric is not capable of being raised to equal that in any other living language – if the Doric has not certain qualities which no other language possesses and qualities at that of consequence to modern consciousness as a whole – then all that can be hoped for is a multiplication of equivalents in the Vernacular to work that has already been better achieved in other languages without any special contribution at all from Scotland to the expressive resource of modern life. The Doric unquestionably has a past and, to a very much more limited extent, a present. The question is whether it has a future which will enable it successfully to compete, at any rate along specialized lines, with other languages. Our interest, therefore, should centre not so much in what has been done in the Doric as in what has not but may be done in it. No literature can rest on its laurels.

> We lack the courage to be where we are,
> We love too much to travel on old roads,
> To triumph on old fields; we love too much
> To consecrate the magic of dead things.

For our part we frankly confess that a living dog is worth any number of dead lions, and we unreservedly accept Thomas Hardy's definition 'that literature is the written expression of revolt against accepted things.'

We have been enormously struck by the resemblance – the moral resemblance – between Jamieson's *Etymological Dictionary of the Scottish Language* and James Joyce's *Ulysses*. A *vis comica* that has not yet been liberated lies bound by desuetude and misappreciation in the recesses of the Doric: and its potential uprising would be no less prodigious, uncontrollable, and utterly at variance with conventional morality than was Joyce's

A Theory of Scots Letters

tremendous outpouring. The Scottish instinct is irrevocably, continuously, opposed to all who 'are at ease in Zion'. It lacks entirely the English sense of 'the majesty of true corpulence'. Sandy is our national figure – a shy, subtle, disgruntled, idiosyncratic individual – very different from John Bull. And while the Irish may envisage their national destiny as 'the dark Rosaleen' and the thought of England may conjure up pictures of roast beef and stately homes, Scotland is always 'puir auld Scotland'. Dr Walter Walsh recently referred to the affinity between the Scots and the Spartans and voiced a deep national feeling when he deprecated material well-being and comfort of mind or body. It is of first-rate significance, revealing that what really does most profoundly appeal to us is not pleasure but pain, to remember what happened at the concert given by Serge Koussevitzki in Edinburgh recently. (It has a bearing on what we are subsequently to say of the mystical relation of Scotland and Russia.) A newspaper critic described it thus:

> He (Koussevitzki) rose to his greatest heights when he came to the modern Russians. There were the introduction to Moussorgski's opera *Khovanschchina*, Rimsky Korsakov's 'The Flight of the Bumble Bee', Rachmaninoff's 'Vocalise' and Tchaikovski's Fifth Symphony. . . . Two of them had to be repeated, but the symphony marked the climax of the concert. Koussevitzki extracted from it *the last ounce of agony and gloom* with which it is charged. It was all very exciting, and at the close there were scenes unparalleled at these concerts. An Edinburgh audience, reputed to be reserved, rose to its feet, cheered and shouted bravos.

– That's us all over! Joy and gladness are all very well in their way – but gloom is what really gets us and we do enjoy agony! . . .

Burns himself had no wish for the increase of mere human self-satisfaction. It is deeply significant that he wrote

> O wad some power the giftie gie's
> To see oorsels as ithers see's

– not 'Oh gie the gift to ither folk to see us as we see oorsels.'

And one of the most distinctive characteristics of the Vernacular, part of its very essence, is its insistent recognition of the body, the senses. The Vernacular is almost startlingly at one with Rabbi Ben Ezra,

> 'Let us not always say
> *Spite of this flesh today*
> I strove, made head. . . .'

In other words, in Meredith's phrase, the Vernacular can never consent to 'forfeit the beast wherewith we are crost.' This explains the unique blend of the lyrical and the ludicrous in primitive Scots sentiment. It enables us to realize very clearly just what Matthew Arnold meant when he called Burns 'a beast with splendid gleams' – and the essence of the genius of our race, is, in our opinion, the reconciliation it effects between the base and the beautiful, recognizing that they are complementary and indispensable to each other.

II

THE Scottish Vernacular is the only language in Western Europe instinct with those uncanny spiritual and pathological perceptions alike which constitute the uniqueness of Dostoevesky's work, and word after word of Doric establishes a blood-bond in a fashion at once infinitely more thrilling and vital and less explicable than those deliberately sought after by writers such as D. H. Lawrence in the medium of English which is inferior for such purposes because it has [an] entirely different natural bias which has been so confirmed down the centuries as to be insusceptible of correction. The Scots Vernacular is a vast storehouse of just the very peculiar and subtle effects which modern European literature in general is assiduously seeking and, if the next century is to see an advance in mental science equal to that which last century has marked in material science, then the resumption of the Scots Vernacular into the mainstream of European letters, in a fashion which the most enthusiastic Vernacularist may well hesitate to hope for, is inevitable. The Vernacular is a vast unutilized mass of lapsed observation made by minds whose attitudes to experience and whose speculative and imaginative tendencies were quite different from any possible to Englishmen and Anglicized Scots today. It is an inchoate Marcel Proust – a Dostoeveskian debris of ideas – an inexhaustible quarry of subtle and significant sound.

As a recent writer on the revival of Irish Gaelic (in which novels as well as poems and plays are now being written) remarks,

> the best work done in Gaelic reveals a part of Irish life that has been long silent, with a freshness due to sources that have remained comparatively uninfluenced by alien imagination . . . Most of the writers of the so-called Irish Literary Revival of a decade or so back were ignorant of Gaelic. Even Synge had probably only a patois knowledge. . . . A school is now arising among young men having the advantage of an educated knowledge of the tongue, and even the distinctiveness of their work in English is more marked. The new generation will doubtless be increasingly bi-lingual and in possession of the literary traditions of Gaelic life.

The revival of Scots Vernacular is being retarded simply because of the fact that the majority of writers in the Vernacular have only a patois knowledge of it – not an educated knowledge – and are not to any useful extent in possession of its literary traditions apart from Burns: while they confine their efforts to a little range of conventional forms.

A writer in the *Glasgow Herald* recently pointed out that reflexly the distinctive humour of our Vernacular fulfilled at least three invaluable functions.

> It stimulates the wits and the descriptive and reflective powers. It keeps alive a spirit of brave and virile gaiety. By pricking the bladders of pride and pretension, and nourishing the independence and self-respect of the step-children of Fortune, it brings all sorts and conditions of men to a greatest common measure of sheer humanity, and is thus a powerful preservative of the true spirit of democracy. . . . The democratic spirit of the Scottish Vernacular speech and literature is strongly allied with an ethical bent which is all the stronger for its fearless

realism and its freedom from didacticism or sentiment, and also with an element of pathos that has suffered somewhat from its dilution and exploitation by certain writers of the Kailyard School.

The writer goes on to say 'jalouse, dwam, dowie, gurlie, mavis, carline, crouse, gawkie, blate, gaucie, and thrawn are chance selections from a long list of fine old words that usefully express shades of meaning which English either ignores or renders very imperfectly.' To that may be added the fact that the Vernacular abounds in terms which short-circuit conceptions that take sentences to express in English. Take only one – Guyfaul. It takes nine English words to convey its meaning. It means 'Hungry for his meat but not very hungry for his work.'

Just as physiologically we have lost certain powers possessed by our forefathers – the art of wiggling our ears, for example, or of moving our scalps this way and that – so we have lost (but may perhaps re-acquire) wordforming faculties peculiar to the Doric for the purposes of both psychological and nature description. There are words and phrases in the Vernacular which thrill me with a sense of having been produced as a result of mental processes entirely different from my own and much more powerful. They embody observations of a kind which the modern mind makes with increasing difficulty and weakened effect. Take the word 'birth', for instance, meaning a current in the sea caused by a furious tide but taking a different course from it – a contrary motion. It exemplifies a fascinating, exceedingly adroit and purely Scottish application of metaphor. Then there are natural occurrences and phenomena of all kinds which have apparently never been noted by the English mind. No words exist for them in English. For instance – watergaw – for an indistinct rainbow; yow-trummle – meaning the cold weather in July after the sheepshearing; cavaburd – meaning a thick fall of snow; and blue bore – meaning a patch of blue in a cloudy sky. Another feature of the Doric which I will not illustrate here is the fashion in which diverse attitudes of mind or shades of temper are telescoped into single words or phrases, investing the whole speech with subtle flavours of irony, commiseration, realism and humour which cannot be reproduced in English. In onomatopoetic effect, too, the Doric has a wider range and infinitely richer resources than English while the diversity of inherent bias is revealed in unmistakable fashion.

Whatever the potentialities of the Doric may be, however, there cannot be a revival in the real sense of the word – a revival of the spirit as distinct from a mere renewed vogue of the letter – unless these potentialities are in accord with the newest tendencies of human thought.

Without in any way committing ourselves to agreement with the writers from whom we quote, let us endeavour to show that just as Burns in a 'Man's a Man for a' That' brilliantly forecasted the spirit of the French revolution, so the whole unrealized genius of the Scots Vernacular has brilliantly forecasted – potentially if not actually – tendencies which are only now emerging in European life and literature, and which must unquestionably have a very important bearing upon the future of human culture and civilization.

Despite the chaos of conflicting opinion on every subject in the world today, there seems to be remarkable unanimity among intellectuals of the type who endeavour to form world-opinions in the view that Western civilization is doomed. Mr H. G. Wells recently wrote: 'I now realize the stupendous instability of the Western world. The system is breaking up. It has neither recuperative nor reconstructive power.' The late Mr Frederic Harrison, in a letter written just before his death, said, 'Every board in civilization is cracking. The British Empire is melting away, just like the Roman in the year 300, and from the same causes,' Following this same line of thought, Professor Graham Wallas, addressing University Women teachers at Bedford College, said:

> The material world – the world that slowly and painfully created itself upon the fragments of Roman civilization – is falling in ruins. Right across from the Pacific to the Atlantic, right across the great Eurasian Continent, the old system has fallen in ruins, and the danger we have to face is greater and more intense than the danger with which the world was confronted at the fall of the ancient civilization. Where there were a few cultivators in the clearings of the woods fifteen hundred years ago, or a few hundred shepherds out in the

plains, now there are millions upon millions of industrialized and concentrated factory workers. The very existence of the present population depends upon organization and to substitute accident and drift and confusion, for organization means to reduce the population to something like what it was at the fall of the Ancient World.

Similar views have been expressed in the books of Samuel Dill and Dr Warde Fowler on the parallels to our own time in the later periods of the Roman Empire and – with immensely greater consequence – by Herr Spengler, the German philosopher, who, in the *Downfall of the Western World* traced the causes of the decline of ancient civilizations and drew an analogy with the present. Spengler's central thesis has already – however ill understood – influenced the literature of every country in Europe: and has given rise to a literature already immense. Spengler is no pessimist: to translate the title of his book, *The Downfall of the Western World*, is to suggest a false idea of it. The idea he seeks to convey is rather 'fulfilment' – the end of one civilization and the beginning of another – the emergence of a new order. Spengler considers the creative element in his writing to lie in the fact that he has proved by the test of concrete experience that universal history is not a universal succession of occurrences, but a group, so far numbering eight, of high civilizations whose life-histories, completely independent of one another, yet present themselves to us with a perfectly analogous development. It follows that he holds each of these civilizations to have an absolute standard, applicable to itself alone. Every vital idea – including Spengler's own, as he admits – belongs to its own age, its own civilization, and in the course of history as a whole there are no false or true doctrines any more than there are false or true stages in the growth of a plant. For the man or nation with a true 'historic view' there are no past models to be imitated; there are only examples of the way in which this or that civilization advanced to its appointed fulfilment. Everything depends upon the way in which men are fulfilling their destiny. He confesses that he discovered his philosophy under the influence of Agadir in 1911, at a time when Darwinian optimism lay like a blight over the European and American world, and ability to face the great tasks implicit in his own civilization was paralysed in the average

West European type of man. Is the position any better today? . . . He sees tremendous tasks awaiting Western culture before its time of fulfilment arrives – in the realm of jurisprudence, for example, of industry, of the practical tasks of government and administration. Only in art and letters can it be said that there are few or no possibilities of achievement. Our literature is bankrupt. All forms of literary and artistic expression, equally with other phenomena of intellectual and spiritual activity, have reached in our Western civilization the point beyond which they can go no further. Western Europe, with America, has exhausted her creative energies as Greece, Rome, Assyria, Babylon, exhausted their energies before her. She can add nothing more to the sum of vitally new human knowledge, of fresh and adequate channels of self-expression. We must wait for the inevitable end or rather the new beginning which will come from a civilization other than ours . . . And he asserts that already in Dostoevsky is to be found the first delineation of that new world.

Of the many antitheses out of which Herr Spengler builds up his thesis – which is destined to have an incalculable influence upon the future of human literature – that which predominates in every chapter is the distinction he draws between the 'Apollonian' or classical, and the 'Faustian' or modern type. The Appollonian type is dogmatic, unquestioning, instinctive, having no conception of infinity – in short, your average Englishman or German – and the Faustian mind, on the contrary, is dominated by the conception of infinity, of the unattainable, and hence is ever questioning, never satisfied, rationalistic in religion and politics, romantic in art and literature – a perfect expression of the Scottish race.

It was anticipated that Spengler, in his second book – which has just been published – would reveal the East as the source of the civilization destined to replace our own, that of the declining West . . . and in this connection it is well to remember in passing that we Scots are Oriental, the descendants of the lost tribes of Israel (*sic*) . . . and so he does but only very briefly. Comparing Tolstoy and Dostoevsky he says 'beginning and end meet here. Dostoevsky is a saint, Tolstoy is merely a revolutionary. . . . The Christianity of Tolstoy was a misunderstanding. He spoke of Christ and he meant Marx. The next thousand years belong to the Christianity of Dostoevsky.' And, immediately, Spengler proceeds to align himself with the very conclusions G. K. Chesterton so very differently arrived at in dealing with the difference of Scottish and English literature. Far from being a fatalist, he is an idealist, in the philosophical sense; far from being a cosmopolitan he is a self-assertive nationalist, and he gives the key to his whole political position when he declares in words that are almost a paraphrase of what G. K. Chesterton said of Scottish literature at the London Burns Club dinner: – 'A nation is humanity in living form. The practical result of theories of world-betterment is, without exception, a formless and therefore unhistorical mass. All cosmopolitans and enthusiasts for world betterment represent fellaheen-ideals, whether they know it or not. Their success means the abdication of the nation within the historical sphere to the advantage, not of world-progress, but of other nations.' What is the cause of Doric desuetude – of the absence of Doric drama and prose – but lack of fulfilment in the Spenglerian sense? What is this distinction between Apollonian and Faustian types, but just another way of phrasing the contrast between the false Scot – the douce travesty, the methodical level-headed self-conscious creature of popular tradition – and the true Scot, rapid in his transitions of thought, taking all things as granted, turning to fun and even to profanity with no misgivings, at his ease in both rooms of life.

The canny Scot tradition has been 'fulfilled' in the Spenglerian sense; and the future depends upon the freeing and development of that opposite tendency in our consciousness which runs counter to the conventional conceptions of what is Scottish. In other words, the slogan of a Scottish literary revival must be the Nietzschean 'Become what you are.'

III

Poet, on people's love set not too high a value,
The momentary noise of frenzied praise will pass
The verdict of a fool, and then the cold crowd's laughter
Thoul't hear: remain unmoved, unruffled and austere,
Thou art a king; live thou alone, the path of freedom
Tread thou; wherever thee thine own free spirit lead,
Perfecting aye the fruits of thy beloved fancy,

Not asking a reward for thine achievement high,
Reward is in thyself – thyself the last tribunal;
More strictly than all else canst thou gauge thine own work.
Art thou then satisfied with it, exacting artist?
Art thou then satisfied? then let the crowd find fault,
And on the altar spit whereon thy fire is burning
And in its childish play thy tripod shake.

— Pushkin

To explore the Russo-Scottish parallelism a little further leads to some interesting points. The condition of British literary journalism today is remarkably similar to that which obtained in Russia after 1855, where a crop of new periodicals appeared, full of vitality and colour. 'This colour,' we read,

> was given them less by their *belles lettres* than by their critical portion, which, indeed, was the outcome of the former but aimed at objects which had nothing to do with it – this is the strength and weakness of Russian criticism – its strength in that the ostensibly 'literary' or even 'aesthetic' criticism became a moral and socio-political power; it delighted in making use of these literary productions which were suited to the spreading of its ideas and deliberately neglected others often far more important in a literary sense; it relegated aesthetics to ladies' society, and turned its critical report into a sort of pulpit for moral and social preaching. This most 'war-like' criticism, one-sided and purposeful, achieved a colossal effect among the young men, to whom the essays of a Chernyshevsky, Dobrolubov, and a Pisarev became revelations, the language of eloquent and fiery agitators, not critics. Therein also lay its weakness, prejudice, and perverseness. One must never let oneself be deceived by its judgments; it extolled or decried the author and his work, as Antonovich did Turgenev in the *Contemporary* because of his Bayarov, not because of the value or no-value of his performance, but for his opinions, his ideas – nay, for the journal in which he published his work. Thus this criticism is often, in spite of all its giftedness, its zeal and fire, only a mockery of all criticism. The work only serves as a peg on which to hang their own views. With a backward society and its mental nonage, its childish dread

of dogmas and authorities, this criticism was a means which was sanctified by the end – the spreading of modern and free opinions, the establishment of new ideals. Unhappily, Russian literary criticism has remained till today almost solely journalistic, i.e., didactic and partisan – True, there was also a literary and aesthetic criticism, but against the journalistic, the 'real', it could not hold its own.

In Britain today, however, this criticism is not 'soldierly' but 'policeman-like'. It is conservative not revolutionary. In Russia the method was necessary and useful: but in Britain, it is not used for the spreading of modern and free opinions, the establishment of new ideals, but in the very opposite direction. Instead of the Russians named we have a 'Claudius Clear', an E. B. Osborn, an Edmund Gosse, and a thousand lesser 'literary' journalists. There are literary and aesthetic critics but against the journalistic and the 'real' they cannot here either hold their own – and, often, indeed the same passage is just as applicable to them, except in so far as the direction of their didacticism and partisanship goes. Scottish literary criticism either of the one kind or the other – as distinct from British (which really means English) – scarcely exists at all.

And – recognizing the necessity and usefulness of the method, while quite aware of its weaknesses – what Scotland needs if a Scottish Literary Revival is to be encompassed is criticism like that which Druzhinin, Annenkov, Dobrolubov, Pisarev and Chernyshevsky applied in Russia.

> Druzhinin was especially noted as the founder of the society for the support of necessitous literary men and scholars. He took up the cudgels above all against the onesidedness of criticism, against its want of consideration, or total ignorance, e.g. of English literature, against the adherence to pattern of its judgement, its dense repetition instead of a due investigation of current and too hasty judgments, and its love for a moral. He greeted the new men of talent, the new poets, and extolled the energy of literature and the soundness of its trend.

Annenkov dwelt in his criticisms on the necessary and natural connection (apart from any set purpose of the artist's) between works of art, and thought and life. – 'He is the founder of "organic" criticism in contrast to the purely aestheticizing and to the "historical" or "realistic". To him a work of art is the organic product of popular life and the historic moment; hence emphasizing of the national principle – the co-ordination of art and the national soil. . . . Above all, he demanded from art sincerity, as being its very life.' Chernyshevsky 'after the rejection of all metaphysics, decides that the beautiful is life; hence Art has only to subserve the illustrating of life and can never replace or come up to reality.' . . . 'Dobrolubov made the young generation enthusiastic, for it recognized in his "realism", his condemning of all "idealism", the only security for successful development.' Then came Pisarev: 'He means his sledge-hammer blows not so much for poetry itself, as for the Conservatives, who made it their pretext, and their reactionary epicureanism.'

Reactionary epicureanism! Scarcely a remark on poetry or *belles lettres* ever appears in any Scottish periodical or book, or anywhere else on the subject of Scottish literature, which does not partake of this nature, allied, also, to Anglicisation, or its more insidious equivalent, 'romantic Nationalism'.

Would that it might be hoped that developing along the lines already indicated by reference to the theories of Spengler and others as inevitable if our latent national potentialities are yet to be realized. Scottish literature might secure a succession of literary critics such as those mentioned, culminating in an equivalent to that moral philosopher and theologian Solovyov (whose religious concepts as the present writer pointed out in a recent article in the *Glasgow Herald* are now being naturalized or re-expressed in Scotland in the writings of Professor J. Y. Simpson of the New College, Edinburgh) 'one of the most interesting phenomena of modern Russia and its mental fermentation – a fearless, fiery proclaimer of the truth, without thought for himself, unselfish, serving only the idea, lastly a contrast to all. His great merit is in times of absolute positivism, nay, indifference to all theory and to metaphysics, to have drawn attention to the "eternal" questions.' Any Scottish Literary Revival worthy of the name must follow in his footsteps:

> In morning mist, with unsure steps, I went
> Towards mysterious and wondrous shores,
> The dawn still battled with the last few stars,

Dreams were still flying, and, possessed by dreams,
My soul was praying unto unknown gods.

In the cold light of day my lonely path,
As erst, I tread toward an unknown land.
The mist has cleared and plainly sees the eye
How hard the uphill road and still how far,
How far away all that was in my dreams,

And until midnight, with no timid steps,
I shall go on towards the wished-for shores,
To where upon the hill beneath new stars
All flaming bright with fires of victory
There stands awaiting me my promised fame.

The attitude which Scottish poets must adopt towards Scotland if the promises of the present juncture are to be realized to the full must be analogous to that expressed towards Russia by the great Scoto-Russian poet, Lermontov:

I love my country, but with a strange love,
This love my reason cannot overcome:
Tis not the glory bought at price of blood,
Nor quiet, full of haughty confidence,
Nor dark antiquity's untouched traditions,
That move in me a happy reverie,
But I do love, why I know not myself,
The cold deep silence of my country's fields,
Her sleeping forests waving in the wind,
Her rivers flowing widely like the sea.
I love to haste through byways on a cart,
And with slow gaze piercing the shade of night
And sighing for night's lodging, on each side
To meet the twinkling light of wretched thorpes.
I love the smoke above the parching harvest,
The nomad train of waggons on the steppe,
And on the hill amid the yellow crops
A single pair of birches shining white.
I see with joy that many cannot know
A well-filled rickyard with a wooden cabin

Straw-thatched with window shutters neatly carved;
And of a saint's day in the dewy eve
Till midnight I am ready to look on
At dancing, with the stamping and the yells
Accompanied by drunken peasants' talk.

As for the period of stagnation which is now passing in Scotland – this present which is giving place to the future daily – it may be described in another poem of the same great writer's:

To good and bad alike disgracefully indifferent,
We starting our career shall fade without a fight,
In face of perils we are shamefully discouraged
And, despicable slaves, bow to the face of might.

The hate and love we feel are both but accidental.
We sacrifice deny to hate and love in turn;
There reigns within our soul a kind of secret coldness
E'en though within our blood the iron burn.

A gloomy visaged crowd and soon to be forgotten
We shall go through the world without a voice or trace;
No fructifying thought, no work begun with genius
Shall we throw forward for the race.
Posterity, as judge and citizen, with harshness
Our ashes shall insult in some contemptuous verse,
As bitter jibes a son, deceived and disappointed,
Over a spendthrift father's hearse.

5   Programme for a Scottish Fascism

This item appeared under the regular editorial column 'At the Sign of the Thistle' in *The Scottish Nation* (no. 7, 19 June, 1923), which C. M. Grieve was editing. MacDiarmid's praise of Italian Fascism puts him in the company of the majority of writers and intellectuals of the period (though his praise of Mussolini predates Ezra Pound's). This 'Programme' followed upon a longer article in the previous number of *The Scottish Nation*, a 'Plea for a Scottish Fascism', in which the success of the Scottish Labour Party was said to depend upon its response to the 'new spirit' of nationalism. 'Scotland today is tinder awaiting the spark of genius to become ablaze with a new national consciousness and will.'

SCOTLAND is not Italy and the political, social, and industrial traditions and conditions of the people of Scotland, and their psychology differ entirely from those of Italy. Nevertheless there is need for a Scottish Fascism just as there was need for an Italian Fascism – and the first plank in the programme of the former would be precisely the same as the first plank in the latter – 'Scotland First' for us as it was 'Italy First' for them. There is no sense in Scottish constituencies sending members to the Parliament at Westminster simply to be outvoted on all matters that vitally affect Scotland by English majorities. There is no sense in a majority of Scottish Town Councils periodically passing resolutions in favour of Home Rule for Scotland – and tamely submitting to the Prime Minister's refusal to consider the question, or as in former Parliaments, to the defeat of successive Scottish Home Rule Bills by English majorities. There is a grotesque anomaly in the great Scottish Churches deploring the menace to Scottish national traditions – and not taking such effective measures as their memberships, which comprise the majority of the Scottish people, would readily enable them to do to conserve them. In Housing – in Education – in Agriculture there is the same tale of ignominy and powerlessness. Can efforts to render effective the declared desires of the great Scottish Churches – to grant the 'hardy annual' demands of the majority of Scottish Local Authorities, the Scottish Trades

Union Congress, and other bodies – to rescue the chosen representatives of the Scottish people from the intolerable predicament which robs them of power – be dismissed as extremist? If so, extremism is a quality of which Scotland stands desperately in need. Mention has been made of only a few of the tendencies in modern Scottish life afflicted with indirection through related causes. Nothing has been said yet of the rapid transformation of the racial basis of the Scottish population – nothing of the alienation of the people from immense areas of the country, capable in the past of supporting a considerable population, and capable in the future of supporting a very large agricultural population, especially if modern intensive methods of cultivation are used (apart altogether from the question of exploiting the possibilities of the areas in question as mountain holiday centres) – nothing of the assimilation of Scots Law to English – nothing of the subordination of Scottish commercial and industrial interests to those of England – and, most important of all, nothing of the moral and spiritual loss involved in the denationalization of Scotland and the destruction of Scottish national culture. In all these directions the same need manifests itself – the need for the development of a new national *will*; the need to overcome in some way or another our present inability to make our representations effective, to get wrongs righted, to devise a reconstructive national policy.

Upon what does the development of such a *force* depend – upon the intensification of everything in contemporary Scottish life that sets the spiritual above the material – that is to say of the majority of the motives that actuate Scottish Labour organizations; of the spirit that is seeking to revive the Gaelic and the Scots Vernacular; of the instincts that are responsible for the contemporary efforts towards a Scottish Literary Renaissance and a Scottish National Theatre; of all the associations concerned to preserve distinctive Scottish traditions and tendencies from absorption and obsolescence. The relation between many of these things may be far from obvious. Superficially considered many of them appear antagonistic even. It is only when each is considered in relation to the idea of Scotland that it acquires proper proportion and reveals its relation to all the others. Too often even the most active protagonist in any of these causes cannot see the wood for his own particular tree.

It is of special significance that the saltatory development of the Labour movement in Scotland, the intensification of Scottish Home Rule propaganda, the awakening of the Churches to a new realization of the moral and spiritual values of Scottish nationality and the need to conserve them, and the recreation of distinct tendencies in Scottish Literature when almost on the verge of complete submersion in English literature, should synchronize. That mere fact of simultaneity shows them as aspects of one and the same force in Scottish life. The danger is that they should not develop proportionately to each other. The Labour movement, owing to the exaggerated importance attached to mere politics, and also to the fact that it has a double appeal – spiritual and material – is conscious of its peril. The lessons of Russia (and by that I do not mean that the Soviet System has failed) are being learned. In Scotland less than in any other country in Europe is Labour contemptuous of culture or inclined to disregard the spiritual factors which alone can consummate its programme. In this connection it is particularly noteworthy that already Labour MPs who were formerly all out for economic change and 'Internationalists' of the old type, have become passionately nationalistic with benefit to their internationalist outlook. The Scottish Labour Movement is already modifying its Socialism as Mussolini modified his. It has got out of the rut of mere theory; and takes service as the touchstone of social values. As soon as it ceases to work for 'Socialism' and makes its goal 'Scottish Socialism', it will have purged itself of the elements which make for false progress and be within measurable distance of complete triumph.

Just as Fascism in Italy must incline to the Left, as has been pointed out, just because nationalism is opposed to capitalist materialism, so already in Scottish literature and religion tendencies are manifesting themselves to meet Labour half-way and make common cause in the interest of 'Scotland First'. It may seem absurd to say, for example, that the revival of the Scots Vernacular depends upon the establishment of some form of Socialism in Scotland; but it will be apparent to all who take the time to go into the matter that this is so.

Programme for a Scottish Fascism

The desuetude of the Vernacular was one of the consequences of that Industrialism of which State Socialism (in the sense in which Hilaire Belloc saw it as the Servile State) may be the apotheosis; but a Scottish Nationalist Socialism will be a very different thing and will restore an atmosphere in which the fine, distinctive traits and tendencies of Scottish character which have withered in the foul air of our contemporary chaos, will once more revive.

Italian Fascism needs most urgently to be almost exactly reproduced in Scotland in so far as agrarian policy is concerned. Its agrarian policy is summed up in the maxim, *the land for those who work it.* Hence it will not attack large properties as such, considering that big scale industry, carried out by those who understand their work, serves a useful purpose in agriculture as elsewhere, but it will expropriate those proprietors who fail to cultivate their property to advantage and thereby lose their claim to ownership by failing to perform some adequate social function. The essential policy with regard to the Scottish Highlands could not be more succinctly and adequately expressed.

> Fascist principles are quite definite in the matter of agriculture. According to them, so long as the agricultural labourer works simply for pay and as a pure mercenary he can have no love for the land, no taste for his own work, no ambition for the perfecting of the agricultural industry. Fascism condemns such a state of things and endeavours to meet it by the proper remedies. These are: (1) To give the peasant a lively affection for the land that supports him, so that he may endeavour to make it more and more productive; (2) To give him a proper interest in his labour by means of a participation in its fruits; (3) To encourage systematically all the most enlightened measures that are the result of changed times, and of this participation on the part of the labourers in agricultural enterprise; (4) To educate the labourers of the soil by full and complete technical, administrative, economic, and financial instruction, so that they may realise their responsibilities in relation to land proprietorship. – Fascism understands the immense social importance of land, hence it condemns absentee and unproductive possession, which leaves vast

tracts of land uncultivated that could be highly productive, and thus fails in its primary mission to society, which is to bring a substantial contribution of labour and production to the common good. According to Fascism, therefore, those landowners who fail in their first duty, which is that of cultivating their own properties, and produce no direct or indirect advantage to agriculture, lose their right of proprietorship, which presupposes categorically some social function on the part of the possessor.

The entire Fascist programme can be readapted to Scottish national purposes and is (whether it be called Fascist or pass under any other name) *the only thing that will preserve our distinctive national culture*. Mere Parliamentary devolution is useless. Every individual and every association interested in anything Scottish can only ensure the success of the particular aim in view by joining with every other individual and every other association interested in anything Scottish.

6 *Art and the Unknown*

This was contributed to A. R. Orage's influential journal *The New Age* (20 and 27 May, 1926), and was included in Duncan Glen's *Selected Essays of Hugh MacDiarmid* (1969). It might usefully be considered alongside Paul Valéry's writings on *Monsieur Teste* and *Leonardo*.

I

COMPREHENSIBILITY is error: Art is beyond understanding.[1]

The function of art is the extension of human consciousness.

Art is therefore the most important of human activities; all others are dependent upon it.

The highest art at any time can only be appreciated by an infinitesimal minority of the people – if by any.[2]

The ideal observer of art at work would be one conscious of all human experience up to the given moment. (The ideal observer of art – as against art-at-work – is God, conscious of all that has been and *will be* achieved.) If consciousness be likened to a cleared space, art is that which extends it in any direction.

The ideal specialist as compared with the ideal observer is conscious not of the whole of human experience up to a given moment, but of its entire development in a particular direction up to then.

---

[1] Cf. Edwin Muir. 'The unnecessary and the inconceivable have been greater friends to man than the necessary and the reasonable. This enigmatical character of art, this ultimate impossibility of making it turn any moral mill, has been noted occasionally in the last two centuries, etc.' (*Latitudes*, London, 1924, p. 143.) The ultimate impossibility of making it turn *any* mill is what is here affirmed.

[2] Cf. Denis Saurat. 'The more complicated beings become, the more subdivided and subtle their desires, the smaller is the group of beings they can collaborate with, until the subtlest artists create, *on the basis of the common languages*, a personal means of expression which we have to learn in order to understand them.' (*The Three Conventions*, London, 1935, p. 89.) The emphasized clause should be excised.

The ideal observer alone can appreciate the value, in relation to art as a whole, of any further achievement.

The ideal specialist can only appreciate an advance made in his particular direction. Artistic experience within the cleared space is only possible in so far as one's range is less than that of the ideal observer and, in any particular direction, than that of its ideal specialist.

Capacity for artistic experience increases in so far as one is making progress in any direction towards the confines of the cleared space.

Ground covered in any direction ceases to be art for those who have covered it, and, for them, lapses into education or entertainment for those who haven't.

However ponderable from other points of view, from the standpoint of art, those bogged in what has lapsed (for those who have passed any given point) into education or entertainment cease to exist. Only those who are further ahead than themselves are of consequence to those who are making artistic progress. Any relationship with others is a waste of time, of life – a betrayal of art.

To halt or turn back in order to try to help others is to abandon artistic progress, and exchange education for art. There is no altruism in art. It is every man for himself. In so far as he advances, the progress of others may be facilitated, but in so far as he is conscious of affording any such facilitation his concentration on purely artistic objectives is diminished.

From the point of view of the ideal observer nothing has value as art which does not add to the area of the cleared space. For him, everything coming within the cleared space automatically lapses into education or entertainment upon its inclusion.

From the point of view of the ideal specialist nothing in any given direction is of value except its furthest point.

All dicta on art are therefore to be judged in relation (a) to omniscience of human experience, or (b) to the appropriate specialism or specialisms.

All that claims to be art therefore is of value *in inverse ratio* to its comprehensibility and to the extent to which it falls into any particular category.

Artists of any degree whatever are recognizable by their intolerance of what they have surpassed.

Art is incapable of repetition.

No artist is great (or really an artist) unless he reaches some point in the unknown outside the cleared space and then adds to the cleared space.

The total addition made to the cleared space is the measure of greatness as an artist – *at the time the addition is made*.

No achievement in art is permanent – as art.

Great artists of the past diminish in so far as the point or frontier of their particular addition recedes from the latest confines of the cleared space.

They cease to be great artists from the point of view of the ideal observer or any ideal specialist, and acquire compensatory importance in the history of art (the highest kind of knowledge).

They remain artists or great artists only in proportion to the appropriate ignorance (i.e. incapacity for experience) of those for whom they are so.

If great art is compatible with a big popular appeal, it can only be in so far as it contains elements unthinkable to the public.

In direct ratio to its popularity (i.e. its comprehensibility) it is not art.

The greatest art at any given time is that which is comprehensible to the fewest persons of competence and integrity, whether as approximations (a) to the ideal observer or (b) to the requisite ideal specialist. For an artist or critic to pride himself on his knowledge of art is to boast – not of his achievements, still less of his powers – but of his tools.[3]

II

The greatest artist at any given time is the creator of the greatest art as just defined in proportion as it defies ideal specialists and demands the ideal observer.

As the cleared space increases the relative importance of each ideal specialist to the ideal observer decreases. The greatest artist is the greatest critic.

Neither his art nor his criticism need be expressed.[4] The

---

[3] 'La mémoire et les sens ne seront que la nourriture de ton impulsion créatrice.' Rimbaud.
[4] 'Kunst ist Gabe, nicht Wiedergabe.' Herewath Walden.

greatest (non-artist) critic is he who feels most intensely the necessity of overcoming the incomprehensibility in question, and that the more intensely in proportion to his intuitive, and correct, realization than the resolution of it calls for the ideal observer rather than for any ideal specialist or any series of ideal specialists.

It is impossible for the artist to achieve the incomprehensible to him, but he may not know how he knows.

The critic may show him that; but that has nothing to do with art.[5]

The critic's function is to make art comprehensible, and so transform it into education and/or entertainment.

His ability to demonstrate his greatness as a critic, therefore, depends upon the extent or difficulty of the supply of art available for his purpose.

A subsidiary function is, therefore, to stimulate an increase of either of these.

His value lies in the rapidity with which he can perform his function for the most incomprehensible art; his greatness on the extent of the circumference of the cleared space upon which he operates.

His value as a critic is not, however, determined in any way by the number of people for whom he makes the art with which he deals comprehensible. The intimate association of the most important criticism with advanced art precludes more than an extremely limited public for either.[6]

Both operate beyond the farthest limit of education, although the ultimate achievement of both is to advance it.

'Popular art' is a contradiction in terms.

'The educative value of art' is a confusion of functions.

Criticism is inferior to art because art is for it a means to an end – the end of the art to which it is applied.

[5]'It is terribly difficult to accept influences which are necessary, and yet use them only as a means toward the end of shaping one's own being from within, and not to keep on carrying these elements as foreign bodies in one's system, however enthusiastically one may have accepted them at first.' Otto Braun.

[6]'A new synthesis of intellect and spirit has become necessary. A synthesis which is directed towards establishing a new balance of the various parts of man, not with the backward, but with the most highly-developed elements.' Hermann Keyserling.

This inferiority is least discernible when criticism confines itself most to the subsidiary function referred to above; or when it co-operates indissociably with the creative spirit in the artist himself.

Herman Bahr quotes Goethe as pointing out, in his *Data for a History of Colour*, that there are sciences which must transcend themselves and become something higher – that is to say, art.

> Since nothing whole can be created either out of knowledge or out of reflection, because the first is lacking in Inwardness, and the second in Outwardness, we are forced to think of Science (*Wissenschaft*) as Art, whenever we expect a sense of entirety from it . . . But in order that we should be able to fulfil such a demand we must exclude no human force or faculty from scientific participation. The profundity of intuition, a firm contemplation of the present, mathematical depth, physical accuracy, the acme of reason, the keenness of intellect, the phantasy moving and full of yearning, a fond joy of the sensuous – none of these can be omitted in order to seize the propitious moment, and exploit it in a live and fruitful sense, that moment which alone can give birth to a work of art, no matter what its content may be.

Appendix. Types of nonsense in criticism. Cecil Gray's contention that poor poetry suits composers better than great poetry. James Agate's statement that Duse's talent 'must be deemed less than supreme in that it needs masterpieces to feed on'.

7 The Waterside

MacDiarmid's short stories and sketches belong to a genre where fact and fiction mix, and fond reminiscence conjures ironic speculation. The master of the form was R. B. Cunninghame Graham, Mac-Diarmid's friend and a fellow founder-member of the National Party of Scotland in 1928. This item was printed in *The Glasgow Herald* (16 April, 1927). It was collected by Kenneth Buthlay in *The Uncanny Scot* (1968) and reappeared in Alan Bold's anthology *The Thistle Rises* (1984).

THERE was faur mair licht and life – o' a' kind – in the hooses alang the Waterside than onywhere else in the toon. The front windas lookit richt into the water wi' nae trees to daurken them, and the lift was clearer and braider there than owre ony ither pairt o' the toon. There were juist twenty hooses frae the Stane Brig to the Swing Brig, and the toon gaed abruptly up ahint them through a patchwork o' gairdens wi' grey stane wa's to the muckle backs o' the High Street hooses and on to the terraces on the face o' the hill. And on the faur side o' the Water there was naething but the Factory. But the river was braid and a' broken up and fu' o' movement there, and, tho' some o' the loons could thraw a stane frae a'e side to the ither, the Factory seemed faur awa' and could dae naething to impose itsel' on the Waterside windas or oppress them in the least. Abune the Stane Brig lang gairdens, dark wi' auld trees, ran doon to the river frae the backs o' hooses that lookit the ither way and formed a continuation o' the High Street, and aneth the Swing Brig there were the heichs and howes o' a lump o' waste grun' in front o' the New Mill that the Toon Cooncil were usin' as a cinder dump, and owre frae them the Murtholm Woods spielin' the braes o' Warblaw.

Juist abune the Stane Brig there was the meetin' o' the waters whaur the Ewes clashes into the Esk and alow the Swing Brig the Wauchope cam' tumblin' in. But in front o' the Waterside hooses the bed o' the river was fu' o' muckle flat shelfs o' rock they ca'd the Factory Gullets that cut up the water into a' kinds o' loups, and scours, and slithers, and gushes, wi' twa-three deep channels in atween them through which the main flows gaed solid as wa's. Gulls were aye cryin' there and whiles there was a heron standin' on a rock when the water was low, or a kingfisher even. Sae, in the simmer time, or bricht winter days, the hooses alang the Waterside were aye fu' o' a licht and life that made the ongauns o' their inhabitants o' as little consequence as the ongauns o' the rats in the cellars were to them, and the dunt and dirl o' the river was in them like the hert in a man, and they had shoals o' licht and the crazy castin' o' the cloods and the endless squabble o' the gulls in them faur mair even than the folk talkin' and the bairns playin'. It wasna sae much a case o' leevin' your ain life in ane o' thae hooses as bein' pairt and paircel o' the life o' the river. Your hoose wasna your ain. It was wind-and-water ticht in a'e way bit no' in anither. A' the ither hooses in the toon were sober and solid in comparison. And the folk that leeved in them had a guid grip o' their lives. But alang the Waterside they were windy, thriftless, flee-about craturs. The sense was clean washed oot o' them. A' the sense – and a' the stupidity tae. It's only some kinds o' birds that ha'e een like what theirs becam' – cauld and clear and wi' nae humanity in them ava.

The folk up the hill lookit doon on the toon and some o' them pitied it and some o' them felt clean abune't, but the taps o' the hills a' roon aboot that they saw frae their windas kind o' steadied and silenced them. They werena like the Waterside folk; there's a queer difference atween ha'en taps o' hills and taps o' waves aye in yin's life. And the folk in the tree-daurkened hooses were different again – they were slow and secret and aften kind o' sad. And the folk on the High Street had naething but themsel's and ither folk in their lives – they were clannish and fu' o' clash and conceit, and aye comin' an' gaen throughither. But the Waterside folk kept skitin' this way and that. There was neither peace nor profit in their lives. They couldna settle. Their kind o' life was like the dipper's sang. It needit the skelp and slither o' rinnin' water like the bagpipes' drone to fill oot the blanks. Withoot that it was naething but a spraichle o' jerky and meaningless soonds.

There was only a narrow cobbled street between the hooses and the water wa' that stude aboot twa feet high, and was aboot as braid on the tap and syne fell frae aucht to ten fit to the riverside rocks. And dae what ye wad, naething 'ud ever content the bairns but to be scramblin' up on the wa' and rinnin' alang't, and their mithers were aye at their doors wi' their hearts in their mooths. They never kent a meenit's peace.

It was only in the winter time that the water exercised its poo'er owre the haill toon. The hills were hidden in mists then and the folk that were aye accustomed to them were at a loss. They were like a puckle water when a jug braks; they'd tint the shape o' their lives. And the folk in the High Street couldna talk lood eneuch to forget the roarin' o' the spate. It seemed to be underminin' the toon. It was level wi' the tap o' the water wa'. Trunks o' trees, hayrucks, and whiles sheep and kye, cam' birlin' doon on the tap o't. The Waterside folk lived in their doors or windas as gin their hooses had nae insides. They could dae naething but look, or raither be lookit at, through and through, for it was the water that did the lookin' and no' them. There was nae question o' thinkin'. It was faur owre quick and noisy for that. It fair deaved them, and every noo and then a muckle wave loupit in through their een and swirled in their toom harnpans and oot again. That's what I mean when I say that the Waterside folk were brainless craturs. Brains were nae use there. To dae onything ava they'd to use something faur quicker than thocht – something as auld as the water itsel'. And thocht's a dryland thing and a gey recent yin at that.

The Waterside folk couldna stop to think. The High Street folk thocht aboot naething bit themsel's, and a' they did was the outcome o' that. The folk on the hillside were like the sailor's parrot – they didna say muckle, but they were deevils to think. The Waterside folk micht ha'e managed to dae a bit thinkin' in the simmer time when the water was low, but low water, they said, gied them a queer feelin' as if the fronts o' their faces had fa'n aff, that fair paralysed them. They were like the man that tell't the wumman he wanted nane o' her damned silence; and sae they juist stottit aboot like a wheen hens wi' the gapes.

I mind a'e Sunday when the water was higher than onybody had ever seen it afore. They were frichtened for the Swing

Brig. But it had stoppit rainin' a wee by dennertime, and the fules o' High Street folks, and a wheen o' the Hillside yins tae, wad send their bairns to the Sunday schule. To get there they'd to cross the Swing Brig. It was weel named Swing Brig that day. It was as crazy wi' unexpectit movements as the flair o' the Hoose o' Fun at the Glesca Exhibition. Every noo and again the rusty contraption wheenged richt abune the clammer o' the spate. Ye could hear nae ither soon' but the roar o' the water and whiles the whine o' the iron.

Juist at skailin' time for the Sunday schule the rain cam' on again waur than ever. It fell haill water. Faithers and mithers cam' rinnin' doon wi' umbrellas and waterproof coats juist as the bairns were croodin' on to the Brig. And a' at yince it brak in twa haufs and skailed a'body on't into the river like a wheen tea leafs in a sink.

The news spreid like lichtnin'. Afore the bairns struck the water the banks at baith ends o' the Brig were black wi' folk. Men that could soom, and some that couldna, dived richt in and brocht bairns oot. Ithers had run to a tongue o' rock that ran oot into the river a bit faurer doon, and were in time to grab a wheen o' the weans there as they gaed whummlin' by. Atween the Brig and the end o' the cinder dump a back swirl had scoopit oot a hole for itsel', and by guid luck maist o' the bairns were spun into that. Men jumpit in wadin' up to their oxters to rescue them, and a wheen wimmen tae. Human cheens were made frae the tap o' the dump to the middle o' the pool. A'e wumman, in particular, was fair awa' wi't; her bairn had been on the Brig, and she slid doon the cinder brae on her hunkers richt into the pool. She grabbit a wee lass frae a man a bit faurer oot, but when she saw it wasna her ain bairn the doited cratur, withoot kennin' what she was daein', pitched it into the water again. She was frae ane o' the hooses on the Hill – a' thocht and nae sense! Nane o' the High Street folk ventured into the water tho' a' their bairns were rescued; and nane o' the Waterside folk's bairns were on the Brig when it brak. Catch them! But they did the feck o' the savin' wi' an air as muckle as to say: 'If the fules 'ud keep their brats at their ain gate-en's they'd be less nuisance to ither folk.' If it had been the faithers and mithers instead o' the bit bairns, I question whether the Waterside folk 'ud ha'e bothered to rescue them, and even as it was I'm no shair they felt in their herts they were daein' richt – especially on a Sunday.

8 Scottish Gaelic Policy

MacDiarmid's concern with Gaelic culture emerges most strongly in the poetry of *To Circumjack Cencrastus* (1930) and in the early 1940s he welcomed the younger Gaelic poets Sorley MacLean and George Campbell Hay with eager enthusiasm (see Item 20). The following article was contributed to *The Pictish Review* (vol. 1, no. 2, December 1927) – a short-lived journal edited by the sculptor and poet Pittendrigh Macgillivray – and shows the confluence of his concerns in social, educational, linguistic and cultural, as well as more specifically literary, fields.

IT is easy to be mistaken in contemporary estimates of literary tendencies, and the fear is already being expressed in certain quarters that the tentative efforts which have been made during the past few years to initiate a new movement in Scottish letters will be discerned in retrospect as having been a mere continuation of the Burns tradition instead of the breakaway from it its promoters imagine. Are these new writers getting down to anything fundamental, or are they merely elaborating, cleverly enough, the established conceptions of what constitutes Scottish pyschology? It is obvious that if they are only achieving the latter they are not providing the basis of a new development of international or even real national consequence. So long as they fail to demonstrate that the Scottish genius contains other and very different elements than have been associated with it and generally thought to comprise it since the Union, superior elements hitherto hidden by the accepted conceptions, no basis has been secured for any major development of Scottish letters. It is precisely the accepted conceptions which constitute the limitations of Scottish literature. How can they be transcended? Technically, of course, the way to begin is to list all the clichés – all the turns of phrase, characteristics of thought, choice of subject, and tone, etc. – which are deemed peculiarly Scottish, and, while concentrating all the more intensely on Scottish life, introspectively and objectively, to rigidly eschew all these 'kenspeckle' features. Another course is to take styles and forms from other literatures and endeavour to naturalize them in Scottish literature.

It will be found impossible to reproduce these styles and forms without abandoning the stereotyped ways of thinking about subjects and treating them, and this will necessitate new usages of language altogether, and entirely different processes of intellection. The danger here, of course, is that the styles and forms chosen may be unsuitable to Scottish purposes, and may lead to a great deal of relatively futile experimentation. There is another course, and the promise of a Scottish Renaissance will increase immeasurably the more it becomes obvious that young Scottish writers are taking it. Already there are promising signs. This is to seek for fundamental values of our own. How is it to be begun? The answer is obvious as soon as it is realized that what is stultifying our efforts is our absence of tradition. We cannot get deep enough down to distinctive grounds to throw up major forms of our own. The reason for this is that we have been cut off from our past. It is this lack of continuity that keeps all our efforts so comparatively provincial and ineffective. A sense of continuity and tradition can only be recovered by 'connecting up' again with our lost Gaelic culture. This is the background to which we must return if we are ever to establish a Scottish classical culture. Without realizing our relationship, however disguised linguistically, politically, and otherwise, to the Gaelic traditions, we will be unable to rise into major forms. The Scottish Ballads, for example, are not our primitive beginnings, but the debris of a lost culture superior and very different to any that has taken its place. As the late Professor W. P. Ker said:

> One of the difficulties about the ballads is that while so much in them seems to be ancient or even primitive, the rhyming ballad verse is comparatively new. Some of the common ballad devices, particularly that of repetition, seem to be as old as anything in humanity, but the form of verse is not old. How did the folklore themes, the ballad habits of phrasing, find expression before the rhyming stanzas and the new sorts of refrains were introduced from France? Where were the ballads before they were made?

And he answers that

an old civilization with an elaborate literature of its own came to an end in the eleventh century, and there is a great division about that time between the earlier and the latter Middle Ages, and great difficulty in understanding the transition. Modern poetry, including the ballads, begins about the year 1100; we are cut off from the time before that, and from its tastes in poetry as we are not from any of the rhyming poetry – French, Provençal, Italian, German, English – from that time onward.

The discipline of the Bardic colleges is what literature most needs today. The Gaelic Commonwealth suggests solutions to many of our major social problems. The so-called Hebridean songs are to the Gaelic culture we must yet recover what Kailyairdism in Scots is to Dunbar. The first step is to abolish the false Highland-Lowland distinction which has been the main obstacle to Scottish unity, and to restore a national balance to Gaelic policy which has become Westernized and non-centripetal. In other words, the need is to stress the Pictish rather than the Gaelic elements in our Celtic culture. They have been ignored for centuries. The position can best be illustrated by considering first the great resemblances and then the significant differences between a Pictish and a Gaelic cross. They are both Celtic. Fundamentally, they are the same, but they differ in detail.

A recent writer in this connection has very well said, with regard to so-called 'Scottish History', that

> there is in the school books a blurred reference to the coming of Caesar to Britain; a very bald mumbling about Picts and Scots, and coracles coming from Ulster to Argyll; the extinction of the Picts and the triumph of the Scots, a Gaelic race from Ireland, who, a few pages further on (so it seems to the bewildered pupil) become Saxons – the Lowlanders, the mainstay and makers of Scotland. The Gael, on the other hand, is pictured as some poor ignorant savage, handy with dirk and claymore, picturesque when not a nuisance to the king and the feudal barons, for whose sole pleasure and profit, it would seem, Scotland was created. No wonder Caledonia is stern and wild! Our Scottish children are kept in ignorance of their Caledonian forbears, and their susceptible hearts are

won by the ennobling of all the Saxon elements in our ancient Scottish Court and aristocracy.

Briefly recapitulating the true facts in regard to the evolution of the Scottish people – so grotesquely travestied in the popular conceptions – he concludes by saying

> the great broad fact remains that Scotland today is overwhelmingly Gaelic in blood. This ought to be brought out clearly in the teaching of Scottish history in our elementary schools, and a less prominent place given to the doings – not always edifying, however romantic – of the kings and queens and the great feudal figures of a Scotland later than the Gaelic age. Let our children be taught that the ancient Gaels were a race with a culture, skilled in the working of bronze and gold, with a soul for poetry. The music, poetry, and legends of the Gael, becoming more popular and even fashionable in these days, proclaim the culture of the race, and give contradiction to the 'wild Irishry' appellative used by various English and lowland writers.

Happily there are abundant signs of this long-overdue *volte-face* in Scottish historiography. As Dr Angus M'Gillivray, of Dundee, said in his recent presidential address to the Caledonian Medical Society:

> Scottish history, as taught even today in our own schools and universities, cannot be regarded as truly national. It is lopsided because viewed largely from one angle – the Lowlands of Scotland. Thanks to the more enlightened policy of the Scottish History Society, the history of Scotland is now beginning to be treated not as the history of any particular part of the kingdom of Scotland, but as a whole. Our Scottish Educational Department and our four universities could materially assist in this laudable attempt to free Scottish history from geographical bias, the former by making Scottish national history compulsory in the leaving certificates, and the latter by encouraging Scottish national history, not only among their ordinary pass degree students, but especially among their honours and research students.

Those who adopt the usual scornful attitude of English-educated people to such a proposal may well be reminded of what Sir Samuel Ferguson replied to like criticisms with regard to Ireland. 'We dare say,' he wrote,

> had it been the policy of any party in ancient Greece to win the thoughts and affections of the Greeks from their own country, so as to make them a safer provincial dependency of some earlier civilized neighbouring nation – Syria, say, or Egypt – this sort of argument or expostulation would have been often employed by them: where is the use of tracing back the barbarous traditions of the House of Atreus? Why waste time on idle enumerations of the pedigrees of Inachus? Turn your thoughts to Egypt. The glorious actions of Sesostris are something, indeed, worthy of men of enlightenment. The sources of the Nile, and the causes of its overflow, you may investigate with profit and delight. Indulge no more in the idle dream of being Greeks – North-West Egyptians, methinks, would sound more proper.

Many generations of Scots have been seduced by like accents. The process has gone so far that it is difficult for Scots today to realize that just as the Greeks would have foregone the power to produce one of the world's greatest civilizations if they had listened to arguments such as these, so by listening to them in respect of England, Scotland has relinquished potentialities no less great. These must be recovered. Only thus can we develop a 'Scottish idea' complementary to Dostoevsky's Russian idea (Dostoevsky's mistake was to imagine that Russia alone could obviate the robotization of Europe), and in so doing demonstrate that Professor Denis Saurat divined aright the larger hope of the Scottish Renaissance movement when he wrote that in achieving its immediate objectives it might do more – it might help to save Europe. But, as Saurat said, to 'burn what we have hitherto adored' is the prerequisite of such a Scottish Renaissance and a great many popular misconceptions of Scottish character and culture must be consumed in the fires of our new purpose.

9 Clan Albainn

'Clan Albainn' (or 'Clann Albann', or any one of a number of variant spellings) was the name given to a group of people who, MacDiarmid claimed, were working as the spearhead of the National Party of Scotland – a 'Scottish Sinn Fein' who were being organized 'specifically in order to act'. After a visit to the Irish Republic in 1928 (where he met De Valera as well as W. B. Yeats), MacDiarmid was convinced that the Irish example should be followed up in Scotland. The National Party of Scotland was founded in 1928. A series of articles which began in May 1930 in the national *Daily Record* discussed the 'Sinn Fein policy' and led to Compton Mackenzie being investigated by the Special Branch. John MacCormick, a founding member and the secretary of the National Party, denied the existence of any such 'secret society' and Lewis Spence, another founding member, criticized MacDiarmid's 'lunatic ideas'. MacDiarmid's response was the following item, published in the nationalist literary and cultural journal edited by J. H. Whyte, *The Modern Scot* (vol. 1, no. 2, Summer 1930).

THE idea that Clan Albainn has been repudiated by the National Party – and that the overwhelming support of the appeal made at the Annual Delegate Conference for a militant policy instead of narrow nationalist and anti-Irish manoeuvres has been exaggerated out of all proportion – can be speedily disposed of – by the publication of the verbatim note taken of the proceedings and the actual figures of the various divisions.

In an article in the Glasgow *Daily Record*, Mr Lewis Spence had the hardihood to say that I had undone much of the good work accomplished by the devoted services and sacrifices of others. I do not intend to reply to this ridiculous charge in the meantime. The actual findings of the Conference and certain of Mr Spence's own speeches (notably one in which he supported my demand for a far more strongly worded new Covenant for signature at Bannockburn) only require to be set alongside that article to expose the true situation. But Mr Spence denounced secret societies as un-Scottish and Clan Albainn as cowardly. I have three replies to make to that. (1) In a more recent issue of the same paper Mr Spence denounces false Celticism and says that 'real Caledonianism'

– which he associates with an alleged secret second Gaelic of which he boasts few Celtic workers know anything and which, with elaborate mystery-making, he refuses to give any clue to – is in no need of revival. Mr Spence can hug his esotericism; I and the others concerned with the Scottish Movement in its various phases do not care a brass farthing for his Secret Second Gaelic or the Horseman's Society. Our secret society of Clan Albainn has no silly mummery about it and is directed to purely practical ends; its 'secret' element is simply like that to be found in all political organizations, no matter how open and above-board they may pretend to be. (2) As to the charge of cowardice, the popping of a toy-pistol in North Midlothian hasn't made panic-stricken pacifists of us all. But the real answer is this – does Mr Spence deny that several years ago he and others who have denounced our militant intentions were actively canvassing forcible and illegal measures? If so, I shall be happy to publish the relevant correspondence in a subsequent issue of *The Modern Scot*. For the time being, I simply assert that Scotland will never secure a measure of independence worth having without being forced to adopt means similar to those taken by the Irish, and that those of us who during the past ten years or so have been actively engaged in the Scottish Movement have never disguised this, but been fully alive to it all along and discussed it repeatedly. (3) Is it more cowardly to contemplate, and organize for, militant action than to blether on in futile protests while ignominiously acquiescing in increasing English control and the progressive evanquishment of Scottish interests? The charge of cowardice can more aptly be brought against the majority of the Scottish MPs who voted for measures of Scottish Home Rule but tamely let the matter drop when the English outvoted them, instead of coming back to their constituencies and organizing a movement which would have rendered it impossible for the Sassenachs to eviscerate their representative functions in this contemptuous and unparalleled fashion.

The organization of Clan Albainn is going steadily ahead. I have had letters of approval and support from all over the country. An Aberdeen friend writes that, judging by the people he has talked to, there will be ten ready to join Clan Albainn for every one who will join the National Party, as soon as the former begins to *act*. All the evidence that has reached me corroborates his view. And so far as the National Party is concerned, its farcical situation is revealed in the editorial notes of the June issue of the *Scots Independent*, which point out that following the sensational disclosures anent Clan Albainn, all sorts of newspapers who have hitherto jeered at or ignored the National Party have now hastened to pat it on the back and assure it that it has an unanswerable case – provided it holds to constitutional methods and eschews extremism! The intervention of the Duke of Montrose is another amusing episode. His Grace contends that Scottish people can look after their own interests without the help of Irish, Poles, English, and other aliens. The answer is – then why haven't they done so? Even His Grace's efforts over many years have failed to stir them up, and Scottish interests have been sacrificed all along the line. In any case, these aliens are citizens of Scotland and their interests are bound up with its condition. Does His Grace propose to disfranchise them – or, like Mr Spence, to evict them? Why can't he face the practical political situation, recognize them for the important, permanent, and increasing factors they are in our electorate, and be ready to welcome any signs they show of identifying themselves with Scottish interests and becoming true citizens of our country? They cannot be worse Scots than the majority of our own people have been, and are. It is high time to stop stammering about the traditional virtues of the Scottish people and face practical realities. Conditions in Scotland today are so desperately bad that help will be welcome from whatever source it comes. His Grace has rendered precious little. At the big St Andrew's Hall Demonstration of the National Party, shortly after the last Glasgow Rectorial, he came on to the platform and spoke along with Cunninghame Graham, Compton Mackenzie, and myself. Prior to doing so all he asked was an assurance that the National Party was independent of all the English political parties. He received that assurance and supported the Party on that basis; yet a little later he supported the Liberal candidate in the North Midlothian by-election against Mr Lewis Spence, the Nationalist nominee. Adversity makes strange bedfellows; it is amusing to see His Grace and Mr Spence making common cause against Clan Albainn now.

Clan Albainn is going on; and in this connection special attention may be drawn to Mr MacDonnell's article on Sinn Fein in the June *Scots Independent*, and to Mr Kennedy's article in these pages. Clan Albainn is well leavened with Douglasites; and even the National Party Conference agreed to an Aberdeen resolution and set up a special Committee to report on the economic policy of the National Party, with special reference to Major Douglas's proposals. *Verb. sap!*

There is one other matter. 'The old gang' are getting the wind up very badly – so badly that Mr Hugh Roberton has been rorting off about 'genius-discoverers', forgetful alike of his own adventures in this gentle art in relation to Mrs Kennedy-Fraser in music, and that great poet, Mr Joe Corrie, and of his complete failure to recognize true merit, while 'Mr Incognito' published an extraordinary article in the *Record* about George Douglas Brown. He said that Brown, if he had lived, would have been ashamed to have had his name remembered in respect of *The House with the Green Shutters*. That may be true; Brown may have been a poor critic – but *The House with the Green Shutters*, however one-sided, is a work of indisputable genius of which he and all his contemporaries and subsequent Scottish writers would have far more reason to be proud than of all the other Scottish novels published since it put together. 'Mr Incognito' did not qualify his denigratory essay with any recognition whatever of its outstanding power and its great, timely, and, alas, still lonely, service to Scottish letters. But an effective reply must wait until such time as 'Mr Incognito's' pseudonym is set aside. His own reputation then will assuredly suffer the injury he attempted to wreak on *The House with the Green Shutters*. It is time these old men ceased their exhibitions of senile jealousy. They have not done anything for Scottish Arts themselves that gives them any title to admonish their juniors: and whatever little reputations they may have secured in this direction or that, assuredly they have no critical stature. With them may be mentioned the fatuous writer on 'The Forcing of Art' in *The Scots Observer*. The contribution was characteristically anonymous; if it had been signed it would have been at once discerned that the writer was a mere nonentity. But its silly arguments showed that in any case. It advocated a

Micawber-like attitude of waiting hopefully for something to turn up in the arts, and declared that tendencious criticism could not engender creative developments. The whole history of arts and letters (as Yeats shows conclusively in one of his essays) proves the opposite. Literary and artistic movements have seldom 'just growed' like Topsy, and in Scotland we have depended long enough in vain on this theory to justify a different effort now. And by comparison with previous periods in Scottish Arts and Letters this change-over has already amply justified itself. But the anonymous writer (like many others of his kidney recently) inveighs against 'coteries' and accuses them of 'self-advertisement', etc. Let him and his like just specify quite clearly in future by name against whom they are making these scandalous charges, and the issues will be speedily cleared.

As Revd W. H. Hamilton and others have abundantly shown, the worst form of self-advertisement is that which denounces (without specifying names or giving any proof) the self-advertising of others; while as to 'general common-sense', the 'general common-sense' of the Duke of Montrose and his like has not achieved so much in any direction as to have any title to any intelligent person's respect. Ideas proclaimed as 'lunatic' and 'impossible' by mediocre conventionalists have justified themselves so frequently and magnificently in human history that it may well be hoped the same will prove true in Scotland's case now. It is Scotland's only hope.

> A further article in *The Modern Scot* (vol. 2, no. 1, April 1931, entitled 'Scottish National Development, Civic Publicity, Tourism and other matters', ended with a section entitled 'Clann Albann'.

. . . [N]othing will be done by the older people. The future of Scotland lies with the left wing of the younger generation, who realize the necessity of 'No Compromise' and have nothing in common with the sort of 'nationalism' now being promulgated by ladies (of either sex) with sweets and lollipops in their mouths, like fledglings being fed on the nest. I see that overtures are being made to induce the Duke of Montrose to join the National Party. Neither he nor any other 'elder Scot' is of the slightest use, and must do more harm than good. The Editor of *The Modern Scot* was right when he said in a recent address that our business is to demonstrate the stupidity of all these people and knock them out of public life. The fact that after decades of public mis-service, during which their country has gone from bad to worse in every direction, they have had to be kicked into a simulation of national purposefulness by a penny daily should be enough in itself to dispose of their claims to attention. It is regrettable that there has not even been any effective group within the National Party to seize the opportunity and drive home the full rigour of the lesson. The Party's methods are wrong. Irish Home Rule, Votes for Women, and other political successes in Great Britain and other countries in recent times have all required militant methods. No degree of Scottish autonomy of the slightest value will be secured without recourse to the same means, by which alone the necessary dynamic to address themselves to anything worth while can be generated in the necessary minority of our people. Once that minority is available we will go ahead – we do not need the others. Despite what is being said in certain quarters that minority is beginning to manifest itself. Clann Albann is surely if slowly growing and maturing its plans. Let there be no mistake about this. *And militant action has already been taken with impunity in one significant instance. The authorities deemed it better not to intervene; the action of the militants was entirely successful and was not subsequently reversed but allowed to stay. But the authorities are so well aware of this militant undercurrent that they prevented any mention of this incident in any of the papers, although steps had been taken by the militants to see that the papers were quickly informed. Subsequent efforts have failed to induce the editors of any of the daily or evening papers to publish any reference to the matter.*

But official steps of that sort have never prevented the development of radical nationalist movements elsewhere and they will not be allowed to do so in Scotland either. The fact that the authorities are acting along these lines show that they have learned nothing from the Irish 'troubles' and other precedents, and that Scotland must take the same hard way to regain that independence without which any talk of

Scottish National Reconstruction is but 'sounding brass and tinkling cymbals'.

After this, the first two points of the 'Summary' of the essay read:

1. Will without power is worthless.
2. Local efforts unrelated to a thoroughly thought-out scheme of national reconstruction are futile.

It is worth noting that 'Clan Albann' became the title for a proposed poem, in which MacDiarmid intended to blend an allegorical vision of Scotland with an account of his own life. This proposal lapsed as MacDiarmid's poetry was published in different forms. But 'Clann Albainn' did not entirely disappear. The 'Clan Albainn Society' is mentioned again in Item 27, 'Knoydart Land Seizures'. The notion of a militant, activist nationalist group was in evidence again in 1948.

10 English Ascendancy in British Literature

This essay was accepted by T. S. Eliot for publication in his highly-esteemed journal *The Criterion* in 1931. Eliot and MacDiarmid met to discuss the ideas raised in the essay in 1930 and MacDiarmid later wrote to the novelist Neil Gunn referring to the publication of the essay as 'carrying the war into the enemies' camp'. The essay reappeared in *At the Sign of the Thistle* (1934). This is the version reprinted here, with the footnotes MacDiarmid added. It was republished in Kenneth Buthlay's anthology, *The Uncanny Scot*, and remains a seminal statement in MacDiarmid's formulation of the political struggle in which literature is engaged.

THE Consultative Committee of the Board of Education has just published a report on 'The Primary School' in which there is a passage stressing the need to realize that there are many varieties of English; that it is not the function of schools to decry any special or local peculiarities of speech; and that a racy native turn of speech is better than any stilted phraseology, especially for literary purposes.

This is excellently said and represents a departure or suggested departure in Departmental attitude which, it is to be hoped, may be speedily followed up in the schools themselves, relieving the children of tomorrow from a subtle but far-reaching psychological outrage which has been inflicted on many generations of pupils and seriously affected the quality and direction of those of them who had literary inclinations. The passage may be commended in particular to the attention of the BBC[1] and to such typical spokesmen of the contrary

[1] This issue, and the whole range of allied issues, with their vital bearings on the arts and the future of civilization, is illuminatingly touched upon in an admirable article on 'Broadcasting' in *The Times Literary Supplement* of 7th December, 1933, where, as against standardization, it is pointed out that 'it may be urged that intelligibility should be attained by a contrary method: of familiarizing the whole nation with the dialects of the parts – a method which might tend to enrich the common language with the more vital regional expressions. . . . Besides, of late the tyranny of print has shown itself stronger; language becomes for many a visual affair; its aural basis has almost been lost. A lack of vitality in poetry may be attributed to this.' I would add that in my view the right way is along the lines taken in his later work by James Joyce, whose multi-linguistic medium, in which elements

spirit as Sir John Squire, who thinks that Burns might just as well have written in English, and Mr St John Ervine, who declares that 'we are resolved to use language for its purpose, the understanding of each other, and not the preservation of quaintnesses or the indulgence of literary idiosyncrasies'.

The essence of Mr Ervine's arguments (and practically the whole case for 'correct English') is given away when he exclaims: 'What would be the use of writing Ulster plays full of dialect expressions if nobody outside Ulster could understand them and there were not enough playgoers in Ulster to enable a dramatist to earn a living? Tennyson wrote in the dialect of Lincolnshire. He also wrote in the language of England. Which Tennyson is known, the first or the second?' That is certainly one question, but it begs many far more important ones, and a Scottish writer may be allowed to give it a Scottish answer by asking another question: 'Which was the better dramatist, Mr St John Ervine when he was struggling to get plays with Ulster dialect elements a London presentation (with a non-success which accounts for the intolerance of his "English ascendancy" attitude now) and producing such comparatively excellent work as *John Ferguson*, or Mr St John Ervine, resolved on the flesh-pots of Egypt, and winning the London success, and international vogue of a kind, denied to his earlier and better work with such a production as *The First Mrs Fraser*?' Burns knew what he was doing when he reverted from eighteenth century English to a species of synthetic Scots and was abundantly justified in the result. He was not contributing to English literature, but to a clearly defined and quite independent tradition of Scottish poetry hailing from the days of Dunbar and the other great fifteenth-century 'makars' – the golden age of Scottish poetry when the English impulse seemed to have gone sterile and Scotland, not England, was apparently destined to produce the great poetry of the United Kingdom. To ask why this promise was not redeemed and why English, a far less concentrated and expressive language, became the medium of such an incomparably greater succession

of at least fifteen languages may be discerned, may be almost unreadable, but becomes generally splendidly intelligible and delightful when read. Nor has the cosmopolitan range of his vocabulary made his medium less Irish – on the contrary, it is far more Irish than ever, as can be appreciated by hearing his own gramophone record reading of 'Anna Livia Plurabelle'.

of poets, involves deep questions of the relationship of literature to economic, political and other considerations and both the causal and the casual in history; but at the moment it is more germane to ask if the potentialities of the Scottish literary tradition can yet be realized? There are signs that they may be. The problem of the British Isles is the problem of English Ascendancy. Ireland, after a protracted struggle, has won a considerable measure of autonomy; Scotland and Wales may succeed in doing the same; but what is of importance to my point in the meantime is that, in breaking free (or fairly free) politically, Ireland not only experienced the Literary Revival associated with the names of Yeats, 'A.E.', Synge and the others, but has during the past half century recovered almost entirely her ancient Gaelic literature. Dr Douglas Hyde tells us that in his early days highly-educated Irishmen were incapable of conceiving that in this whole corpus there was anything worth recovering, let alone an entire classical tradition, with its own elaborate technique, its own very different but (if only because incomparable) not inferior values which maintained itself intact – in active intercourse with all contemporary European developments, but unadulterated by them in the integrity of its own modes – for at least two thousand years, and has (as has Icelandic literature) an alternative value of prime consequence when set against the Greek and Roman literatures which are all that most of us mean when we speak of 'the Classics'. One may well speculate what the results today would have been if this great literature, instead of being virtually proscribed by the 'English Ascendancy' policy and practically forgotten, had been concurrently maintained with the development of 'English Literature'. Would such a synthesis or duality of creative output (each element of it so very different that they could have complemented and 'corrected' each other in a unique and invaluable fashion) not have been infinitely better than the sorry imperialism which has thrust Gaelic and dialect literatures outwith the pale and concentrated on what has become to use Sir William Watson's phrase, 'scriptive English' – with consequences which may yet result in a drastic relegation of all the modern English poetry from, say, Wordsworth down to the Georgians? There are already signs of that; Mr H. P. Collins in his *Modern Poetry* dismisses almost all the modern English poets as of no abiding value, and draws special attention to the comparative stature of Charles Doughty, while acutely emphasizing that Doughty failed, not because he used a species of Anglo-Saxon, but because he used it archaically. Mr Robert Graves, in his *Contemporary Techniques of Poetry*, deals illuminatingly with the interrelations of poetry and politics, and in a particularly suggestive passage emphasizes the extent to which English poetry has lost its native rhythms and joined itself to strange gods. And Mr G. R. Elliott, in his *The Cycle of Modern Poetry*, contends that

> Wordsworth short-circuited the life of poetry. That is why she has such a 'short uneasy motion' today. She is still caught in the round of naturalistic theory and emotion into which the magic of the greater poets of the past century conjured her; and that circuit, *always limited enough*, has now become (in Hobbes's phrase) 'nasty, short, and brutish' – or, at best, vivaciously galvanic. No wonder quite a few of our younger writers, especially in England, show symptoms of wanting to break away desperately from that antarctic rotation. They have impulses toward Greek humanism on the one hand or medieval religion on the other.

He goes on to say:

> These two great traditions, however, are vitally united in Milton. Our poetry cannot have a second real renaissance, a forward movement taking with it the social consciousness of the English race – which the eighteenth-century poets reflected shallowly and the nineteenth-century poets overrode – until Milton shall have for us as full a significance, relatively, as Homer had for the Greeks on the eve of the Periclean Age. Of course, civilization in the Renaissance had come to such a complexity that Milton (unlike Homer) had to have his Shakespeare, by way of complement, and Shakespeare had to have his Milton.

I think we want to cast our eyes in many other directions, as well as towards Milton, in the present plight of poetry, which he admirably defines when he says:

Many critics agree that poetry today has come into a kind of dilemma, but their opinions differ as to the kind. Most of the views I have read seem to me either too exclusive, considering the comprehensive nature of poetry; or too contemporaneous, considering that the main impulsions of our present poetic movement are at least a century old. The outstanding fact is that the great poetic impulse that rose in the later eighteenth century and culminated in the nineteenth, the Romantic or Naturistic impulse, or whatever one wishes to call it, is now pretty well exhausted. The wheel has come full circle; a cycle is ending. Poetry today, in England and America, is groping for a fresh direction. Many sharp tangents have been tried during the past twenty years; but they have proved to have a sharp *recurvous* tendency. Meteors hailed as heralding a new system, a twentieth-century poetry, have proved to be rockets. In short, poetry has not yet hitched her wagon to a new star. She is still caught in the dying orbit of the nineteenth-century mind and art. . . . Our poetry from Blake and Wordsworth on has continually believed itself to have the 'clearest call and veriest touch of powers primordial' when, really, the 'call' was a distant echo and the 'touch' was a passing breeze of naturistic or spiritistic doctrine – for these two varieties of absolutism foment each other, and now that electrons are beginning to look like angels, God knows what variety of the Unseen All may come next! That is why modern poetry, with its remarkable array of poetically gifted persons, from Wordsworth to Hardy, could not come near the highest level of the Renaissance on the one hand, nor make a sustained appeal to common sense on the other. Whitman intended, more than any poet had ever done, to represent common humanity – and he became the prophet of an esoteric aesthetic cult.

It is not only writers like Messrs Collins, Graves and Elliott, who show 'how the wind is blowing' amongst those mainly concerned with the traditions and future of English letters, no less than amongst those of us in Ireland, Scotland and Wales, who, to put it frankly, see no reason why the whole English tradition from Shakespeare to the present day should not be as completely lost to British, and world, consciousness as Ancient Gaelic Literature was little more than half a century ago. In contradistinction to Mr St John Ervine most of the recent writers on the English language – e.g. Dr J. Y. T. Greig in *Breaking Priscian's Head* and Mr Basil de Selincourt in *Pomona* – are concerned with the exhaustion of English and the prospect that, as it becomes more and more of a world-language, it will become progressively useless for higher literary purposes (which, *pace* Mr Ervine, have never had much to do with whether their practitioners could make a living at them or write for more than 'a little clan'), while, in the preface to his *Poems of Thirty Years* Mr Gordon Bottomley expresses similar ideas and refers to the increasing difficulty of writing poetry in so-called 'standard English'. It may be noted also, as, at least, a curious coincidence, that Dr Laurie Magnus in the preface to his *Dictionary of European Literature*, Herr Spengler in the *Downfall of the Western World*, and Count Keyserling in *Europe* all look for the next great impulse and development in European culture – not to any of the countries which use a great world-language and have already a major literary tradition – but to one of the smaller countries. The use of a little-known language has little or no effect either in keeping products in it (owing to the lack of sufficient criticism) to lower standards than those operating in great literatures where competition is keen, or in debarring its writers from international influence, as is shown by such cases as those of Ibsen and Strindberg. (I first heard of Padraic O'Conaire, the Irish short-story writer, though his inclusion in a Danish anthology.) Most modern European literatures have been, and are, very differently resolved from Mr St John Ervine in regard to the use of language, as is shown by the creation of Landsmaal in Norway, the revivals of Provençal and Catalan, the vast amount of linguistic experimentation that has been going on in recent Russian literature, with the progressive de-Frenchification and de-Latinization of the Russian tongue, the use of *skaz* (the reproduction of accentual peculiarities) and *zaumny* (cross-sense, as in Lewis Carroll), the invention of new words by writers such as Remisov, in profound sympathy with the creative genius of the language or of an *ad hoc* new language for each new work, as in Kruchonyk, not to mention, nearer home, the employment of slang by such writers as Aristide Bruant or Carco in France (to cite the first two names that occur to me), or the multi-linguistic work of James Joyce.

Literature, so far from manifesting any trend towards uniformity or standardization, is evolving in the most disparate ways; and there are few literatures in which dialect elements, and even such extreme employments of – and plays upon – them as render them permanently untranslatable and unintelligible to all but a handful of readers in their own countries, are not peculiarly and significantly active. On this account (as isolating it from general contemporary tendency which must have some deep-seated relation to the needs of modern, and prospective, consciousness) it is a pity that English literature is maintaining a narrow ascendancy tradition instead of broad-basing itself on all the diverse cultural elements and the splendid variety of languages and dialects, in the British Isles. (I do not refer here to the Empire, and the United States of America,[2] though the evolution of genuine independent literatures in all of these is a matter of no little consequence and, already clearly appreciated in America, is being increasingly so realized in most of the Dominions, which is perhaps the cultural significance of the anti-English and other tendencies in most of them which are making for those changes in the Imperial organization which will deprive England of the hegemony it has maintained too long.) To recognize and utilize these, instead of excluding them, could only make for its enrichment. It is absurd that intelligent readers of English, who would be ashamed not to know something (if only the leading names, and roughly, what they stand for) of most Continental literatures, are content to ignore Scottish, Irish, and Welsh Gaelic literatures, and Scots Vernacular literature. Surely the latter are nearer to them than the former, and the language difficulty no

[2]'Before 1880 American Literature was, on the whole, dominated by Europeanism; by 1930 it had, on the whole, freed itself from that domination. . . . No nation has yet produced a great literature until it found a new voice to express a new vision, and a new interpretation of the universal kaleidoscope' – *American Literature, 1830–1930*, by A. C. Ward. See also V. F. Calverton's *The Liberation of American Literature*, reviewing which, Professor Herbert Read says: 'All this has its bearing on the question of a Scots literature. A Scots literature for Scotland is one thing, and such literature must, in accordance with these views, be based on a native Scots language – that is to say, the remoter it is from English, the purer as literature it will be; at the same time, its appeal will be confined to those who know Scots, but the more purely national it is, the more likely it is to be universal and translatable. Anything else is a local inflection of English, and as such a departure from purity and universality.'

greater.[3] These Gaelic, and Scots dialect poets were products of substantially the same environment, and concerned for the most part with the same political, psychological, and practical issues, the same traditions and tendencies, the same landscapes, as poets in English to whom, properly regarded, they are not only valuably complementary, but (in view of their linguistic, technical, and other divergencies) corrective. Confinement to the English central stream is like refusing to hear all but one side of a complicated case – and in view of the extent to which the English language is definitely adscripted in certain important moral and psychological directions, and incapable of dealing with certain types of experience which form no inconsiderable part of certain other European literatures, and may well be of far greater consequence to the future of humanity as a whole than the more 'normal matters' with which it is qualified to deal, becomes a

---

[3] It must be remembered, of course, that it was only with the utmost difficulty and against precisely the same sort of opposition and arguments as we are now contending – that Elizabeth Elstob succeeded in preventing English treating its own Anglo-Saxon background (and where would English studies be without that now?) in precisely the same way as it has treated the other minority elements in our midst. The attitude is not a new one; as Dr Laurie Magnus points out in his *History of European Literature*, Molière's enemies said 'he could not write, because his characters spoke the language of their class: we remember how Sir Philip Sidney "dare not allow" Spenser to frame his style "to an old rustic language, since neither Theocritus in Greek, Virgil in Latin, nor Sanazar in Italian, did affect it." ' A common way of trying to meet the case is that suggested by Professor H. J. C. Grierson when, writing of Robert Henryson, he says: 'At Columbia University this year Professor Krapp brought out a complete translation in modern English of *Troilus and Criseyde*. I have not, I confess, read it, and am a little afraid to do so. But it is worth while to let a wider audience become familiar with one of the greatest of English narrative poems. Might it not be worth while trying a rendering in the Scots of today of some of the best of Henryson's fables, as an experiment? I will leave it at that.' Professor Grierson's fear is better justified than the experiment he suggests. Probably in such a case what would happen would be akin to those feats whereby the American anthologist, Mr Louis Untermeyer, amongst many similar achievements, modernized the line in Chaucer's 'Wife of Bath', 'Housbondes at chirche-dore she hadde fyve' into 'She'd had five church-door husbands'; omitted verses 14, 16, and 17 entirely in 'The Twa Sisters of Binnorie', ran verses 10 and 11 together, and added a charming ending of his own; and reduced 'Sir Patrick Spens' from 22 verses to 13, conveniently drowning Sir Patrick on the way out to Norway instead of on the way back, and in the final verse transformed 'half-owre, half-owre to Aberdour' into 'O forty miles off Aberdeen'!

sort of self-infliction of an extensive spiritual and psychological blindness. Few literatures offer within themselves so rich a range of alterative values, of material for comparative criticism, as does, not English, but British, meaning by the latter that common culture – in *posse*, rather than *in esse* – which includes not only English (and English dialect) literature, but the Gaelic and Scots Vernacular literatures as well. This can be seen at a glance. To institute certain comparisons in English literature one has to compare the present with the past. But if one takes in Gaelic literature, the ancient technique, even the tone, is practically unchanged; the comparison is with the changed English present and the unchanged Gaelic present. The point need not be pursued.

It is time, so far as Scottish literature in particular is concerned, to do as the Irish have done in their case, and reverse the attitude that has hitherto prevailed – exemplified by the late Professor J. H. Millar, who began his *Literary History of Scotland* with the disconcerting remark: 'With the Celtic literature of the Highlands we have here no concern. Our business is with the literature of the English-speaking Scots.' The phases of Scottish poetry – the lets and hindrances of its evolution – cannot be properly understood if the fact that great poets like Alasdair MacMhaighstir Alasdair, Duncan Ban MacIntyre, and Iain Lom wrote gloriously of Scotland and Scottish matters in a language of which the great majority of Scottish people know nothing, but against which they are still deeply prejudiced, is not taken into consideration and, along with it, the facts that at a certain period the best Scottish poets wrote in Latin, and that, again, later, even those who were continuing or interested in Scots Vernacular poetry were practically ignorant of the 'Auld Makars' and unable to see its distinctive course in proper sequence and perspective, while, on the other hand, modern Scots Vernacular poetry has been sadly parochialized by a tendency to regard 'Scottish' and 'Kailyard' as synonymous and to stigmatize the work of a John Davidson, or a John Gawsworth, or a Frederick Branford as 'un-Scottish'. Let us have an all-in view of the literary production of our country for a change. Sectionalism has not helped our cultural development; the broader endeavour may. Apart from that, there is no other way in which Scottish writers can contribute proportionately (in quality) to the common stock, for, as Edwin Muir has pointed out, no Scotsman writing in English has done first-class work, indispensable or even relevant to the main line of English literary evolution. The Scottish contribution could be completely excised and leave English literature practically unaffected. Or, as Professor Gregory Smith puts it [in *Scottish Literature*]: 'The Scottish contribution will remain eccentric, fantastic, whimsical – never essential.' In other words, Scotsmen must remain creatively inferior unless their own line lies in a different direction than a mere subsidiary to English letters. My attitude is that of an English music critic who recently wrote:

> As a nation we cannot keep time; we cannot play the 'cretic dactyl' at the beginning of the seventh symphony, or the broken triplet for strings in the Tannhauser March, nor can we sing the triplet in Bach's 'Et resurrexit' clearly. And we take no shame, because we didn't write that music. But let us then study and absorb the music that we did evolve and write music of our own, for 'we can do no other'.

It is time each of the British elements – English, Irish, Welsh, Scots – realized that.

There is nothing in an all-in attitude to prevent us from 'distinguishing and dividing'. Rather will it enable us to do so more completely and effectively. It will preserve us from the absurd limitation of Mr Graves's outlook on Scots poetry – a limitation due to just such a superior and uninformed attitude as led another recent English critic to hail a translation of Brian Merriman's 'Midnight Court' as a *rara avis* in Irish Gaelic literature in singular and refreshing contrast to the 'Celtic Twilight'. If he had troubled to learn more about Irish Gaelic Literature he would have known that hard realism and sharp satire were far more typical of it than the stars and shadows of Yeats. Above all, it will rid us of the fallacy to which Mr Graves gives further currency when he attributes the alleged conservatism of Scots verse to the fact that 'English is the normal language of those who write it'. Even if this were true, and did not raise the question: 'Yes – but which English?' we would draw his attention to the case of Sir Walter Scott and remind him of the shepherd who wrote (see *The Private Letter Books of Sir Walter Scott*, page 321): 'I cannot help telling you that I am astonished, perfectly astonished, how ye have acquired the Scottish dialect and phraseology so exactly. Certainly neither your education not studies could have discovered ought of that antiquated language; yet when ye chose to adopt it ye have it as truly as if ye knew no other, but had lived in the most sequestered nook of the Forest all your life.'

The differences of Scottish and English poetry have been very inadequately studied. In his essay on the Ballads in *Latitudes*, Mr Muir has very effectively brought out and commented on the profound differences between Scottish and English ballads – the tremendous concision and imaginative strength of the former; the comparatively domestic character of the latter. They are entirely different in kind, and the best of the Scottish ballads move on a far higher plane. Professor H. J. C. Grierson in *The Background of English Literature*, in the title essay and in certain passages of the essay on Byron, has also made a number of useful points with regard to the differences between English and Scottish mentality, while in Mr Daniel Corkery's *Hidden Ireland* – that fascinating study of the Munster bards of the Penal Age – there is a detailed analysis of the differences between Scottish and Irish Jacobite songs which should not escape the attention of anyone contemplating any constructive critical effort on behalf of Scottish poetry. More research of this kind is long overdue and necessary. Above all, care should be taken not to force consideration of the course of Scottish poetry into a purely English mould, in the same way that Scottish history has been harmed by being forced into the mould of English constitutionalist conceptions – a distortion from which the new school of Scottish researchers is only beginning to liberate it.

In his *Defence of Ryme* Samuel Daniel very well said: 'Every language hath her proper number or measure fitted to use and delight. All verse is but a frame of words confined within certain measure – which frame of words consisting of Rithmus or Metrum, Number or Measure, are disposed into divers fashions according to the humour of the composer and the set of the time.' Nothing need be said here of the profound linguistic differentiation of Scottish and English people; the most amazing thing about the Scots Vernacular is not its decline but its persistence and the extent of its currency still, while the subtleties of Gaelic speech, and the extent to which they are removed from English, need no comment. It is Daniel's second point on which attention must concentrate – 'the set of the time'. And the trouble here is that few, if any, of our people have a sufficient sense of the difference in historical incidence between Scotland and England. As Mr Donald Carswell says:

> There are few contrasts in history more remarkable than that which prevailed between North and South Britain in the eighteenth century. For England the character of the eighteenth century consisted, not in its events, important as these were, but in its culture. It was not so much an epoch as a philosophy. Its guiding principle, equilibrium, was applied vigorously to every department of life (except perhaps the convivial) and with conspicuous success to the business of government. Englishmen felt secure; and if this security engendered self-satisfaction, it did at least allow them to cultivate their gardens to some purpose. Unfortunately, the philosophy of equilibrium was unable to cross the Tweed. For Scotland the eighteenth century had an entirely different meaning and content, which are reflected even in the romantic idealizations of the period that are current today. To the English mind the eighteenth century conjures up an agreeable picture of Beau Nash, Dr Johnson, fox-hunting squires, bottle-nosed parsons, and hearty innkeepers. To the Scot it is the century of Rob Roy and Prince Charlie – an unstable, adventurous, even heroic century, full of bitter-sweet memories. It was in fact an era that, far from being static, was marked by violent and bewildering change.

Similar contrasts – even deeper, if in some respects less obvious – differentiate the whole course of English and Scottish history, and a clear view of the difference between English and Scottish literature, and their very different possibilities today, can only be had if this is kept continuously in mind.

Unfortunately for the great majority of Scots today such a clear view is very difficult, if not impossible, to come by. The essential differences between the English and Scots have been very largely hidden by the increasing Anglicization of the latter, but their assimilation to the English has been very superficial, and deep-seated and unalterable psychological differences remain. Only the 'surface minds' (in the Bergsonian sense) of the Scots have been Englished; beneath the crust of imitation there remain potentialities of incalculable difference, and it is these the so-called Scottish Renaissance Movement today is attempting to bring into renewed manifestation, not without a certain measure of success, but, so far, in a very 'hit-and-miss' and unscientific fashion. The conditions for the success of a Renaissance movement have not yet been secured. There are three main ones. The first has perhaps already been secured or is likely to be, and that is a rising tide of Scottish national consciousness. The second is a thorough-going reconcentration, in our schools and universities and elsewhere, on the study of Scottish Literature. A well-known Scottish critic recently confessed how, as a boy and young man, his knowledge of Scots literature was confined to the Ballads and Burns and a few popular songs. It was only in later life that he came to read Dunbar and the other 'Auld Makars' and discovered James Hogg and other more recent writers in Scots, and belatedly secured something like a complete view of the evolution of Scots poetry as a separate literary tradition. I was speaking the other week to another Scottish critic who was in somewhat similar case and found he knew nothing of Duncan Graham, the 'Skellat Bellman', and had never gone through any good collection either of 'Pasquils' or 'Bothy Songs'. Neither of these gentleman knew anything of Scottish Gaelic poetry. In other words, their tardy attempt to secure an all-in view of Scottish poetry still remained hopelessly one-sided.

No other people in the world have ever preferred an alien literature to their own, and practically excluded the latter from the curricula of their schools and universities, in this way; and it is not to be wondered at that English literature, which has never suffered from any such neglect, should have acquired an importance out of all proportion to Scottish. The disparity between the two today may yet be redressed to some extent if anything like the same attention is given to Scottish literature in Scottish schools and elsewhere in Scotland as is presently given to English.

The third point is the necessity to bridge the gulf between Gaelic and Scots. Both have been tremendously handicapped by circumstances, and yet in their evolution, thus miserably attenuated and driven underground by external factors, they have continued to complement and correct each other in the most remarkable way. I am not going to make use of the terms 'Romantic' and 'Classical', although these dubious counters do roughly correspond to the Scots and Gaelic traditions in poetry respectively. But the failing of the former in modern times has been formlessness, while the latter has been choked by an excessive formalism. They have a great deal to learn from each other.

In addition to their equal and opposite needs (and they have so profound a bearing on the position of literature as a whole today, in its search for 'a new classicism', that if Scottish poetry could effectively bridge this Gaelic-Scots gulf it might well lead the way in the great new movement in poetry which is everywhere being sought for) both Gaelic and Scots poetry have this in common – the need for a prolonged and exhaustive preoccupation with their own languages. 'What Gaelic needs,' says Donald Sinclair, 'is a tremendous recovery of idiom. A great deal of the language has gone dead through disuse. It must be revived.' The problem in Scots is precisely the same. The language has been allowed to disintegrate into dialects and these have gradually lost all the qualities befitting them for major expressive purposes rather than for homely, local uses.

If, to this intensive concern with the problems of the two languages, can be joined a dignified concern with making a creative contribution worthy of Scotland, the conditions of a real Renaissance will perhaps be available. Mr Collins well says:

> When we consider how profound is the inherent significance of poetry to the human soul; how deeply suggestive should be the impression left by any poetry that is really expressive of a very important epoch of the consciousness of man, and consider the effect of one, or the cumulative effect of many, of the numerous contemporary poets of wide repute, the sense of incongruous deficiency is too great. The present writer has gone scrupulously through the whole of a widely-acclaimed volume of 'Georgian Poetry' not without pleasure, and afterwards reflected with consternation that never for an instant had he the sensation of being in contact with the serious creative intelligence of a great modern nation. The quality of the thought embodied seemed immeasurably inferior to that which goes to the making of a high-class review of letters

or philosophy or scholarship. There was nothing to recall or suggest the impressive intellectual and moral traditions of English literature.

Once a worthy and adequate ambition can be disseminated among young Scottish writers, they will address themselves naturally to the serious deficiencies in the structure of their literary tradition. Mr John Buchan's observation in the notes to his anthology of Scots Vernacular poetry *The Northern Muse* that, despite Scottish religious traditions – or perhaps because of them – there is an almost complete lack of poems on the plane of 'divine philosophy' since Dunbar – is a case in point. Our nature poetry is still very vague and unenterprising, and a great extension of exact notation is highly desirable, while the elaboration of effective national myths is another matter essential to the creation of great Scottish poetry. The role of our race in history – the special qualities and functions of Scottish nationality – have not yet been voiced by our poets; the prevalent conceptions are all out of date or too puerile and sectional, and lack the necessary dynamic force. In actual technique – traditional verse forms, and, above all, Scottish versus English and other rhythms – there is no less need for research.

Finally, too much may have been made in certain quarters of the failure of Scotland to provide, like England and France, a constant succession of new schools of poetry. Poetry in Scots is still widely popular. Mr Charles Murray's *Hamewith* and Mrs Jacob's *Songs of Angus* sold splendidly – in salient contrast to the great bulk of modern poetry – and, to go further back, 'Hugh Haliburton's' poems were cut out of the papers in which they appeared and treasured by humble readers all over the country, while the contemporary popularity of Burns was tremendous. Another case in point is the wide, popular delight today in 'The Whistle', 'Tam o' the Kirk', 'The Lum Hat wantin' the Croon' and many other poems. There is not the divorce between poetry and popularity in Scotland that is to be found elsewhere. This is a vital matter and one of the real foundations for hoping for a great Scottish literary revival. 'How can the modern poet,' asks Mr Herbert Read, 'find a means of reconciling his world and his art?'

The only literature which is at the same time vital and popular, is the literature of the music-hall. There is no poetry in 'Tipperary' and 'Keep the Home Fires Burning' – there is only sentimentality. But it is just a possibility – and no more than a possibility – that the music-hall song and its allied forms – music-hall patter and revue libretto – contain the germ of a new popular poetry. It is significant that the only poems which suggest such an art are some of Mr T. S. Eliot's recent poems.

This crucial problem has not yet arisen in Scotland, where it is still possible to write poetry in the native tradition and secure a wide measure of popularity. I am not, of course, suggesting that any such poetry is yet, or can be, modern in any other sense than contemporaneously produced, but neither is more than a moiety of current English (or, for that matter, French, German, or any other) verse, and that moiety is not yet accepted of the schools or the people, but an object of attack and derision outside very small 'ultra-modern' circles. It is nonsense to say that there can be no revival of the Scots Vernacular because it is 'essentially bucolic'. All languages were until recently, and the Scots Vernacular actually has a far smaller percentage of its vocabulary referring to technically agrarian matters or even to Nature in the broadest sense than English, while it has a higher percentage of words (most of which have no, or no exact, equivalents in English) of the sharpest psycho-physical significance or the subtlest shades of mental discrimination, all of which can be adapted, directly or metaphorically, to the most modern uses. The word-making resources of Gaelic are more than equal to all requirements.

In this connection the English ascendancy bias is particularly noticeable, for although English has drawn its vocabulary from practically all the languages of the world, it has almost wholly eschewed both Gaelic and the Scots Vernacular, yet the latter in particular is full of words, linguistically akin to the basis of English and readily familiar to most Englishmen through their correspondence with English dialect terms, for which English has no equivalents at all to which it can only approximate by the most lumbaginous licences of circumlocution. This means, of course, that English is adscripted in ways antipathetic to the genius of

Scots, and turns a blind eye to certain fields of consciousness.[4]

In these discursive notes, which only touch the fringes of far-reaching issues, I need not attempt any summary of the evolutionary courses, or outstanding treasures, of the Welsh, Irish, or Scottish Gaelic literatures. But there is unquestionably a tremendous loss involved in that centralization of literary journalism and studies generally in Great Britain on the 'English mainstream', which leads *The Times Literary Supplement*, *The Observer*, *Sunday Times*, and the cultural reviews, to devote their principal articles week after week to 'small beer', such as Churchill, Cyril Tourneur, Colley Cibber, Otway, Godolphin, and all the rest of the stand-bys of doctrinal theses – and compels successive generations of school-teachers throughout the British Isles to teach, not only English, but Irish, Welsh, and Scots school children and university students about minor English poetasters and dramatists – while ignoring such relative 'giants' alike in the quality of their work, their influence on successive generations of writers, and the interest of their personalities and eventfulness of their lives as Alasdair MacMhaighstir Alasdair; Mary of the Songs (the only woman who has had a decisive influence on the evolution of any literature) or Aodhagan O'Rathaille, the Dante of Munster, to name only three of a score deserving mention even in such an essay as this.

The literary output of these islands has been artificially forced into certain limited channels (while not extirpating in Scotsmen, Irishmen, and Welshmen psychological qualities capable of, or requiring, under their superficial Anglicization, expression in very different forms), and, as a result, the reading publics of Great Britain have been blinded to four literatures full of very distinctive values, of absorbing technical interests, and of very diverse potentialities, and the further development of these four literatures have been practically inhibited. Surely all this represents an enormous loss. Can it not still be made good? What has happened in Ireland can also happen in Scotland and Wales. The Gaelic literature of Scotland is still practically a *terra nullius*. We have no study of it a thousandth part as good as Corkery's or

---

[4]In Ireland's *Contribution to the English Language* (Studies, Vol. XXII, No. 88), Mr P. J. Irwin points out the surprising fact that, apart from familiar Anglo-Irish dialect terms, the English language, as it is now written and spoken, contains fewer than twenty Irish loan-words.

de Blacam's or Douglas Hyde's or Eleanor Hull's books on Irish Literature; and non-Gaelic readers can still only approach the best Scottish Gaelic poems through such inadequate and distorting translations as were those, in Ireland, of Sir Samuel Ferguson and the beginners of the Irish Literary Revival, which have only to be compared with the re-translations, far 'harder' and truer to the original Gaelic spirit and free of the 'Twilight' nonsense, of such recent translators as Professor Bergin, Mr Robin Flower, or Mr James Stephens, to show how much has still to be done.[5]

Space does not permit me to indicate here what interrelations of Scots Gaelic and Scots Vernacular are today leading writers in the latter to the former again and causing them to realize that they cannot get back to major forms until they recover their lost Gaelic background; nor can I discuss the kindred movement in Wales that is proceeding under the leadership of Professor Saunders Lewis. But in both Wales and Scotland the services of such re-translators and literary historians as I have named in connection with Ireland are still sadly to seek; and it may be further suggested that the whole movement will not take its proper shape or get into effective grips with the English Ascendancy tradition until the

[5] A good start has been made towards rectifying this during the past two years. I would draw attention in particular to J. L. Campbell's admirable *Songs of The Forty-Five*, and to *The Owl Remembers*, an anthology of Scottish Gaelic poems, drawn from all periods since the eighth century to the present, selected and edited, with notes, by the Revd John MacKechnie, with an introduction and English versions by Dr Patrick McGlynn. By far the best and most comprehensive account of the whole Scottish Gaelic situation yet written is the series of articles, 'Cuis Na Cànain', contributed to the *Free Man* during 1933 by Fionn Mac Colla. The appalling backwardness of Scottish Gaelic studies of all kinds, the utter worthlessness of what passes for knowledge in An Comunn Gaidhealach and other spheres, and the importance of what is actually there to study, given a competent approach, is best illustrated by comparing the usual views on bag-pipe music with Mr Francis George Scott's masterly and most vitally important lecture on 'The Music of the Pipes', in which he pointed out: 'The piobaireachds of the Golden Age, like plain song, transcended the time factor in music and became unmeasured music, literally and metaphorically timeless. Later piobaireachd writers, working unsuspectingly against a background of tonality and harmony, had given a "tuney" flavour to their productions, and this was the distinguishing feature of the period of decadence. To such a point had we come today ttha most people understood music to be tunes and tunes to be music. A similar criterion, applied to poetry, taking lyrics as the standard of measurement, would cancel out Milton, Shakespeare, Dante, and all the major names in literature.'

younger groups in Ireland, Scotland, and Wales make common cause. The attitude of the Irish Bards of the Penal Age to that 'easier mode of writing' – the abandonment of the strict rules and elaborate technique of the Colleges – is at least an influence which would be a salutary importation into the contemporary literary atmosphere. All I would add is that the two deepest issues involved in this matter are (1) the possibility of 'getting back behind the Renaissance', and (2) its bearing on the 'Defence of the West', or Conservation of European Civilization. Mr Corkery outlines the first of these when he writes:

> It has to be insisted upon that Renaissance standards are not Greek standards. Greek standards in their own time and place were standards arrived at by the Greek nation; they were national standards. Caught up at second hand into the art-mind of Europe – thus becoming international – their effect was naturally to whiten the youthfully tender national cultures of Europe. That is, the standards of a dead nation killed in other nations those aptitudes through which they themselves had become memorable. Since the Renaissance there have been, strictly speaking, no self-contained national cultures in Europe. The antithesis of Renaissance art in this regard is national art. To some it may seem as if the Renaissance has justified itself in thus introducing a common strain into the art-consciousness of all European countries. That common strain was certainly brilliant, shapely, worldly-wise, strong, if not indeed gigantic, over-bounding in energy, in life. Yet all the time there was a latent weakness in it, a strain, a sham strength, an uneasy energy, a death in life. It always protested too much. Dissembling always, it was never single-hearted enough to speak plainly, and, so, intensely. It therefore dazzles us rather than moves us. If it has justified itself, then should we swap Rheims cathedral for St Peter's and Rouen for St Paul's! 'One would, however, swap Dante for Shakespeare?' – Yes, but what did Shakespeare's native wood-notes wild know of the Unities? Happy England! – so naïvely ignorant of the Renaissance at the close of the sixteenth century. Unhappy France! – where even before Shakespeare was born they had ceased to develop their native Christian literary modes, had indeed begun to fling them aside for those of Euripides and

Seneca.... The Renaissance may have justified itself, but not, we feel, either on the plane of genuine Christian art or genuine pagan art. It is not as intense or as tender as the one, nor so calm, majestic, and wise as the other. A Romantic movement is not usually thought of as a violent effort to rediscover the secret power that lay behind Greek art; yet in essence that is what every Romantic movement has been.

And that most romantic of all movements, the search for a new classicism today, is not a quest for any mere neo-classical formalism, but an effort to get down to *Ur-motives* – to get back behind the Renaissance!

As to the second point – 'The Defence of the West', or the Conservation of European Civilization – the old balance or conflict between the North and the South has been violently disrupted by the emergence of Russia and the Soviet concept of things. That constitutes a third side; where is the fourth to come from – not from England; but whence else if not from Gaelic culture – the fourth side upon which European civilization can re-establish itself, just as, to switch the argument into other terms, the old duality of Man versus Nature having been disrupted by the emergence of the Third Factor – the Machine – balance can only be re-secured by a fourth factor, the effective emergence of 'disinterestedness'.

11 The Scab

This originally appeared in *The Glasgow Herald* (15 August 1932) and was collected in both the anthologies edited by Kenneth Buthlay and Alan Bold.

IN the very heart of these beautiful policies there is a malign piece of ground, called The Scab; and, talking with others who come here, I have been interested to discover how obscurely but overwhelmingly important it is. This is no peculiarity of my own temperament; it is shared by many others different enough from myself. Willy-nilly, all steps gravitate thither oftener than to any other part of the grounds. The beauties of the setting become negligible in the light of that abject gem, a jewel of horror whose rays, as it were, annihilate the rest of the world, and can destroy the heavens themselves. Its fascination (for we are conscious of the element of pleasure even when we are most insistent upon describing our feelings as repulsion) remains almost entirely a secret to us; we can hardly begin to explain it. Anything we can say seems inept and absurd. We have, moreover, a constraining consciousness of our ingratitude, a sense of shame; the grounds are so magnificent, so perfectly laid out. We are ashamed to prefer the canker to the rose. It is difficult to admit that all loveliness goes for nothing as against this appalling eyesore; that ugliness, naked and unashamed, is a far more potent magnet than beauty. But it is so. I have been amused to see how some of the visitors have sought at first to hide the fact that it attracted them so irresistibly, but gradually shed their pretence – one or two with unrestrained terror of the lure that had so inexplicably enslaved them, as if it had revealed some evil predisposition of their souls – as no doubt it had. Others of us never attempted any dissimulation; we were hurried, open-eyed, to this patch like flotsam is to the heart of a whirlpool. It is our Sargasso Sea.

The Scab is unnatural. Any grave is soon covered over; fields champed out of all semblance into obscene messes of mud bestuck with blasted parodies of trees are very soon recaptured by the green grass and the wild flowers. Nature lies just round the corner, ready to seize the first opportunity to recover any territory that is taken from her. But Nature does not lie round the corner here. It is as if Nature recognized that this had never belonged to her and never could, or had been somehow compelled to give it up as forever irreclaimable. There is an invisible barrier beyond which no blade of grass, no runner of a weed, no thread of a root, attempts to pass. Chance of wind may deposit a seed there from time to time, but without result. Nothing grows there. I think that nothing has grown there since Time began, or ever will – that it might be ploughed and replonghed as deep as the centre of the earth and filled with fertilizer, to no end, and that, even were it possible to remove that sterile soil, such of it as was transferred elsewhere, in bulk or in separate particles, would there again produce sterility, in patches or in specks according to proportion, while the place from which it had been taken would remain a ghastly pit which nothing else could fill. I may be wrong: I am of a fanciful disposition, but that is how I feel about it, and others who know it as I do share my feelings despite the most radical differences of temperament.

So far as I can ascertain, it has no particular history. There is no reason why it should be thus infamously differentiated from the rest of the world. It had a common origin with spots which are now gardens or glades or green fields. In the beginning of things no one could have foretold that it would become so unlike these, or, witnessing the stages of its alienation, if there were any such, could have suggested any reason for its monstrous and unparalleled development. While Nature holds aloof, however, and, so far as human eye can see, attempts no reconciliation, the Scab is stealthily but incessantly encroaching on Nature. Even in my experience it has extended perceptibly, and Nature, while falling back inch by painful fraction of an inch, never attempts to regain the ground she so loses. This is unlike Nature, unlike her infinite patience, her inexhaustible resource. One would expect some sudden sally, some surprising circumvention. But no. Things take their course. Nature knows when she is beaten! – and the Scab apparently has her beaten. All that she can do is to yield

The Scab

only by degrees as infinitesimal as the eternal concentration of her enormous opposition can contrive.

In putting matters thus I am only too conscious, of course, of the inadequacy of language to deal with such a situation. I have called the Scab unnatural, and spoken of it as impervious to Nature. But that is not quite true. It is to green life. But there are forms of life which infest it (apart from the fact that it is a kind of living death itself). Ants, for example! They have succeeded in forming intricate establishments in that sinister and inhospitable soil. They maintain a perpetual traffic on and, to some undetermined extent, within it. Seeing them following their incomprehensible courses (a vicious circle if ever there was one) – which they support upon nothing found within that desolate circle, but upon material they abstract from Nature, to and from which they journey incessantly, without let or hindrance – an extraordinary similarity presents itself to one's eyes between them and this barren soil. They are simply like mobile particles of it, well-nigh indistinguishable from it. Not so is an ant that one may encounter in Nature. The foil of greenery, of infinite variety, sharpens such an ant to our sight, and endows it with lively qualities of enterprise and dexterity and even a tiny burnished beauty these sordid insects entirely lack as they pass and repass (to no other end than the multiplication of their kind) on this wretched surface mechanised to so unendurable a degree that the sight of them going and coming afflicts the conscious but baffled spectator with a sense of meaningless and endless motion alien and repugnant to the human soul. Other insects and tiny reptiles are found here too. The evidences of their existences uncorrected by the diversity of Nature assume a hideous relief: their *formes*, and other commotions or indentations of the earth, are an unsightly testimony to insensate activity. The whole plot has been mined and honeycombed and corrugated throughout the ages, in countless ecstasies of futile ingenuity: the product of a mindless itch.

And some of those with whom I have discussed the phenomenon believe that the Scab will, slowly perhaps, and perhaps at an incalculably accelerated rate, but surely, spread over the whole earth, and that in the end the blessed light will fall only on an immense panorama of empty 'workings', established in their time by myriads of ants and other insects and tiny reptiles the last of which are dead.

12 Life in the Shetland Islands

> MacDiarmid removed to the island of Whalsay in the Shetland archipelago with his second wife and their young son in 1933, in conditions of great personal poverty and stress, broken in health and exhausted by years of literary and political activity. In the Shetlands he was to undergo a crisis of spirit and a critical test of his courage which are evident in the great philosophical poems of this period, most notably 'On a Raised Beach', and others from the 1934 volume *Stony Limits and Other Poems*. This essay is from *At the Sign of the Thistle* (1934), and was later republished in Kenneth Buthlay's *The Uncanny Scot*.

I

IF the real Robinson Crusoe had the good luck to land on an island where tropical conditions obtained and the problems of securing shelter and food were accordingly at a minimum, I felt justified in preparing for staging my first venture at such a life where both these problems are exceedingly acute by selecting an island which, though uninhabited, is within easy enough distance of other inhabited islands to make it reasonably likely that the waving of a coat would attract attention.

I went further. The adjacent islands, if inhabited, are only sparsely so; a coat or something might be waved for weeks without being seen; besides, my jacket and my raincoat are of a colour that would be practically indiscernible. My shirt is brighter, but the weather would prohibit any undressing for the purpose of removing it and waving it as a flag. I did not trust to such chances of rescue. I arranged with the boatman who took me over from the inhabited island of Whalsay to the uninhabited island of Linga to train his telescope on a given spot on the third day afterwards in the early afternoon, and, if I was seen standing there, to come over and fetch me. If not, to keep on doing so every afternoon thereafter until I was so seen – if I ever was. The boatman suspected that I might commit suicide, but he did not communicate his suspicions to anyone else; he did as he was told; he trained his telescope on the arranged spot in the early afternoon of the third day, but he was a bit of a Nelson. I was not there, as a matter of fact, but, even if I had been, he could not have seen me, for a thick wall of fog (one of the many little matters I had not foreseen or provided for in the arrangements I made). Nevertheless, he came, and I returned to Whalsay with him.

I took no food with me to Linga, but I took a good supply of the thick black tobacco which is my habitual smoke and plenty of matches. I felt justified in doing this, since it was past the season when birds' eggs are to be found all over the island and even the later period when young birds can be caught by the hand among the rocks. It would be extremely difficult to bring down any of the birds still about. I suppose a more resourceful fellow than myself might have managed to collar one or two of them in their nests during the night, but they nested in places that are precariously enough accessible even by day to one who is less sure-footed than one of the local sheep, and, apart from the perils of rock climbing, I suffer from night-blindness. I had decided if I did catch one to cook it in the way I had heard of gipsies cooking hedgehogs in Dumfriesshire in my boyhood: cover it – feathers, intestines and all the rest of it intact – in a nice thick coating of mud, and put it in the middle of a good-going fire until the mud was baked hard and had begun to crack. Then I would poke the ball out of the fire, let it cool a little, and break off the fired-clay covering, which would bring the feathers and skin away with it and disclose the flesh, done to a nicety.

The contingency did not, however, arise. So far as a larder was concerned then, I was restricted to the chances of rabbits or fish. There are black and blue rabbits on the island, but they are very scarce. As a boy – in a place where rabbits were far more plentiful – I had succeeded in coming up to them and bringing a stick down upon them. I wondered if I could repeat the feat. I never saw a rabbit to attempt it upon, however. There were plenty of nice, fat 'sillocks' (first-year saithe) close in to the shore; at times the top of the sea was quite solid with them. I caught four – with a piece of string I found among the flotsam and jetsam in one of the little coves, or 'gios', as the Shetlanders call them, and a bent pin. I had not brought the pin of *malice prepense*; it was a pure accident that I happened to have one in the bottom seam of my waistcoat.

But for that I should probably have had nothing to eat these three days; the four 'sillocks' were all I did have. Catching them with bent pins is common practice in the Shetlands. They are so easily caught; they practically jump into your hands at times if you hold these an inch or thereby above the surface of the water. Occasionally I saw the dark patches in the water close in, indicating the presence of shoals of mackerel; but you cannot catch mackerel with a bent pin. Nor can you catch a dog-fish with a bent pin; there were any amount of them hard in to the shore. The Shetland people do not eat them; but, under the name of 'rock turbot' and other fancy appellations, they sell well in the South of England, and are, as a matter of fact, quite good eating.

I said that, failing birds, I was restricted to the chances of rabbits or fish; there was one other possibility. I feel certain now that I would have killed a sheep (one of this year's lambs) rather than have gone a day or two longer than I actually did without food beyond the four 'sillocks'. The Shetland lamb season had just begun; one could buy a lamb for five or six shillings. I thought a little of the practical problems involved – I have never seen a lamb butchered – and decided they were not insurmountable. I am not so certain now, however, as I am that, given a day or two longer, I would have killed a lamb, that I would have surmounted the difficulties of killing and skinning and cutting it up quite so easily. My only instrument would have been my pen-knife, which I keep for the twin purposes of cutting up my plug tobacco and digging the dottel out of the bottom of my pipe. I am afraid it would have been a very gruesome business. However, as I have said, the boatman came on the third day. So the contingency did not arise after all.

I slept in a cave in the rocks. It was very cold, and in any case I should say 'lay at nights' instead of 'slept', because I found the glug-glug of the water against the rocks and the roar of the tides in a little bed of shingle away up at the top of the cave very annoying. There are no trees in the Shetlands; so it was impossible to find any sheltered spot on the surface of the island to lie in; and there is no bracken or long grass, so it was impossible to gather anything to make any sort of bed on my ledge of rock. A little earlier on it would have been possible to read in the open until well after midnight; indeed, there is practically no night. But by this time the long light of the summer-time had given way to the opposite conditions when there is a very short day. I had brought with me a volume of Rilke's poems and Theodora Bosanquet's little book on Paul Valéry; but I did not open either of them. I was too busy; lying for the most part on that rocky ledge with the sound of the sea in my ears and the darkness of the cave (broken only by the yellow flashing of innumerable matches and the red glow of my lit pipe) grateful to my eyes, doing nothing – but what I intended to do, which was sufficiently engrossing to keep me from being lonely or conscious very much of either cold or hunger; for I am a poet myself, or think I am, which explains the whole thing. All the same, I would have killed a sheep. I will yet – and stay on the island till I have eaten the whole of it. Poetry must be served. But it will be a few weeks earlier in the year, and I will also have an eider duck or green cormorant or two and a plentiful supply of mushrooms.

II

The Shetland Islands are fighting (in a curious fashion, as will appear as this article proceeds) a losing battle. The fishing, upon which they principally depend, is in a bad way; the population is rapidly declining; crofts are falling into desuetude and the ground is being increasingly acquired by big sheep-farmers. It is a significant fact that as soon as Shetlanders abandon the calling of the sea they begin to wear an extraordinary excess of clothes and to live in more and more oven-like homes with sealed windows and big fires. A couple of pairs of thick drawers may be necessary for a fisherman, especially in the exposure of the small boats prosecuting the haddock-fishing; but the superimposition of fifteen sets of underclothing on a schoolboy is another matter. Yet a school MO found that in one case; and remonstrance with the elderly aunts with whom the boy lived only evoked the obstinate answer that he was a Scotsman and did not understand how cold it was in the Shetlands. As a matter of fact it is much less cold in the Shetlands than it is in Edinburgh, or in the Thames

Valley. There is a sharp differentiation in physique and health between the children of those who are still fisher-folk (the vast majority) and those who are not. The former are by far the healthier. It is, indeed, impossible to eke out a decent living in the Shetlands by crofting alone. That is the difference between the Orkneys and the Shetlands. The Orcadian is a farmer with a boat; the Shetlander is a fisherman with a croft.

The Shetlanders know perfectly well that there is no real reason why they should not have a very prosperous fishing industry. But they have never had it. In the old days they lived under conditions of virtual slavery; the laird had to get his share of all the fish they caught, then the minister had to get his, and between them these two gentlemen got the best of the fish. The Shetlanders had to live on the balance and the similarly-taxed crops of their small crofts. Bad seasons put them into debt to the lairds, and they never got their feet clear; nor were the lairds sufficiently enlightened in their self-interest to equip the fishermen in the most effective fashion. They had to work with craft and tackle inferior to that being introduced elsewhere; and any offence meant their expulsion from the islands. Such conditions induced a secret radicalism and an external sycophancy – characteristics which survive in the Shetlanders today in the forms of a hidden preservation of their real lives and an outward accessibility to current conventions generally. This duality makes the Shetlanders very difficult to know to anyone who does not actually live long enough in the Shetlands to win the native confidence and secure acceptance as if island-born. The power of the lairds has almost entirely disappeared, of course; they are poorer than many of the fisher-folk and virtually dependent in many ways on their charity; and it is amusing to observe how the old bland dealing with them on the part of the fisher-folk, masking their true feelings under an even amiability, persists in the present attitude to these superiors in reduced circumstances – an attitude of affected humility and readiness to help, backed with the clear realization that if the wheel of fortune should restore them to any measure of power the gentry, now so innocuous, would instantly manifest again their predecessors' old characteristics of ruthless exaction and injustice. Happily their wings have been shorn away; a 'revenge complex' never manifested itself in a subtler and more patient form; the sons and daughters of the victims of an age-long oppression of almost unparalleled savagery know how the heirs of the oppressors are now placed and afford themselves the luxury of being sorry for them, but do not avail themselves of any opportunity of taking political or practical measures at variance with a species of lip-service to the shadow of the ancient status. This negativeness is the outstanding feature of life in the Shetlands. It would almost seem as if the psychology of it were a sense that the traditional oppression had vanished, but that a definitive move in any direction might incur other oppressions still more dire. And there is a great wisdom in that. Poor though they may be, and hard though they may have to work, they have now a certain independence – they are self-subsisting in regard to the staples of life; they lead a kind of all-round life rare in these days of the greater and greater division of labour, farming, fishing, building, cobbling, butchering, knitting and what not each household for itself; their time is their own to make of it what they will and can. All their intromissions with organized industry and commerce, and with life as it arises in the form of education, newspapers, radio and other contacts with the outside world, and everything that does not spring directly out of that core of island economy, are marginal to that substantial body of free living, within which they maintain themselves not only materially but spiritually. They may profess the same religious and political and other views and interests as people elsewhere, just as they talk English and not their own old Norse language; but all such professions are only a protective camouflage. On that level they give visitors an impression of quiet candour and good nature; but visitors must not attempt to probe below that to the real nature of their lives. They do not want the latter discussed in any way. So long as writers confine themselves to a rehash of the traditional lore, stories of the Vikings, general descriptive matter, and mere tittle-tattle, they will approve; but they resent any writing that slips below the surface. They do not want to be 'disturbed in their warm corner'. For that is the essence of the matter. Given the measure of independence they have, the island economy is in curiously surreptitious enjoyment of a measure of Douglasism – of economic nationalism within the present framework of international interdependence and high finance. The degree to which the latter impinges upon them does not, in their particular conditions of living, deprive them of a

Life in the Shetland Islands

sufficient field of self-reliance which that system cannot touch. Their fishing industry is a mere fraction of what it might be, thanks to trawler combines, poaching within the three-mile limit, the rigging of the markets by alien financial interests, and the interposition of middleman parasitism of all kinds. But where a Douglasite might contend that an immense access of prosperity was immediately practicable, what the Shetlanders are concerned about is the really extraordinary degree of comfort and well-being obtainable under the existing system in conditions such as theirs where this measure of independence obtains and self-subsistence as the first call on their activities is practicable. They are not going to risk anything that may deprive them of that; they know perfectly well that strangers watching their toilsome lives and little externally-poor cottages have no idea of the degree of comfort that actually obtains in their homes; they have a not-unnatural fear – akin to that which leads a certain type of well-to-do person to dress quietly and avoid ostentation – of 'giving the game away'. They do not believe they could in essentials be a great deal better off; but for certain easily specifiable lets and hindrances they could be as well off with a great deal less exertion and hardship – but there are perhaps worse things than such exertion and hardship, and a mere increase of monetary wealth without a proportionate enrichment of their actual lives does not attract them – does not, at all events, counterbalance the danger of any active endeavour to secure it. So they argue. Who can say that they are wrong? Who dare advise them to risk anything that might, whatever else it brought them, diffuse or dilute the deep integrity of their lives? Who can assail the shrewdness that realizes the brevity of individual lives in a way that disencourages any attempt to envisage the remote benefits that might accrue from present sacrifices, or the relative unimportance of the few thousands of Shetlanders to those world-affairs that breed the over-riding factors that, in the last analysis, so largely determine the precise width of the margin on which the island economy can continue to operate? They have a real autonomy in basic matters; so they refuse to respond to any denunciation of that centralization of their affairs in London which in all other matters stultifies their local initiative. 'Faithful in small things', they are not to be shaken in their allegiance to them by hopes that they could do as well in greater.

Behind these economic matters there lies a very interesting life, in the various aspects of which not dissimilar tactics in dealing with the outside world are discernible. They may speak of the Shetlands as 'the Viking Isles' and recall old traditions; but they have really little or no history, and have allowed the old Norse language, which would have differentiated them superficially from the Scots and the English, to lapse. Yet whilst sacrificing the obvious signs of separate raciality, and under a surface appearance of practical at-one-ment with the people of Scotland and England, with whom they share the same language, the same religion, the same education, the same newspapers and broadcast programmes, and other apparent interests, their social spirit is profoundly different. This deep difference does not manifest itself externally; it does not issue in cultural or political movements – it concerns the very texture and inmost essence of their lives. They belong, nominally, to the Church of Scotland, which dispenses them from any necessity to discuss religion; they have allowed themselves to forget their history and ancient speech because they know that by thus converting positive things into negative things they do not weaken them but render them less susceptible of recognition and attack; but their deep hold upon their own essential tradition is maintained in many ways, as for example, in their sexual and matrimonial customs. How can one prove the latter? They will blandly deny that any such difference exists. Nothing in their appearance – at least nothing at all easy to discern – in the tone of the island life – discloses the fact that in these intimate relationships they pursue a course which would be repudiated everywhere in Scotland and England as 'immoral', 'dangerous', or 'unthinkable'. Yet it is so. On certain nights in the week the lads go to their lassies' homes and to bed with them, with the full knowledge and approval of the parents. It is understood that 'if anything happens' marriage will follow; and it almost invariably does. As in other peasant communities, where similar customs are known, this simple resolution of the complications of adolescence seems to induce a forthrightness and understanding between the sexes and a complete lack of furtiveness, pretences, discomforts, and general cant and humbug. Or perhaps it is the simplicity of the people which makes the custom possible. Once a young islander goes with a girl he is – almost invariably – with her 'for keeps'. None of the other girls would have anything to do with him if, after once committing himself, he attempted to 'change over'. The Shetland practice puts the relationship of the sexes on a natural basis. It is true, of course, that one man may be more suited to a certain woman than to any other woman; but under their system he is perhaps as likely to hit upon his 'true affinity' as under any other. What is certain is that the individual differences between men and women who live in hearty contact with hard and essential labour are relatively unimportant set beside the possibility of any average man and woman making an average good job of the business if, having once come together, they determine to play their part by each other. And that is what happens in the Shetlands. Romance in the sex-relation is replaced by a general realistic co-operation which can well dispense with it. And as a matter of fact Shetland couples are extremely faithful and affectionate, and have, moreover, that essential equality which comes from being mutually indispensable in the given way of life, for the degree of independence of which I have spoken is dependent in almost equal measure on the exertions of both partners. Much of the work of the croft devolves upon the woman, while the man is at his fishing. They are literally tireless, these Shetland women, carrying their loads of peat in the 'kishies' (as they call the peat baskets) resting on their backs, and knitting as they go. Here too, as everywhere, the 'law of compensation' is at work, for the effect of 'kishie' carrying on the woman's back is said to ease child-bearing.

These brief notes touch only the fringe of a difficult and little-known subject, and have communicated nothing of my love for these island people amongst whom I live. The few aspects of Shetland life upon which I have commented are only pointers to a 'way of living' which, so far as I am personally concerned, makes the Shetlanders by far the most interesting and attractive people in that congeries of very varied groups which constitute the people of Scotland, of whom a recent writer has said: 'Though Scotland is a small country, yet there are many Scotlands; South Uist differs more from the Merse, let alone from Motherwell, than Rochdale from Dorset, or even Lille from Béarn.'

III

'Scotland's greatest exclave.' The claim involved in so describing the Shetland Islands will, no doubt, be hotly contested by the Hebridean enthusiasts, though there can be no challenge if the term 'greatest' is taken to mean in superficial area, in present or potential economic value, or in historical interest. But I mean rather more than all that even. I am using the term 'greatest exclave' in its strictest sense as well, meaning that the essential traditions, life, problems, and potentialities of the Shetlands are at the furthest remove from the general conceptions bound up in the term 'Scottish' and that the greatest ignorance about them prevails on the Scottish mainland itself. They are the greatest of our unrealized possessions – a province capable of greater regional planning than any and of a more distinctive cultural development. My point can be readily established by comparing the tourist traffic to the Hebrides with the almost negligible tourist traffic to the Shetlands; the scantiness and poverty of books or articles about the Shetlands with the constant succession of volumes about the 'Immortal Isles' and newspaper and magazine articles on Iona, Skye, Hebridean song, and so forth; the relative familiarity of the Gaelic language to the Norn; and the history and character of the land problem and traditions of the western islands to the general ignorance of the udal system and the very different but not less chequered and tragic history of *Ultima Thule*. The appeal of the Shetlands is not so facile as that of the Hebrides, nor has it been eked out with so many adventitious aids. This is not altogether a misfortune. If the Shetlands are much less known they have at all events escaped the dangers of superficial and generally false enthusiasm and have nothing to correspond to 'Celtic Twilightism'. If the fake-glamour of the Hebrides has become a weariness to the flesh and a real obstacle to their true appreciation, an insistence on the claims of the Shetlands may now prove a useful corrective and help to establish a properly balanced conception of Scotland as a whole. A sense of actuality will serve us better than any artificial allure.

It is all the more regrettable that so few holiday-makers come to the Shetlands since the essence of a holiday is a complete change, and this the Shetland Islands offer to mainland dwellers to a far greater extent than is obtainable anywhere else within easy reach, which is to say, at moderate cost. Superficially even, the Shetlands are quite unlike Scotland, and, unless the visitor has been prepared in advance, he or she may find it difficult to account for the sense of something very different – the sense of something wanting. It may take them a little time to realize that what is affecting them is the total absence of trees and of running water. But one quickly gets accustomed to that, and appreciates that, even if trees and singing streams could be introduced, they would be no improvement; they would simply make the Shetlands like other places we know, whereas, without them, the Shetlands are complete in themselves, and the absence of these usual features of the countryside does not involve any deficiency or monotony. There is no less variety of form and colour; just as we find it difficult in other connections to imagine how we could get on without certain things we are accustomed to, so here it surprises one to discover how easily even the presence of trees and rivers can be dispensed with and how, instead of a sense of loss, we soon realize that their absence throws into relief features we seldom see or underprize because of them – the infinite beauties of the bare land and the shapes and colours of the rocks which first of all impress one with a sense of sameness and next delight one with a revelation of the endless resource of Nature albeit in subtler and less showy or sensational forms than we are accustomed to appreciate in regions of more profuse development. It is in fact the treasures and rich lessons of a certain asceticism the Shetlands provide, and these offset in an invaluable way our normal indulgences in scenic display. But the spirit of the Shetlands is not easily or speedily apprehended; one must accustom oneself patiently to a different aspect of the world, a different rhythm of life, before one can fully understand how its variations from what we have been used to are counter-balanced by its own essential qualities. The lack of ostentatious appearances, the seeming bareness and reserve, make the Shetlands insusceptible of being readily or quickly understood; one must steep oneself in them, let them grow upon one, to savour them properly. It is a splendid discipline.

Though frank and kindly, the Shetland people are like their

country; their distinctive qualities and traditions are not seen at a glance, but must be carefully studied to be truly gauged. It is not because they are 'clannish' and debar the incomer from intimacy, but simply that the essential differences of their racial and cultural background and mode of life are in themselves elusive and easily missed by the hasty observer. You will hear little of the old Norn speech; you will hear little of the strange beliefs in the trolls and so forth; you will be able to detect still less of the lets and hindrances of their secret adhesions to old customs and ways of thought still effective in their vital practice but seldom consciously admitted, or attributed to their true origins, even by themselves under their quiet but friendly exteriors. They are a secret people, not by active concealment, but because they are so natural and unselfconscious in their unobtrusive but very real differences that these habitually escape the observation of the impatient and uninstructed, and because nowadays most of the Shetlanders themselves have lost most of the obvious manifestations – in language, costume, social habits, and so on – of those essential differences which are as potent as ever in their intimate selves. Outside Lerwick and one of two other small townships which are in no wise typical, one of the signs of this different life and different attitude to life is to be seen in the fact that the cottages, instead of being grouped into little villages or clachans, stand separately, each on its own croft. This does not mean that the people are unsociable – they are far from that – but simply that they are independent and self-reliant; they do not need to stand shoulder to shoulder either for gossip's sake or mutual support against the danger of bogies. This may seem a small thing, but it is very significant, and an understanding of the Shetlands can only be got by slowly and carefully piecing together such little signs and symbols. Another illustration may help to make my meaning clear. Southern city people looking out over a grey Shetland landscape dotted with these little isolated cottages, each by its own scanty patch of vegetation, might conclude that these were the outward signs of a very hard, stoical, and niggardly life, destitute of all the amenities of civilization; but to go into these seemingly poor cottages is to appreciate at once that, despite appearances, there is a 'routh of gear', an unexpected degree of comfort, a rich family and social life. So it is with all the outward appearances in the Shetlands; a very vivid and generous life lies behind them, and whatever may be missing of what is taken for granted elsewhere, this different tradition of existence has its own fullness and ample compensations in every respect.

In one respect, however, the outward signs are not misleading. The Shetlands are going steadily downhill; the population is decreasing; there is a passive attitude to adverse conditions, a lack of local initiative or a realization that alien over-control and centralization in London make any attempt at local initiative vain. This negative attitude – this capacity for endlessly tightening the belt and yet preserving a tranquil and apparently contented mien – has, of course, a long and tragic history, and dates back to the times of feudal oppression and Shetland's deprivation of the old Norse laws and liberty. They have at least a strong subconscious feeling that their present affiliations are hopelessly wrong – that their problems and potentialities are being posed against a wrong background and cannot therefore be seen in proper or useful proportion. They are fully alive to their situation both in regard to the fishing industry and the other aspects of their island economy; they know the remedy – but they feel that under present conditions it is inapplicable; they will do nothing. But they entertain this feeling without much, if any, sense of grievance; they are not embittered, only they are used to disappointment and hardship, and (this is the point) accustomed behind the scenes, at their own firesides and in their own personalities to triumph over them with a resource and a quiet puissance of character which is apt to seem incredible to the outsider discerning enough to catch a glimpse of it.

Their case, however, is what that of the Faroe Islands was seventy or eighty years ago. The Faroes were then on the verge of destitution. Since then they have risen to comparative affluence, built up a prosperous and progressive fishing industry and developed a vigorous national renaissance in every aspect of arts and affairs. The Faroes did this by breaking off alien ties opposed to their true national development; and by putting their activities once more upon their natural basis and developing them in accordance with the dictates of a true local economy, they have risen to their present healthy and happy condition. The

Shetlands could do likewise, given like courage and enterprise and an effective re-orientation on their true basis. But there is no sign of any such attempt so far. If it does come, the Shetlands may become the theatre of an exceedingly interesting politico-economic-cultural movement; but till it does they will remain Scotland's greatest exclave, the neglected of the neglected, a sphere of lapsed traditions and unapprehended possibilities, a congeries of islands of a forlorn fascination which is to be found nowhere else.

13 The Last Great Burns Discovery

> This formed part I of an essay on 'The Burns Cult' in *At the Sign of the Thistle* (1934). It was republished under the above title in Kenneth Buthlay's selection *The Uncanny Scot* and reappeared in Alan Bold's anthology *The Thistle Rises*.

SO Charlie Crichton has gone to his reward! Well, he will rank for all time as one of the Great Burnsians, in the direct line of Duncan MacNaught and Thomas Amos and John Muir. Their like will not be seen again. The whole field of Burns lore has been 'redded' with a small-tooth-comb – there is no scope left for the development of such Titans now. Crichton was the last of them. Only minor gleanings, the veriest *minutiae*, remain; these cannot feed the indomitable will of such men. What pigmies in comparison are even the best of our Burnsians today! There is no help for it. It is 'beyond remeid'. Yet even when Crichton first became prominent in World Burns Circles over thirty years ago the same might have been said – it seemed almost equally unlikely that he could find anything sizeable either or be destined to do more than stroke the t's and dot the i's of his distinguished predecessors. Those who thought that reckoned without their host however. The secret perhaps is just that Crichton knew better than anybody else all that had been done already. Heavens, how he applied himself! He had the whole thing at his finger-ends. He wasted no time on false trails. He knew the whereabouts of every scrap of holograph and every relic of Burns himself and his family and his relatives and everybody mentioned in his poems or letters or in any way connected with him, and the birth-places and various dwelling-places and last resting-places of them all. Yet he did not give up hope; he was sustained, I can only suppose, in addition to infinite tenacity of purpose, by some premonition of his high calling, of the momentous discovery which, despite all the probabilities, had eluded the myriads of indefatigable searchers who had gone before him and been reserved for his humble self.

I stress the adjective – his *humble* self; since his natural modesty must have had a great deal to do with it – that, and his profound common sense, as the direction in which his researches finally took him, and the very nature of his discovery, show. If he subsequently – and most naturally – became less humble the question is whether he did not remain to the end infinitely more humble than anyone else would have done in like circumstances. I think he did.

All this, of course, is an old story now. It is nearly twenty years since he gave to the world what I feel amply justified (there are certainly no indications to the contrary) in calling the Last Great Burns Discovery. It came at an opportune moment. The Burns Movement had fallen on lean years; and there was a ridiculous attempt in certain would-be-clever quarters to switch it off its traditional lines and concentrate attention on highbrow stuff and nonsense like the 'intellectual content' of the poems, the verbal texture, the rhythms, stanzaic forms, and the like. Crichton put an end to that.

I know what I am writing about because of a fact which I have never disclosed before, simply because, for his own good reasons at the time, he asked me not to. *I was the first man to whom Crichton disclosed his epoch-making discovery*. I divulge this at last with a full sense of the title to immortality Crichton thus – I think deliberately – conferred upon me; and am, of course, in a position to prove it up to the hilt. The time was not ripe then – nor for another couple of years – to make it public. Crichton judged it unerringly; those of us who remember the effect of his disclosure, the worldwide furore, when he decided that the moment had come, can vouch for that. It was a veritable bombshell; the biggest thing in Scottish literary history since the Kilmarnock Edition itself – and probably the last big thing Scottish literary history will register!

Few men could have kept the secret of having been Crichton's first *confidant* as I have done, and I have frequently in these intervening years laughed up my sleeve at nobodies bragging of some petty detail and posing as Great Burnsians without knowing that, like little Jack Horner, I too had had my finger in that pie and had pulled out such a stupendous plum!

I remember that evening as it were yesterday. We had been sitting in Crichton's parlour discussing some teasing, if very trivial, points in current Burnsian controversy – on the musicology side. He worked up to it very gradually; probably afraid of the effect a too-sudden disclosure might have upon me. Finally: 'Now I've got something to show you,' he said, 'something really big. We are going for a walk before the light fails. It isn't very far.'

Off we went; across a field and over a medium-sized hill and through the valley on the far side of it, until we came to the 'larach' of an old cottage, and, beside it, a patch of jungle running down to a little burn. That patch of jungle had been the cottage garden once upon a time. Now, even then I knew my Burns topography as well as most so-called expert Burnsians, and my excitement began to rise. I suspected what Crichton was leading up to; I was right up to a point – Burns *had* lived for a while in the cottage that had stood on those old founds. But Crichton – though I saw him noticing out of the tail of his eye that I had already jumped to that conclusion – had something far greater to show me. He plunged breast-high into the tangled growth of the old garden and I followed him until, close by the burnside, he threw aside a last swathe of rank vegetation, as if it had been a curtain, and said: 'There!'

What I saw was a little ruined old dry closet. There was no door to it; but the roof had been recently repaired, and the seat inside, though rotted away in parts, was wonderfully preserved.

'You don't mean . . .?' I cried.

He nodded solemnly.

It was an august moment – the most impressive moment of my life – as we stood there in the gathering twilight, and he told me the slow but sure steps, the ten years' unremitting study, that had led to his discovery and his final and absolute proof that (though, alas! there was no scrap of writing on the walls, no carved initials on the woodwork even) Burns himself had used that very place, that very seat; the only convenience he had used that was still extant – Burns himself, and Jean Armour.

'Since then,' he said, with a break in his voice, '. . . You will understand. . . . It has become a sort of temple to me; a Holy of Holies. I am not a rich man, as you know, but I have bought this property . . . to preserve it for all time.'

What a wonderful thought! That strip of semi-decayed wood bridging the years and bringing one into almost direct physical contact with our national Poet – and on no adventitious grounds but on the immutable basis of common human necessity, of constitutional at-one-ment! Darkness was descending upon us but I felt a glow of supreme exaltation and looked with awe into my friend's eyes.

We stood silent together in unspeakable communion for a little while.

Then swift upon the rapture of revelation came the tragic cry which showed the real genius of the man – his power of thinking of *everything*; literally nothing escaped him – and the way in which the achievement and failure are hopelessly twined together even on such great occasions.

'But the pail,' he cried, 'the old pail wasn't there. If only . . .'

We left it at that.

14 The Burns Cult

This formed part II of an essay of the same title in *At the Sign of the Thistle* (1934).

THE Burns cult must be killed stone-dead – and would be instantly if a single lightning flash of the spirit of Burns were alive in Scotland – home or colonial.

The whole *raison d'être* of the Burns Club is to deny that Burns was Burns – and to make him instead acceptable to conventional standards that would have found in him their most powerful and persistent enemy, and to middle-class 'buddies' whom he would have flayed alive.

What an organization the World Federation of Burns Clubs could have been – could even yet become – if it were animated with the true spirit of Burns and fulfilling a programme based on his essential motives applied to crucial contemporary issues as he applied them while he was living to the crucial issues of his own time and generation! What a true Scottish Internationale that would be – what a culmination and crown of Scotland's role in history, the role that has carried Scotsmen to every country in the world and given them radical leadership wherever they went!

Are the young Scots of today – the Free Scots – going to tolerate any longer this infernal insult to Burns, this base betrayal of the historical function of the Scots spirit? Scotland will signalize that it has come to itself again and resumed its proper attitude to world affairs when it makes a bonfire of all the worthless, mouldy, pitiable relics that antiquarian Burnsians have accumulated at Mauchline, Dumfries, and elsewhere and reconcentrates on the living message of Burns's poetry the world-wide attention devoted today (at least once a year) to the mere man and his uninteresting love affairs and the ramifications of the genealogies of his acquaintances and the poor bric-à-brac of his *lars* and *penates* and the witless lucubrations of the hordes of bourgeois 'orators' who annually befoul his memory by the expression of sentiments utterly anti-pathetic to that stupendous element in him which ensures his immortality.

An element – it cannot be overstressed – utterly and forever irreconcilable with the political, religious, social, and all the other bearings and elements of the personalities and lives of 99.9 (repeater) of his yearly panegyrists.

Burns cult, forsooth!

It has denied his spirit to honour his name.

It has denied his poetry to laud his amours.

It has preserved his furniture and repelled his message.

It has built itself up on the progressive refusal of his lead in regard to Scottish politics, Scottish literature, and the Scottish tongue.

It knows nothing about him or his work – or the work that should be done in continuance of his – except the stupid and stereotyped sentiments it belches out annually.

It is an organization designed to prevent any further renaissance of the Scottish spirit such as he himself encompassed, and in his name it treats all who would attempt to renew his spirit and carry on his work on the magnificent basis he provided as he himself was treated in his own day – with obloquy and financial hardship and all the dastardly wiles of suave Anglicized time servers and trimmers.

It has produced mountains of rubbish about him – to effectively bury the dynamic spirit – but not a single good critical study, not a single appreciation above the literary level for which a first-year Higher Grade schoolboy would be thrashed if he so dealt with some petty English novelist or poetaster.

It has failed (because it never tried – it has been numerically ample to succeed if it ever had) to get Burns or Scottish literature or the Scottish language to which Burns courageously and rightly and triumphantly reverted from English, taught in Scottish schools.

Its gross betrayal of the Scots language – its role as a lying agent of the Anglicizing process Burns repudiated – was well seen in its failure to support the great new Scots dictionaries.

Its money is for no such cause, but for its own gobbling gluttonous throat and the swollen paunch over which its hypocritical fingers are apposed like a five-bar gate when it rises to propose 'The Immortal Memory'. Immortal fudge!

Burns knew what he was doing when he repudiated all the canting Anglicizers and reverted to the Scots tongue and the Scots spirit – and the need to follow his lead at long last is today a thousand times greater than when he gave it.

We can – if we will. We can still rescue Scotland from the crash of England's collapse and the ruins of an Empire vitiated by England's infernal Ascendancy policy. We can still affirm the fearless radical spirit of the true Scotland. We can even yet throw off the yoke of all the canting humbug in our midst. We can rise and quit ourselves like men and make Scotland worthy to have had a Burns – and conscious of it; and we can communicate that consciousness powerfully to the ends of the earth.

We can if we will – if we don't, if we won't, the Burns cult will remain a monstrous monument to Scotland's refusal to follow Burns's lead – a monument to the triumph of his enemies.

Until then, Scotland remains –

> A nation which has got
> A lie in her right hand and knows it not.

– the fit land of our Burns 'orators' but a scandal and a disgrace to the spirit of Burns himself.

15 A Plan for the Unemployed

This was the final essay in *At the Sign of the Thistle* (1934).

THE whole problem of unemployment is radically altered by the realization that an ever-increasing proportion of the population will become surplus to industrial and commercial requirements. Science is tending to eliminate all kinds of human drudgery that have hitherto employed masses of workers, and this is a tendency capable of immediate and infinite acceleration as soon as the lets and hindrances to the introduction of new labour-saving and production-increasing devices imposed by the existing economic system (which is based on the necessity of people 'earning their livings') are removed, as they soon must be. The Leisure State is within sight and from this point of view, as Lloyd George says, it is high time to cease thinking of unemployment in the traditional way and begin regarding it as a great opportunity. This is admittedly difficult in a transition period when practically everybody is feeling the economic pinch. It is particularly difficult for the unemployed themselves to realize that they are the vanguard in a great process which will progressively relieve mankind from the necessity of drudgery, as long as they themselves must exist on allowances which debar them from enjoying their leisure. That again, however, is only an unfortunate, and it is to be hoped very temporary, aspect of the transitional period. I am not concerned here with the ways and means whereby the economic system is to be altered, though I have my own very definite views on the matter, and certainly think that these should be the prime concern of all well-disposed persons and particularly of the victims of the present phase themselves. There is, happily, evidence that the latter are concentrating increasingly on the subject. The use they are making of the time on their hands is reflected in the augmented issues of the Free Libraries – and particularly of the issues of books on economic subjects. The main thing perhaps is that they – and other people – should clearly realize that unemployment is a permanent and progressive phenomenon and that there is no possibility, let alone desirability, of the reabsorption of the workless into the productive system. A thorough understanding of this will clear away all manner of absurd arguments and anticipations. That is a necessary preliminary to an adequate view of the phenomenon and the advancement of any useful proposals for dealing with this new state of affairs. Towards public speakers, and others, who are still thinking, talking and writing in terms of a state of affairs which has passed and can never return there ought to be an organized intolerance on the part of all who have a clear view of what is happening, for their obsolescent dogmas only serve to complicate the issue and make comparison worse confounded.

Nor do I intend to deal here with the other type of person who is gravely alarmed at the prospect of people having so much spare time at their disposal and declares that they will not know what to do with it and will inevitably waste it in ways less desirable than the old drudgery and become hopelessly demoralized. I do not believe anything of the sort. The average morale of the lower-paid workers was never very high even when they were fully employed, and I see no signs of any great deterioration due to unemployment. The unemployed, it seems to me, are pretty much the same sort of people as the employed and not a bit worse than the latter in regard to crime or vice of any kind. Any demoralization that is going on is not due so much to the actual fact of unemployment as to its concomitants of insufficient purchasing-power and equivocal social status in their present state of affairs. As soon as they realize that their unemployment is permanent and will in time be shared by the vast majority of the workers, and that they are no longer going to be financially penalized on this account, but on the contrary are to have ample purchasing-power allocated to them, most of the alleged demoralization will disappear. In any case, no one should want to prevent scientific progress or impose needless labour on moral grounds; that is to enforce personal prejudices in an altogether unwarrantable fashion. The proper thing is to trust humanity with all the new opportunities available to it. These may be misused by some people; there may be an interval of chaos and readjustment; but the faculties of humanity will sooner or later achieve an effective equilibrium under the new conditions.

My concern is with the unemployed themselves during the transition phase. I believe that the majority of them are just as diligent and capable and public-spirited as any other section of the population. Footling self-help schemes are a mere evasion of the realities of the situation and not only affect the standards of organized labour on the one hand and enter into competition with established tradesmen on the other, but, taken by and large, represent an effort to re-enter the existing economic system by the back-door and regain and maintain a precarious footing there. Such a manoeuvre is not good for the morale of those concerned either. They are not meeting the implications of their position fairly and squarely and doing man-sized jobs. Expedients such as these will only delay the inevitable reckoning and prolong the agony that comes from a failure to confront the whole situation and deal with it in a rational and adequate manner. What, then, are my proposals?

I think the worst feature of unemployment is the feeling amongst the unemployed that they are regarded by others as failures and a burden on the community. They are nothing of the sort. They are the heralds of a new economic order, and like most pioneers have to suffer for it. But they ought not to conceive their position in terms of a superseded and unreturning condition of affairs. Literally they should realize it as a great opportunity and make the most of it. Freedom from unnecessary toil and ample leisure should be recognized and utilized as great social assets. The unemployed should neither be sensitive about getting – or not getting – 'something for nothing', or about giving it! The idea of others that they ought not to get a decent living unless they work for it, and their own notion that it is unthinkable that they should do anything free, gratis, and for nothing, spring from the same basic misunderstanding, and should cancel each other out. In this transitional phase there are abundant ways and means by which the unemployed can seize their new social opportunity, vindicate themselves against the charges of indolence and demoralization, rehabilitate themselves in the eyes of their fellow-men (and in their own eyes!), and signalize their changed status. The way is not by means of a little amateur tailoring or cobbling on their own behalf, not by petty schemes of mutual assistance, not by a reversion in certain directions to the processes of primitive barter. But the way is by a thorough mobilization of their abilities of all kinds and the application of these in a systematic and disciplined fashion to general public needs. I am referring to purely voluntary work on schemes of real value for the common weal. All manner of important improvements and desirable schemes are at present hung up indefinitely on the plea of economy or because money is not available to carry them out. Resources and amenities of all kinds are going to rack and ruin for the same reason. Let the unemployed, without abating one iota of their claims to proper maintenance, rise above their personal troubles and organize to effect these improvements or discharge these neglected services free, gratis, and for nothing. They have ample ability. It will be a magnificent gesture which cannot fail to impress and win over sections of people who presently regard them with distrust and misunderstanding. It will be the best possible earnest that they themselves, the unemployed, realize their great opportunity and are ready to make the most of it. The schemes they actually carry out in this way will be to their own advantage as well as other people's. The all-important thing is to destroy the habit of measuring everything in terms of money value. If they gain nothing financially, at least they will lose nothing – and they will gain a great deal in self-respect and general goodwill. And they will hasten the general process of discerning an immense social asset in the liberation of humanity from all preventible drudgery, and with that hasten the substitution for the present economic system, founded on the gospel of the need to work, of a new and more generous system, based on a realization of the role of Science in ushering in the era of leisure and freedom. The speedy, if not the ultimate solution of their present problems of poverty and hardship depends very largely upon the way in which they recognize and use their present chances.

Let them go to those territorial magnates who are bewailing their inability owing to high taxes to look after their lands properly and startle them by offering to do for nothing at all what properly considered is a service to communal property

– the great public asset of our forests and rural areas. Let them embarrass public authorities by offering to do gratuitously all the desirable things these bodies allege they are unable to do owing to the cost. They will speedily reduce to absurdity the upholders of the present financial system. They will exemplify a new spirit in keeping with the coming order, and prove themselves conscious heralds of the greatest advance in the history of humanity.

16 Five Bits of Miller

This was privately published by MacDiarmid in an edition limited to forty numbered copies, in 1934. It was collected in both Kenneth Buthlay's and Alan Bold's anthologies.

FIRST of all, there is my recollection of a certain fashion he had of blowing his nose: the effect of the sound mainly, and my appreciation of the physiology of the feat. A membraneous trumpeting. Fragments of a congested face, most of which was obliterated by the receptive handkerchief. Like an abortive conjuring trick in which, transiently, certain empurpled and blown-out facial data meaninglessly escaped (as if too soon) from behind the magic cloth which, whipped off immediately after, discovered to the astonished gaze not the expected rabbit or flower pot but only Miller's face as it had been before the so-called trick (the trick of remaining the same behind that snowy curtain when literally anything might have happened) or, rather, Miller's face practically unchanged, for the curious elements that had prematurely broken out of their customary association were to be seen in the act of reconciling themselves again, of disappearing into the physiognomical pool in which they usually moved so indetectibly. – I had invariably present in my mind on such occasions moreover a picture of the internal mechanism, the intricate tubing, as if Miller's clock-face had dropped off, disclosing the works. I never really liked the way his wheels went round; the spectacle offended some obscure sense of mechanical propriety in me; I felt that there should have been a great deal of simplification – that there was a stupid complexity, out of all proportion to the effects for which it was designed. I was in opposite case, regarding Miller, to the guest who took for a Cubist portrait of his host a plan of the drains that hung in the hall.

Then the condition in which this weird aggregation was kept revolted me. It was abominably clogged up. What should have been fine transparencies had become soggy and obtuse: bright blood pulsations had degenerated into viscid stagnancies; the tubes were twisted, ballooning or knotted in parts and taut or strangulated in others. Miller could never hoist his eupeptic cheeks with sufficient aplomb to hide this disgraceful chaos from me or dazzle my contemptuous eyes with lardy effulgence of his brow from which his hair so precipitately retired. 'Yes, yes,' I would say to myself, 'a very fine and oedematous exterior, but if you were all right behind instead of being so horribly bogged – really lit-up from within, instead of disporting this false-facial animation – man!; if your works could only be completely overhauled and made to function freely and effectively, what a difference it would make!'

Then there was his throat. I hated to hear him clearing it. He was top-heavy as I have just shown. That appalling congestion behind his face consumed practically all his energy. The consequence was that any movement of his throat sounded remote and forlorn, a shuttle of phlegm sliding unaccountably in a derelict loom, the eerie cluck of a forgotten slot, trapping the casual sense that heard it in an oubliette of inconsequent sound. It was always like that; like the door of some little windowless room, into which one had stepped from sheer idle curiosity, implacably locking itself behind one. A fatal and inescapable sound, infinitesimally yet infinitely desolating. How many stray impulses of mine have been thus irrevocably trapped! I feel that a great portion of myself has been really buried alive, caught in subterranean passages of Miller's physical processes as by roof-falls, and skeletonizing in the darkness there. Miller clearing his throat was really murdering me bit by bit; blowing bits off me with those subtle and unplaceable detonations of his, of which his over-occupied head behind that absurdly bland face must have been completely unaware –

Thirdly he had a way of twirling his little fingers, almost as if they had been corkscrews, in his ear-holes and withdrawing them with lumps of wax in the nail-ends. Uncorking himself by degrees. But his brain was never really opened: it remained blocked, or rather it had coagulated – his hearing never flowed clear into one. Just an opaque trickle devoid of the substance of his attention. – One felt always that one was receiving a very aloof incomplete audition. The wax itself was inhumanly stodgy and dull – not that bright golden vaseline-like stuff one sometimes sees, silky skeins of it netting the light, flossily glistening, a fine live horripilating honey. But orts of barren comb that had never held honey; dessicated fragments of brown putty that made one sorry and ashamed.

Even yet I cannot trust myself to do more than suggest in the most elusive way the effect his cutting his fingernails had upon me. He did it so deliberately and his nails were so brittle and crackling. Dead shell. His finger-tips under them were dry and withered. Shaking hands with him was like touching dust and deepening reluctantly but helplessly into the cold clay of his palm. – But meanwhile I am speaking of his nails. They literally exploded. He affected to use scissors like the rest of us: but, watching him closely, I was never deceived. It was not by the scissors that he cut his nails. He blew them off with his eyes. I know that sounds absurd and impossible. But if you could only have seen the way in which he looked at his finger-tips while he was engaged in this operation, and the extraordinary crepitation and popping-off that ensued –

Lastly, there was the way in which he used to squeeze a blackhead out of his chin. He was the sort of person who more or less surreptitiously permits a horde of these cattle to enjoy his cuticle for a certain length of time for the queer sport of killing them, and, at the appointed time, he slew them with amazing precaution and precision. I think this process gave him some strange dual effect of martyrdom and ceremonial purification. I cannot attempt to describe here the rites with which he was wont to sacrifice a blackhead of the proper age on the altar of his complexion. For the outsider the ceremony was to a great extent masked by the fact that he only obliquely faced any congregation through the medium of a mirror. In a fragment of it that eluded the blocking back of his head and a thin slice of side-face decorated with a whorl of ear, one saw all that one might, heightened in effect by the liquid light in which such a reflection was steeped. The squeezing-out process was a delicate and protracted one. Blackheads do not squirt out under pressure like paint from a tube, but emerge by almost imperceptible degrees. A very slim yellow-white column (of the consistency of a ripe banana) that ascends perpendicularly and gradually curves over and finally, suddenly, relapses upon its base again.

Yes! I think that perhaps the most vivid recollection of Miller I still retain is that of some knobbly fragment of his chin on which under the convergent pressure of two bloodless, almost leprous, finger-tips the stem of a blackhead is waveringly ascending; and then of the collapse – lying there, thready, white, on a surface screwed and squeezed to a painful purple, like a worm on a rasp!

You remember the big toe-nail in one of Gogol's stories? Well, I have only these five somewhat analogous bits of Miller left – mucus, phlegm, wax, horn, and the parasitic worm – five unrelated and essentially unrepresentative bits of the jig-saw puzzle that I used to flatter myself I could put together with blasphemous expertise. All the rest are irretrievably lost. But see what you can make of these five.

17 Major C. H. Douglas

MacDiarmid collaborated with the novelist Lewis Grassic Gibbon (James Leslie Mitchell) to produce *Scottish Scene: or The Intelligent Man's Guide to Albyn* (London: Jarrolds, 1934). The book was divided into sections with stories, poems, 'newsreel' items (collections of cuttings from contemporary newspapers) and essays. Two 'studies' were headed 'Representative Scots': one, on James Ramsay Macdonald, was subtitled, 'The Wrecker' and written by Gibbon. The other, on Douglas, was named 'The Builder'.

I DO not propose to give any of the particulars here concerning Major C. H. Douglas's birth, antecedents, career as a civil engineer or subsequent missions to various countries as a witness in regard to economic issue. These, together with the long list of books which he has published since he first set out his proposals in collaboration with Mr A. R. Orage, are to be found in *Who's Who* and other reference books. A year ago – or even six months ago – the great majority of people in Great Britain had not heard of Major Douglas's name and any knowledge of – let alone understanding of – his 'New Economics' was confined to an exceedingly small percentage of the population. Now his name, together with some notion of what he stands for, is known to intelligent people everywhere and it is almost impossible to pick up a newspaper or weekly review either in Great Britain or America or the British Dominions which does not contain references to him and to his proposals. That is not altogether a good sign perhaps; it means that the powers responsible for keeping all mention of his name and discussion of his ideas out of every paper and periodical except these little-known periodicals of extremely limited circulation which existed for the specific purpose of promulgating Douglasism, for a period of some ten years have at last decided to 'lift the ban'. Whatever their motives may be in doing so, however, the lifting of the ban discloses this hitherto generally-unknown Scottish engineer occupying a position of altogether unusual and world-wide importance. He is disclosed as one of the few leaders in the world today – and the only one acting simply and solely as an individual 'off his own bat', and not vested with Government power. Although his name is only now becoming known to the masses in this and other countries, it has been known for more than a decade to all the financial and political chiefs. It is no common achievement to flutter such dovecots all over the world simultaneously, and to have associations and study circles and active propagandist journals in all the Continents. Douglasism today is a live issue confronting every civilized government; it is pushing its way ahead and numbering its adherents by thousands in the United States, in Australia, in Canada. Look over history; how many times do you encounter a single man building up a movement against all the strongest vested interests in the world? It is ample proof of Major Douglas's genius for leadership that he has shown an amazing power of adapting himself to all the complicated circumstances affecting the promulgation of his discovery and has stuck to his point, undeflected, 'with cool understatement' despite one of the most rigorous and prolonged press boycotts in the history of journalism and without compromising his position one iota piloted the biggest revolutionary project in the history of humanity into a foremost place in the councils of every civilized country. For that is what it is. Short-sighted opponents are still apt to declare that the two alternatives before civilization are Communism and Fascism. Neither Communism nor Fascism can last long in any modern country without a tremendous repudiation of the tendency of science to the Leisure State and a corresponding reversion to barbarism. There is no alternative to Douglasism compatible with the maintenance and furtherance of existing civilization. One of the parrot-cries of nit-wits is that Douglas is the 'Einstein of economics' and that the reader must go to his books prepared to think in terms of algebraic formulae. A Scottish lady – Lilias McCrie, of Johnstone – in a recent letter to the press provides the best reply to this:

> There are only three pages (out of 212!) in Major Douglas's *Social Credit* in which these occur, and the author always brings us right up to the door of his argument in clear

English before taking the leap into a world whither only those with the necessary education can follow. The more I read these books the more admiration and respect do I feel for the imaginative insight and practical genius which brought them into being; although I do sometimes feel a strong maternal impulse to chastise the author for being content with such a cool understatement of his case. However, if I were not so constantly reminded of the engineer's hand on the slide-rule I could not trust so much this new hope which he has given for an unhappy world.

Not only is Douglas a true Scotsman, frequenting Scotland as much as he possibly can, but his proposals afford the only technique for assuring absolute national – or absolute individual – independence, and he paid Scotland the undeserved compliment of setting forward his concrete outline for the immediate application of Douglasism in any country in the form of a Draft Plan for Scotland; the only document of the slightest political or economic consequence produced in relation to Scotland since the Arbroath Declaration of Independence. That Draft Plan for Scotland has been the storm-centre of the world's controversy on the most crucial issue confronting civilization ever since it appeared; but it has secured relatively little attention – and still less appreciation and understanding – in Scotland itself. This is the measure of our appalling provincialization, backwardness, and impotence.

When the Scottish Nationalist Movement started I immediately realized that there could be no Scottish Movement of more than petty local consequence unless it was related to some substantive manifestation of the Scottish genius which would signalize Scotland's re-emergence into the arena of world-affairs with a contribution of consequence to all humanity. It was not difficult to find that master-idea. It lay in Douglasism and it was inevitable in any sound view of Scottish history that it should do, for Scottish genius had been disproportionately embodied in engineering on the one hand and economics on the other – so much so in the latter respect that the 'Aberdeen story' had become the world symbol of the Scottish character. Douglas fused and transcended these two in an unmistakable fashion; and I found that the few intelligent people associated with me in the early days of the Scottish Movement had all come to the same view. Unfortunately the majority were not to be won over and the subsequent history of the National Party of Scotland had been a progressive repudiation of 'the big idea' and a relapse upon the footling anachronisms of provincial politics. The only two organs in Scotland which have any appeal to the intelligent reader and have been associated with any of the creative development of contemporary Scotland, however – the *Modern Scot* (quarterly) and the *Free Man* (weekly) – are both Douglasite and have Major Douglas and myself and many of the leading propagandists of Douglasism among their contributors. I am perfectly convinced that within a very few years all that has appeared in any Scottish paper, except these two, on the present so-called 'economic crises' and on the basic principles of the present money, political, and industrial-commercial system, will seem as pitifully ludicrous to any intelligent person as the most grotesque notions of Middle West fundamentalists in the sphere of religion. Douglasism does not entertain the myth that nothing can happen anywhere unless it happens everywhere simultaneously; and Douglasism must be applied first of all in some specific country. That country ought to have been Scotland; it would have been Scotland – it could not have helped being Scotland – if we had really had point one per cent of the hardheadedness, enterprise and business nous claimed by us and generally ascribed to us. That, however, is a myth, belied by every fact in Scotland today; and so we have missed our great opportunity and forfeited a historic role which would have given us the honour of world-leadership in the greatest development in the history of humanity – a big enough change surely from being merely the 'northernmost and most neglected county in England'. The Duke of Montrose and Sir Alexander McEwen and Mr John McCormick and all the rest of the ridiculous gang of so-called Scottish Nationalists may fiddle away as long as they like with their puerile constitution-mongering; Scotland has missed Destiny's cue once again and is condemned to a mere walking-on part – but Scottish genius acting independently of all but a tiny minority of Scots has not been similarly remiss. Douglas will rank as the greatest of all Scotsmen and his tremendous achievement – so intimately related to all that is most vital in Scottish genius as to have been almost predictable and certainly inevitable – will, despite the defection of the vast majority of his race, have had, at least, the quick recognition and unwearied advocacy of the tiny minority of his countrymen who have any claim to be regarded as 'fully alive in their own time'. The remainder resemble the occupants of a town that has been long and sorely besieged who when the siege is raised fail to recognize the fact and continue to live on rats. It remains, of course, for some other country to have the honour of first applying Douglasism. The future of Scotland will depend upon whether it can speedily evoke from the national genius that has been lying fallow so long some other master mind which will be a significant contribution, not only to the solution of Scotland's own problems, but to humanity at large. There is no sign of that so far, and until there is Scotland must continue to pay the penalty of failing to recognize a prophet in his own country by a further spell of relegation to the small change of provincial politics and parish-pump culture. In the meantime Douglasism has at long last begun to make rapid headway even in Scotland itself, and Douglas groups are to be found from one end of the country to the other. The bulk of the population, however, are still in the grotesque position of regarding Ramsay MacDonald as a great man.

The true relationship of Major Douglas to Calvinistic Scotland – the necessity of his emergence at this juncture – are reflected by himself when he says:

> There probably never was a time in which disinterested legislation was so rare, just as there probably never was a device which was so effective in silencing criticism of interested legislation as this idea that self-interest on a worldly plane must necessarily be wicked. I would therefore make the suggestion, in order to add to the gaiety of nations by creating a riot at once, that the first requisite of a satisfactory governmental system is that it shall divest itself of the idea that it has a mission to improve the morals or direct the philosophy of any of its constituent citizens – Sir Walter Fletcher said: 'We can find safety and progress only in proportion as we bring our methods of statecraft under the guidance of biological truth': I think that this is one of those remarks which illuminate a subject much as the skyline is illuminated upon a dark

night by a flash of summer lightning. We *know* little *about ourselves, and less about our neighbour, and almost nothing at all about the nature of a healthy Society. Nor do we display any particular anxiety to increase our knowledge in these directions.* Yet there is, nowadays, none so poor that he is not prepared to produce at short notice the plans which will put every human being in his place, within the space of a few short weeks. Preferably with the aid of a few good machine-guns. It is no less than a tragedy, that *the inductive method, for which in particular the English temperament is specially suited,* is not in itself a reliable instrument in this emergency. The physical scientist who wishes to obtain a sure foundation for the formulation of laws, begins his investigation by standardizing his reagents. Temperature would be meaningless if we had not something we call 'zero'. But in regard to the biology of the State, we are in a difficulty. We do not even know how unhealthy we are, though we have a strong suspicion that we are very sick indeed. To those, then, who are anxious to make a definite contribution to the salving of a sick world, it may not be impertinent to suggest that the natural creative forces of the universe might plausibly be expected to produce at least as good results if left alone to work themselves out through the agency of the individual, as may be expected from planning which is undertaken without any conception of the relation of the plan to the constitution and temperament of those who are affected. If all history and all observation has not been misread, there is implanted in the individual a *primary desire for freedom and security, which rightly considered are forms of the same thing.* There is no such thing as a freedom and security which is held upon terms, whether these terms are dictated by the State, by a banking system, or by a World Government. Until it can be shown that, with the resources which science has placed at his disposal, the individual is incapable of making freedom and security for himself, the multiplication of organizations whose interference he cannot avoid will only make a world catastrophe the more certain.

The phrases I have italicized regarding freedom and security represents what has all along been the keynote of the Scottish genius, while the reference to the English partiality for the inductive method shows clearly where we stand *vis-à-vis* our Southern neighbours in this crucial matter.

The policy of orthodox finance is puritanical. It is founded on distrust of men and the assumption of scarcity. It has been crystallized in the stern injunction: Work More – Consume Less, Work and Save. It satisfies the will-to-power of a certain type of man, and its drive is towards a super-central bank of which the Bank of International Settlements is a precursor and towards a world-state in which the external preserves on men will be severe. It is an effective policy, since it is associated with a system of rewards and punishments imbedded in modern industry. It is, in a phrase, the policy of centralizing financial initiative in the hands of a very few private individuals. Or, in other hands what we are suffering from is the maladjustment of Finance to Industry; or financial system is derived from a scarcity-obsession, whereas thanks to the Machine our industrial system holds aloft a cornucopia of Abundance.

The policy on the other hand of the heterodox finance advocated by Major Douglas has (to quote Gorham Munson) been termed 'economic democracy' because by socializing credit it aims to decentralize financial initiative (to decentralize it down to the individual in fact and establish the economic independence of the individual). In the light of this policy the aim of industry is simply to supply goods to the people who want them. 'Morals' are to be removed from industry in the sense that industry is to be judged by a criterion of efficiency and not asked to provide employment or to function as an instrument of social coercion and moral governance. The values to be safeguarded in the Douglas Commonwealth are Liberty, Leisure, and Culture. The will-to-plenty of the inviduals is to be given satisfaction, and *the whole business and industrial life of society relegated to a subordinate place, somewhat as in the economy of the human body many biological processes proceed automatically or semi-automatically, leaving the psychology of the human being free to develop its interests.* Systems were made for men, not men for systems, declared Major Douglas in the first chapter of his first book and the interest of man, which is self-development, takes precedence over all systems, economic, political, and theological. A ringing statement to come from an economist!

A ringing statement to come from a Scotsman – the first since

Burns whose was the first since the Arbroath declaration of independence! What are commonly regarded as the typical Scottish virtues, ever since the Reformation and the Industrial Revolution, have certainly been on the contrary anti-Scottish, and the dominant characteristics almost wholly products of English domination. What is to be noted about Douglasism is not only its significance as the latest, and by far the most stupendous, manifestation of the essential genius of Scotland, but its sheer modernity, its concordance with the crucial needs of all mankind, by contrast with which all the other politico-economic and corresponding theological and social views in Scotland today look like material which has somehow overflowed on to the country at large from the Royal Scottish Museum. Or, perhaps it would be even truer to say from our Lunatic Asylums, for all non-Douglasites are committed to the logical but insane financial doctrine that the cure for an unsaleable surplus is more production or economy. Our fools, madmen, or sinister sadists in authority are rejoicing even as I write this that Scotland has no fewer than 1600 Saving Associations in schools, but, alas, only three or four hundred in industrial establishments. If the boy is indeed the father of the man, everything that can be done is being done to make the coming Scotland safe for universal cretinism; but perhaps the relatively small number of these organizations amongst our adults as compared with the number forced upon the helpless children under an educational system that would be involved in a terrific uproar if any teacher was found inculcating Socialist propaganda, shows that already the 'gospel of thrift' is ceasing to 'cut much ice'. Those responsible for its propagation ought to be corralled and confined in some remote institution where they can spend the remainder of their days impressing its beauties upon each other. They include all our 'leading Scots' – even Sir Harry Lauder.

It is a poor testimonial to those who would guide Scotland's destinies for them to have to admit that they cannot understand Major Douglas's proposals – that they do not want to worry about fundamentals, but are content to appeal to that mythical figure 'the man in the street' and make average newspaper-created ignorance and incompetence (and the habit of waiting for the lead to come from other countries) the foundation stone of 'the new Scotland'.

They are not in earnest. They have not begun to get down to the subject. All they want is what they said twenty years ago or what Gladstone said in Midlothian. They simply want a continuance of the same old game with the same old pawns. It is monstrous that in a matter of this sort 'national newspapers' should have recourse so largely to the opinions of men of a type who occupy prominent positions in every age but whom history invariably shows to have been figureheads of no real value. What have these highly-placed persons ever done or tried to do for Scotland? Can it be claimed in any quarter that their intelligence is proportionate to their influence? Isn't it part and parcel of the present disorder of civilization that *people like these* should have their opinions quoted, and that our Parliamentary system – and public life generally – should be practically insulated against real brain power and creative ability?

No form of devolution (and any form of devolution is an insult to Scotland – it is not for England to give us back 'control of our domestic affairs' but for us to assert our independence and take our own course regardless of England) which brings these precious legislators back from Westminster to Scotland is worth a damn. *They will remain the same on this side of the Border as on the other.*

All the Nationalist Party motives – and the motives of the newspapers affecting an interest in the 'new Scotland' – are belated applications in Scotland of methods that have been tried and have failed or are failing elsewhere, and are therefore only an aspect of that standardization which a true nationalism must combat. The National Party ideas are drawn from English political practice; all the forms of reorganization it is proposing for Scotland have been tried elsewhere and found futile. They all hate true ideas – ideas in the dynamic, creative sense. They are too busy grinding their little axes to think. The hatred of intellectual distinction is their chief characteristic. But Scotland is not to be rehabilitated by being decked out in any other country's cast-off political or economic clothing. In minor matters, we are told, we may look after ourselves; but in the major matters – which after all condition these minor matters too – we will leave the initiative in other hands. Was ever such idiocy? It is precisely where the crucial issues develop – at the very heart of the conflict – that everything worth a rap in modern Scotland must concentrate: and the future of Scotland, and of more than Scotland, will depend upon the ability of these elements in our nation, and these elements alone, to evolve ideas and forms of a distinctive character, substantive or our national genius, and contributive in due proportion to the development of human affairs.

And the first step to that is to recognize the significance of the fact that it is precisely this neglected, provincialized Scotland which, at the very threshold of its renaissance, has given the world in Major C. H. Douglas a son of immense genius, who has hit upon ideas which will solve civilization's most pressing problems – ideas at that which could only have been discovered by a Scotsman, related as they are to essential factors alike in the old Gaelic commonwealth and in subsequent pre-Union Scottish policy and financial practice, and overturning, as they do, the vicious 'commercial Calvinism' which has been so largely responsible for Scotland's decline. In view of the vistas opened up by Major Douglas's proposals – the fact that they are utterly incontrovertible and that all the incompetent and lazy can do is, not to pretend to refute them, but to moan that 'they are incomprehensible' – and the obvious facts of the existing position all over the world towards the betterment of which no other proposals of the slightest value have been offered – it is farcical to ask us to think about the silly Rotary Club notions of the Scottish Development Council and those guilty of such a derogatory view of Scotland's potentialities are condemned out of their own mouths as incapable of contributing to the Scottish Nationalist Movement in precisely the same way as the disease cannot contribute to the cure. The whole mentality – or lack of mentality – of these people is, in fact, our problem; and the sole value of the official Nationalist 'literature' and its journalistic support is to reveal that mentality again in all its ghastly complications of hoary platitude, sales promotion stuntism, inveterate prejudice, and helpless anti-intellectualism.

A handful of us must still be less concerned with a mission ship to Canada (the next should be sent to Timbuktu), tartan souvenirs, and sprigs of white heather and all the rest of the stock-in-trade of the people who believe that the more fools get together and pool their inanity the better we shall be, than with the forces which have compelled mankind

> To build a pyramid of plenty
> And faint with hunger at its base.

18 Charles Doughty and the Need for Heroic Poetry

In an interview with Catherine Kerrigan, MacDiarmid claimed he had been reading Doughty as early as 1904 (at the age of twelve!) and in this essay, published in *The Modern Scot* in 1936 as a review of Barker Fairley's edition of *Selected Passages from 'The Dawn in Britain' by Charles M. Doughty* (1935) and Anne Treneer's *Charles M. Doughty: A Study of his Prose and Verse* (1935), MacDiarmid concentrated his argument on the idea of heroic or epic poetry. The essay is crucial to the argument about the formal shift in MacDiarmid's own poetry, from lyric to epic. It points forward to his appraisal of Ezra Pound in 'The Return of the Long Poem' (Item 28). Doughty (1843–1926) remains neglected and unread; his enormous prose work *Travels in Arabia Deserta* (1888) and his volumes of poetry, despite MacDiarmid's claims for its achievement in bringing together scientific, geological, etymological and mythic fields of knowledge, have been found turgid and impenetrable. Yet Doughty stands behind Tennyson and Palgrave, a shadowy figure in the dark hinterland of Victorian English literature and a monumental precedent for epic poets of the twentieth century, whose project has never been adequately assessed.

ONLY in the USSR today is the trend of poetic effort towards epic – in keeping with the great enterprise afoot in that country, and as a natural consequence of the linguistic experimentation in recent Russian literature, the liberation and encouragement of minority languages and literatures, and the de-Latinization and de-Frenchification of the Russian language. For the condition of any language which has deserted its native basis and over-adulterated its vocabulary, and been devoted to all sorts of tasks save only the expression and elucidation of the Ur-motives of its people, must unfit it for any effort of like magnitude – for, that is to say, in other words, a form equal to the perspectives of modern life and the horizons now opening before us. That was why Charles Doughty – his genius lying in the direction of epic – had to abandon modern English and use a large infusion of Anglo-Saxon words and native syntactical forms. Robert Graves and others went 'back to Skelton' and used the old native rhythms, and Auden and other young poets today are following that lead, and that accounts for their communist tendency. But the far greater enterprise of Charles Doughty has gone unrecognized or obstinately opposed. It is dismissed (in *The Times Literary Supplement*) as a 'reversal of language' – which is on all fours with the fact that Wagner's *words* are generally dismissed as of no consequence. Yet Wagner was right, not wrong, when he spent years studying word-roots. He knew (as Charles Doughty knew) that we were coming to another of the quantitative – as against accentual – periods in culture. It is that lack of historical knowledge which disables no Marxist that is wrong with our mere impressionist commentators on such a phenomenon. (It is this question of quantity as against accent that distorts to most Scots the nature of our pibrochs of the great period. These knew no 'bar'. They were *timeless* music – hence their affiliation with plainsong, with the neuma. Barred music – accented music – finds its ultimate form in symphony. Unbarred music – quantity music – expresses itself in pattern-repetition; hence the idea that the Celt has no architectonic power, that his art is confined to niggling involutions and intricacies – yet the ultimate form here is not symphony; it is epic.) It is epic – and no lesser form – that equates with the classless society. Everything else – no matter how expressly it repudiates these in the mere logical meaning of what it *says* as against what it *is* – belongs to the old order of bourgeois 'values', to the nebulous entities described by terms like 'spiritual' and 'soul'; in short, it stands for the old romantic virtues, which is to say, pragmatically, for nothing. Doughty, as against Auden and Day Lewis, say, is the only English poet who belongs to the new order, that is to say, to our own time. His significance today dwarfs all the other English poets since Elizabethan times into utter insignificance, and the failure of contemporary English literati to recognize that is only another confirmation of the communist diagnosis of the present phase of English literature (it is significant that D. S. Mirski had no difficulty in recognizing the overtowering quality of Doughty) as being thoroughly in keeping with the imminent fatal crisis of a degenerate capitalist society. To those of us who are concerned about a Scottish renaissance, Doughty's unique preoccupation with – and marvellous imaginative penetration into – ancient British (Celtic) consciousness[1] is as convincing a 'pointer' as Wagner's devotion to the study of word-roots.

Dawn in Britain is a great storehouse of the history, fact, legend and romance of the Celtic peoples', truly observed one of its earliest reviewers. That sealed its fate. How the English ascendancy policy treated Irish Gaelic literature, Dr Douglas Hyde shows us. How then could it tolerate Doughty's attack from inside – from within the English language itself? Never!

When two new books on Doughty recently appeared,[2] all the host of contemporary little English reviewers hastened to deny that Doughty is a great poet and to dismiss his work as hopelessly archaic, mere obstinate linguistic pedantry and a 'reversal of language'. Despite these, Doughty will yet come to his own:

> For while the tired waves, vainly breaking,
>   Seem here no painful inch to gain,
> Far back, through creeks and inlets making,
>   Comes silent, flooding in, the main.
>
> And not by eastern windows only,
>   When daylight comes, comes in the light.
> In front, the sun climbs slow, how slowly,
>   But westward, look, the land is bright.

It is not through the English that due recognition of Doughty can come. It is significant that the authors of these two new books on Doughty are a Scotsman (a Shetlander) and a Cornishwoman. The trouble with all the little English reviewers is their inability to realize that 'the stone the builders rejected' may well 'become the cornerstone'. The whole development of modern English

---

[1] A complete account and examination of Doughty's sources is now [1936] under weigh. Until that is published we will not know in any detail the means whereby Doughty came to this extraordinary understanding of the ancient British element.

[2] Anne Treneer, *Charles M. Doughty: a study of his prose and verse* (Cape, London, 1935); *Selected Passages from* The Dawn in Britain *of Charles Doughty*. Arranged, with an introduction, by Barker Fairley (Duckworth, London, 1935). Readers should also consult Professor Barker Fairley's *Charles M. Doughty: A Critical Study* (Cape, London, 1927).

literature has gone hand in hand with an ascendancy policy that has belittled and discouraged literary effort in its own dialects, done its utmost to stamp out Irish, Scottish and Welsh Gaelic and the Scots Vernacular, thinks (with Sir John Squire) that 'it would have been much better if Burns had written in English'. As I pointed out in *At the Sign of the Thistle*, 'it must be remembered that it was only with the utmost difficulty – and against precisely the same sort of opposition and arguments as we are now contending – that Elizabeth Elstob succeeded in preventing England treating its own Anglo-Saxon background (and where would English studies be without that now?) in precisely the same way as it has treated the other minority elements in our midst.' Doughty was a great English national poet in the same sense as Bjørnson was a Norwegian one – 'to name the name of Bjørnson is like hoisting the Norwegian flag'. As Bjørnson put it:

> A poet's is the prophets' call:
> In times of need and travail-throe
> His faith the gleam they seek can show
> To those who strive, and striving fall.
> Now ringed by champions from of old,
> Now marshalling the new-enrolled,
> Mid whispering hopes, he hears the cry,
> He sees the dreams, of prophecy.
> In song the spring-sap of his nation
> Breaks forth, and is its inspiration.

As a writer on Bjørnson has said:

> In the lines in which he pictures himself appealing alternately to the heroes of old and the contemporary generation, as well as in the metaphor, to which he was so fond of recurring, of the spring renewal of life, he discloses one of the key-points in his philosophy – his ever-present sense of the continuity of national existence, which viewed future and past with a correlated faith and pride, and looked upon the great figures of Norwegian history as collaborators in his task no less than his contemporaries . . . It was with a just appreciation that Ibsen saw in his rival the model for King Haakon in his *Pretenders*,

the character in whom this ideal of union is so central.

What English poet but Doughty could be cast for any similar role in a drama of English history? And assuredly it is of prime importance at this great crisis, this watershed, in English history that we should have Doughty sending Brennus and young Sigamer and Caradoc and all the rest of his great characters out into our streaming streets today instead of letting English poetry leave it to Blake to send Albion's Angel, driven howling from Westminster by the fires of Red Orc, to go

> Grovelling down Great George Street, and
> thro' the Park Gate.

It must be realized that one cause for his countrymen's repudiation of England's most comprehensive understander – the only English poet of whom, in Matthew Arnold's famous phrase (criticizing Byron as 'so empty of matter, Shelley so incoherent, Wordsworth even, profound as he is, yet so wanting in completeness and variety') it cannot be said that 'he did not know enough' – is the fact that Doughty was not 'a prophet of easy things', but came with what their misguided spirits regard as bad news. English literati are still babbling about English as a 'world language', and following the 'pure English' lead of the BBC. Doughty alone foresaw and understood it all thoroughly and realized that the English ascendancy policy must go – that England must relapse on its native basis and let its dialect and minority language elements at long last resume their proper function after the tremendous misdirection of a policy by which England had gained the whole world and lost its own head. Great Britain, or better still, England might inspire an epic, but not the British Empire. And so, just as, during the war years, it was government policy to represent Ramsay Macdonald (destined for the highest political honours) as a dangerous man in order to hide the fact that John Maclean was really the dangerous man, we have today all sorts of little rhymsters hailed as revolutionary poets (as if real revolution would not involve far greater technical changes than any they affect) and Doughty, the real revolutionary, ignored. Doughty and Wagner; real revolutionaries – Wagner with the *Nibelungenlied*, Doughty concerned to give the ancient

British (Celtic) the due they are denied in the official story and in the consciousness of the vast majority of Britons today. Wagner 'wasting his time' among word-roots, and Doughty emphasizing aspects of English history generally and best treated as non-existent and dragging out hosts of obsolete words too – sad spectacles both for contemporary 'common sense'! The sinister opportunism which prevails amongst us is in significant contrast to the spirit of Lenin's admonition: 'We do not know and we cannot know which spark – out of the innumerable sparks that are scattering around in all countries as a result of the political and economic world crises – will kindle the conflagration, and therefore the most seemingly hopeless, musty and unfrequented directions are not to be taken for granted and overlooked but diligently explored.'

The general rejection of Doughty by these English reviewers is only a ridiculous belated insistence on a poetic diction – on the employment of a certain English and not any other. It is the same 'quaint survival' of an idea that dismisses my 'synthetic English' experiments in *Stony Limits* as 'unfortunate', that denies, not only the urgent and unescapable necessity of the poetic use of the full range of modern scientific terminology, but the experiments in linguistics of James Joyce, and Ezra Pound's use *as a language* of multifarious references to all periods of history and all phases of human activity. This is the great stumbling-block which compels every modern creative writer in English to use lots of unfamiliar and often technical words – and compels each of them (Meredith, Hardy, Patmore) to use different ones. It is this stumbling-block, too, which is responsible for the failure to incorporate in the canon of our speech the ubiquitous out-of-the-way words constantly being used, not by such creative writers, but in the ordinary course of contemporary English journalism and conversation (e.g. from one recent newspaper, snickersnee, finnimbruns, and ipsissimosity). Yet Edward Garnett, in the *Sunday Times*, had to take severely to task for his egregious utterances Mr Basil de Selincourt, the *Observer* reviewer of the recent books on Doughty. This provided the only refreshing feature of a dreadful exhibition of ineptitude, prejudice, and the complacency of reviewers so immersed in the cataract of current tittle-tattle and coterie disputes that they are completely incapable of any objective view. Forgive them; they do not know what they are talking about. As a friend of mine writes: 'In this hopelessly introverted world you can't expect any response from the gang-leaders to a great *out-going* spirit. They blink like owls in the strong sunlight.' And the most owlish blinking of all was not even de Selincourt's but Geoffrey Grigson's – and that is the right measure of *New Verse* and its young hopefuls. Montagu Slater, in *The Left Review*, clearly understands the 'back to Skelton' movement and the partial return to a native basis in rhythms and words of Graves and Auden and others, but I have not yet been able to study the effect of Doughty's 'strong sunlight' on any communist critic; I eagerly – and confidently – await the spectacle. My friend writes to me:

> How little sense there is anywhere of his (Doughty's) being in any way a new vision, a radical genius, something to approach from the inside, not the outside . . . What needs rubbing in strongly now is the importance of this heroic poetry for the new ideal in Europe. England, being the least progressive country at present, has the sort of poetry that goes with it: Eliot, Auden, etc., all ironists, using the old forms and calling themselves revolutionaries. But there has been no revolution yet. A real revolution would affect technique more.

I ought to make it clear that in referring especially to Doughty's significance for communists I do not mean he belonged to the Communist Party. I remember the following passage from the obituary notice in the *Cambridge Review* by his friend G. G. Coulton:

> Once or twice Alfred Ollivant, the novelist, made a third with us; but his rather extreme socialism met Doughty's extreme conservatism without the least friction. Doughty with his characteristic slight turn of the head, but far more definite sidelong turn of the eyes towards the man he was talking with, would blast Socialism and all kinds of Liberalism in a single Elizabethan phrase, but with such impersonal detachment, or even personal cordiality, that Ollivant would appreciate the utterance almost as much as I did.

And I think of how Professor B. Ifor Evans says that Bridges, in his poem 'To a Socialist in London', expounds 'a sort of spiritual *laissez-faire*, which is not unsavoured with self-complacency', and how Mr R. L. Megroz says:

> Only a long succession of academic praises of Bridges by people suffering from very similar mental restrictions derived from the old-fashioned English class educational system could have culminated in the extraordinary chorus of excited eulogy which greeted this scholarly minor poet's verbose *Testament of Beauty*. What was said about this prosaic and rhetorical but skilful metric exercise in unoriginal uplifting thought in the English Press, if exhibited in a collection, would supply a most damning illustration of the meaning of 'middle-class culture'.

The people who hailed Bridges in this egregious way are the same people who are now denouncing or rejecting Doughty at the same time as they are belatedly revelling in the slight achievement disfigured by exaggerated Marianism and other unpleasant and singularly untimely and undesirable traits of Gerard Manley Hopkins (whose technical achievements are all to be found equalled and excelled in Doughty, as Professor Fairley pointed out in an admirable article in the *London Mercury*, June 1935). They are the same people, too, as those who are now reviewing Thomas Lovell Beddoes favourably and at great length apropos the three new books which have just appeared about him and his work. Hopkins and Beddoes accepted; Doughty rejected. 'It's a mad world, my masters.' *And they chose Barabbas*.

I feel sure it will be a long time before any of these little writers – even those of them plying most assiduously such catchwords as 'a sense of one's own time' and 'economic awareness' – achieve or find any better passage to their professed purpose than this of Doughty's:

> I saw the travail-stained hammer-men stand;
> Sons of the daily labours of their hands:
> Idle, at corners now of shot-crazed streets:
> Toilers, for whom, those daylong murky hours,
> The vital air was a pernicious breath;
> An headstrong, handstrong, hungered, impotent

> Pale multitude, with thick curses on their lips.
> Cumbered dejected wretches the town paths.
> Some were, that only shades of manhood seemed.
> (Those startle, at the coming of a Stranger!)
> Their joyless mills, and chimneyed factories,
> Blackened by fire; be broken down and waste.
> Shut were the iron gates, behind their backs!
> Drudges of steel! that giant, ere few days were,
> Reciprocating stride of wheeling engines;
> Which wrought, with panting breaths, for human
>   livelihood
> Hath ceased!

As Miss Treneer says: 'I can think of no modern picture of a machine which surpasses this of the giant drudge. A line like "Reciprocating stride of wheeling engines" makes a reader wish that Doughty had more often tried to write in this condensed and pregnant way. Metaphor is exciting. The leap of our imagination gives something of the same satisfaction to the mind, as speed to the body; it is exhilarating, and daring and dangerous. Simile is more sedate.' And this, in this particular connection alone out of the immense range he establishes (one of the greatest of English poets alike in range and mass, in concentration and variety, in historical imagination and proleptic power) is the poet they are dismissing as a dull pedantic archaicizer!

There are precedents in literary history for the precise position in which Doughty has been placed – and precedents of special interest to us Scots at that.[3] But let me quote Miss Treneer's admirable passage on this archaic business:

> Recently we have been able to hear the voice of Gerard Manley Hopkins, who did not live to see Doughty's verse, and probably tasted the prose only in extracts, raised emphatically against the principle of archaism. While admitting that

---

[3] See 'Sixteenth-Century Humanism as illustrated by the life and work of George Buchanan', *George Buchanan: Glasgow Quatercentenary Studies* (MacLehose, Glasgow, 1907), where the same charge of 'archaism', on similar entirely superficial grounds, against this great Scottish revolutionary are brilliantly repelled in terms that almost without alteration would equally stand for Doughty's case.

Victorian English is a bad business, he 'cannot away with any form of archaism' or any diction 'sicklied o'er' with Elizabethan English. 'But come now,' he writes to Bridges who had recommended *Arabia Deserta*, 'is it not affectation to write obsolete English? You know it is.' What Hopkins could not realize was that Doughty was engaged on a process for which the word 'archaism' as applied, say, to the poetry of William Morris, is unsuitable . . . Of the diction of Doughty's poetry it is hard to say a final word. For myself the words rejoice me, and I do not think this is merely because I am, to use a phrase of Hopkins, weathered to the style. Doughty's language accords with what he says in his *Notes* language should be; 'wine of a good vintage', 'words of a good stock', of 'honest ancestry', 'hale'. 'It is rich of a golden simplicity, antique, of singular efficacy, distinct'. I have examined numbers of his words in relation to the sources from which he drew them, and have lingered to admire the rightness of his usage of forgotten words, and, even more, his skill to re-brighten known words by calling to the surface their overlaid tones. The work he did for words often corresponds to what a new owner will do for an old room; he will strip off layers of shoddy paper or plaster to show the genuine panelling beneath. In addition Doughty was able to make his words carry the force of his conviction in a way which annuls Hopkins's objection to the use of obsolete words as tending to 'destroy earnest'. Earnest is only destroyed if a writer is concerned preciously with words instead of with what he has to say. Doughty was not thus concerned; though he sometimes uses his old words merely for colour as in the Saxon episode in *Mansoul*, or for glee as in the faerie poems, or for rusticity as in the pastoral scene in *The Titans*, or for pageantry as in some parts of *The Dawn*. To criticize his diction as though it were everywhere alike and always 'quaint' is like applying a common measure of criticism to Spenser's *Hymnes*, to his *Shepherd's Calendar*, and to *The Faerie Queen*. Thenot may ask Hobbinol what 'garres him greete,' with perfect fittingness, but this 'rustical rudeness' would not be fitting to *The Four Hymnes*. So in Doughty, Goodfellow Pipit may 'play pluck-buffet in the hazel scrogs,' but the diction is very different in the loftier parts of *Mansoul* or of *The Dawn*. The 'eclectic' used by Doughty in these parts is merely an extension of common practice, not what he called 'a whistling, windy singularity.' All speech is an eclectic; Doughty merely extended the bounds of choice, while at the same time making the conditions of choice more rigorous.

We Scots ought to remember with pride how Doughty was influenced by a Scottish book – *The Effect of the Mis-use of Familiar Words on the Character of Men and the Fate of Nations* (1856), by David Urquhart. Like David Urquhart, says Miss Treneer, Doughty

> held that the English of his day and the mode of thinking which the preponderant use of abstract terms implied was thoroughly bad. Urquhart, who had been much in the East, praised the concrete qualities of Turkish, and contrasted with it unfavourably the generalities too current in English . . . Doughty studied words no less as a moralist than as a poet, believing that the right use of vital language was essential to the health of individuals and nations. 'Words are almost the elements of human thoughts,' he wrote in his *Notes*; and on another page he jotted, 'The old manly English, full of pith and stomach.' One of the duties of a poet was to preserve the elements from decay, and keep the notation clear, warring against loose use of words as a thing perilous to thought and feeling, and as an insidious means to undermine the integrity of individual persons and finally of whole peoples.

Charles Doughty was advanced, generally, far ahead of his times. Professor Fairley is right in claiming that in inner chronology Doughty is later than T. S. Eliot. As the following note appended to *The Dawn in Britain* puts it '. . . it is the prerogative of every lover of his country to use the instrument of this thought, which is the Mother-tongue, with propriety and distinction; to keep that reverently clean and bright, which lies at the root of his mental life, and so, by extension, of the life of the Community: putting away all impotent and disloyal vility of speech, which is no uncertain token of a people's decadence.'

Doughty's idea was to make a fresh channel for English direct from the upper reaches, from the vernacular as it was before the

Renaissance, and so freshen and purify the corrupt main flood . . . Not that the revival of obsolete words is of main importance in Doughty's experiment. Much more important is his scrutiny of known words, and his close fitting of word to sense. He did not fall into what Bacon calls the first disease of learning, that men hunt words rather then matter; but neither did he neglect the warning of his favourite Ascham, 'Ye know not what hurt ye do to learning, that care not for words but for matter, and so make a divorce betwixt the tongue and the heart.'

I have only space left in which to say that Professor Fairley's book is a model of selection and arrangement – an invaluable introduction for 'weaker brethren' – and that Miss Treneer's study is beyond praise in its tact and thoroughness. They should be carefully read by all who are concerned with the problems of the Scottish renaissance, as showing in detail how all the difficulties involved in the reintegration and full modern use of Scots were solved to great poetic purpose in a kindred medium; and bearing no less effectively on the issues involved in the future use and development of Scots Gaelic as a literary medium.

19 The Great McGonagall

> This item was published in *Scottish Eccentrics* (1936), a collection of essays on expected figures such as Lord Monboddo, who believed that all men were born with tails and a world-wide conspiracy of midwives amputated them at birth, and Sir Thomas Urquhart (few literatures in the world can claim as a major writer one who died laughing!), and others less expected, such as the miniaturist William Berry, and Elspeth Buchan, an eighteenth century religious guru. The book builds into a cavalcade in which the uncommon and uncanny qualities are prized in the wayward, antinomian, versatile, erudite, wandering Scot, the type of person given to going beyond the frontier where the might of general, common-sensical ideas ceases. With McGonagall, we have the inverse of everything this praiseworthy character might be. The shorter version of this essay which is given here comes from Kenneth Buthlay's selection *The Uncanny Scot*.

CONTRARY to the general opinion – in Scotland at all events, for I am not sure that he is much known in the English-speaking world outside Scotland – William McGonagall was not a bad poet; still less a good bad poet. He was not a poet at all, and that he has become synonymous with bad poetry in Scotland is only a natural consequence of Scottish insensitivity to the qualities alike of good poetry and of bad. There is so much that is bad in all poetry that Scots people know and admire that it is not surprising that for their pet example of a good poet they should have had to go outside the range of poetry, good, bad, or indifferent, altogether. McGonagall is in a very special category, and has it entirely to himself. There are no other writings known to me that resemble his. So far as the whole tribe of poets is concerned, from the veritable lords of language to the worst doggerel-mongers, he stands alone, 'neither fish, flesh, nor good red-herring', and certainly his 'works' will be searched in vain for any of those ludicrous triumphs of anti-climax, those devastating incongruities, which constitute the weird and wonderful qualities of bad verse. This, of course, is recognized by experts in this peculiar department of literature. Hence, although it may be true enough of McGonagall that, in his own way,

> O'er all the Bards together put,
> From Friockheim to Japan,
> He towers above, beyond dispute,
> Creation's greatest man,

he, rightly, does not figure in such an anthology as *The Stuffed Owl*. As Wordsworth says:

> Yet, helped by Genius – untired Comforter,
> The presence even of a stuffed owl for her
> Can cheat the time . . .

But McGonagall had no such help, and the last thing his incredible sincerity sought to do, or succeeded in doing, even to the tiniest extent, was to cheat time.

It is laid down in the above-mentioned anthology that 'good Bad Verse is grammatical, it is constructed according to the rubrics, its rhythms, rimes, and metres are impeccable. Generally the most distinguished poets – from Cowley to Tennyson – provide the nicest pieces in this anthology. The first quality of Bad Verse which the compilers have aimed at illustrating is bathos; other sure marks are all those things connoted by poverty of the imagination, sentimentality, banality, anaemia, obstipation, or constipation of the poetic faculty . . . and what Mr Polly called "rockcockyo".' McGonagall stands outside all these requirements. His productions know nothing of grammar, the rubrics and the accepted devices of versification. Bathos is a sudden descent from some height – a manoeuvre of mood of which McGonagall's dead levelness of utterance is quite incapable. Poverty of the imagination is a different thing altogether, and produces quite different effects, from that utter absence of anything in the nature of imagination at all in which he stands sole and supreme. His invariable flatness is far below mere banality; sentimentality and 'rockcockyo' of any sort are entirely foreign to his stupendous straightforward seriousness alike of intention and expression; and anaemia is a term that suggests a human character of which his inspired work is completely devoid. Take his stanzas on 'The Famous Tay Whale':

> 'Twas in the month of December, and in the year of 1883,
> That a monster whale came to Dundee,
> Resolved for a few days to sport and play
> And devour the small fishes in the silvery Tay.

He describes the efforts made to harpoon the whale, and how it was finally towed ashore at Stonehaven, and ends:

> And my opinion is that God sent the whale in time of need,
> No matter what other people may think or what is their creed;
> I know fishermen in general are often very poor,
> And God in His goodness sent it to drive poverty from their door.
>
> So Mr John Wood has bought it for two hundred and twenty-six pound
> And has brought it to Dundee all safe and all sound;
> Which measures 40 feet in length from the snout to the tail,
> So I advise the people far and near to see it without fail.
>
> Then hurrah for the mighty monster whale,
> Which has got 17 feet 4 inches, from tip to tip, of a tail;
> Which can be seen for a sixpence or a shilling,
> That is to say, if the people are all willing.

What this amounts to, of course, is simply what quite uneducated and stupid people – the two adjectives by no means necessarily go together, for many uneducated people have great vitality and a raciness of utterance altogether lacking here – would produce if asked to recount something they had read in a newspaper. It is almost exactly of material of this kind that the consciousness of current events consists so far as most people are concerned. In their retailings of, or comments upon, such matters, the *hoi polloi* would also reflect their personal feelings as is done here, by the tritest of emotional exclamations. If this is not quite all they are capable of 'carrying away' of what they hear, see, and read, it is, at any rate, a very fair specimen of their powers of articulation.

    The deviations from this stuff of common consciousness, or rather common conversation, are two. In the first place, there is the organization of the material not only into some regular succession of sentences but into verses if only of the crudest kind. This is to be explained partly by the fact that McGonagall was trying to write up to a very vaguely conceived, or misconceived, level; he was trying to be 'litt'ry': a similar laboriously unnatural organization manifests itself very often when uneducated people try 'to talk polite' rather than in their natural, much racier, if quite ungrammatical and disjointed way – and partly by the fact that a kind of rude rhyming is a very common knack and comes much more easily to many such people than any similar attempt to 'rise above themselves' in prose would do.

In the second place, there is the insistence on giving the exact figures. This was a special characteristic of McGonagall's. It is just possible that it was due at the outset to a vague Biblical reminiscence, but his constant use of it is due to his incorrigible laziness. In these circumstances the precise numbers were a veritable stand-by to him. They fascinated him; there was no getting past them – they clinched the whole matter. If his work gave him a real thrill at all it was when he came to such figures. Apart from that, however, his use of them was due to his laziness because he found them where he found his themes – in newspaper reports, which he did little but hammer out till he got rhymes at the end of his sprawling lines. What set McGonagall off on this tack was a combination of three factors – his laziness, his peasant conceit (carried, of course, to an absolutely abnormal length), and the fact that he lived in Dundee. Dundee was then and has since been the great home and fostering centre of the cheapest popular literature in Scotland, and huge fortunes have been built up there on precisely the chief ingredients of McGonagall's art – mindlessness, snobbery, and the inverted snobbery of a false cult of proletarian writers. So far as literature has been concerned, the idea of Burns as a 'ploughman poet' has been fatal. Scotland has suffered since from an endless succession of railwayman poets, policemen poets, and the like. The movement was in full swing when McGonagall was caught up in it. It culminated in the collection and publication by a gentleman who lived near Dundee of the work of scores of utterly worthless rhymers, in no fewer than sixteen volumes, with a table showing the occupations of the contributors. It is not surprising that McGonagall thought – or was easily persuaded by one of his friends or more likely one of his tormentors – that he could do as well as any of these. Having once performed the miraculous feat of knocking a bit of journalese into rough rhyming verses, he naturally conceived an inordinate admiration for his own powers – and so far as any question of comparative worth arose it naturally seemed to his type of mind, with its almost inconceivably complete absence of intellectual background, that this was only a question of one man's opinion against another's, and McGonagall was not the man to cry stinking fish. He was, indeed, genuinely incapable of realizing or being persuaded that his poems were not at least as good as any ever written – with the possible exception of Shakespeare's – and he did not hesitate to proclaim the fact. It may have been his persistence in this, the realization that he really believed it and was prepared, if need be, to become a martyr for genius's sake, that led to his subsequent shameful baiting. For though the great majority of his contemporary Scottish rhymsters were exceedingly vain, and believed, no matter how belauded their contemptible productions might be, that far greater praise was their real due and would be accorded by posterity, it was their fashion to pretend to be humble. There was no pretence about McGonagall – a fact which in no way runs counter to his cunning understanding that most of those who praised him so egregiously did not believe what they said, though for the sake of a few coppers it paid him to accept their bogus attentions and finally allow them to 'give him the bird' to their hearts' content. Where McGonagall differed from all these other working-men poets was that he knew nothing of poetry – nothing even of the execrable models they copied, nothing of the whole debased tradition of popular poetry in which they operated. He was quite incapable of all their stock *clichés*, their little flights of fancy, any indication whatever of play of spirit, anything like their range of subject-matter, and, above all, of any humour. He, in fact, heartily despised them and all the common attributes and graces of their verses, which he regarded as trivial and unworthy of his portentous Muse. But he stuck fast by the fundamental ingredients of the great Dundee recipe for sound family literature – a love of battles and an incontinent adoration of kings, queens, members of the royal family, the nobility, and the leading officers of the army and the navy; in short, the recipe which has made modern Scotland what it is. Knowing his own perfect loyalty and integrity in these great matters, the 'slings and arrows of outrageous fortune' to which he was continuously subjected were incredible to him. He deserved better – in fact, there was nothing that he did not deserve. He was sustained through all his miserable career by this unwavering consciousness of his high deserts and enabled to regard all his calamities as a series of monstrous and inexplicable injustices. His 'poems' were, in truth, little worse than those of the vast majority of Scottish poets whom the very type of people who baited him regarded with affectionate interest and approval; his 'poems' were, in truth, little worse than those the vast majority of the Scottish people, now as then, regarded as very poetry – but, in both cases, how little and yet how much it is! If, however, 'extremes meet', there is no little justification for McGonagall linking his name with Shakespeare's, and indeed the course of literary history shows countless such linkings with that great name.

The connection between versification and mendicancy is a very old one. The writers of the old broadsides required a livelier turn of language, some faculty of satire or invective, and a sense of news values, all of which McGonagall conspicuously lacked. Neither had he the social address which was such an asset to Dougal Graham, the Skellat Bellman of Glasgow, for example. His affiliations are rather with the melancholy individuals, purporting to be ex-soldiers, who hawk terribly bad sets of verses from door to door today. I have no idea how this line pays these gentlemen, but a slightly higher type of tramp poet, selling little pamphlets of verse, seems to do fairly well, judging by several of these men I have known personally, who, little though they made by it, at least wrung a livelihood out of it and in so doing made a great deal more than all but one or two of the genuine and really gifted poets of our time. Even in Scotland today some of these tramp poets are faring none too badly. McGonagall would have been exceedingly glad to have had a tenth of what they earn.

At first – living in one of the vilest slums of Dundee – he secured a regular clientele for his penny poems, but he also fancied himself as a tragic actor. His appearances in various public halls in the city led to his being pelted with refuse of all kinds and generally mishandled, and the police warned the lessees that he must be given no further engagements. McGonagall justly enough protested against this, declaring that he was the innocent party and yet he was being punished and deprived of a source of livelihood. The police would not listen to his complaints, however. His appearances on the streets next became signals for all manner of baiting and hooliganism. It became impossible for him to try to sell his broadsides at street corners or in the shops, or even to go round his regular clientele. He was made the prey of practical jokes and hoaxes of all sorts and sent off on wild-goose chases to London and to America. Forced to leave Dundee, he lived for a little in Perth; but Perth was too small to yield even the minimum number of poem-purchasers at a penny a time to keep him (and his wife) in the barest necessities. So he went to Edinburgh (where he died) and there, and in Glasgow, was subjected to extreme ill-usage and baited unmercifully by students and others who organized mock dinners at which he was crowned as the world's greatest poet and decorated with bogus honours. The small collections taken up at these affairs, as the price of his ignominy, and frequently of his acquiescence in physical assault and battery, were his main – almost his only – source of income. He became a national joke. His claims to be superior to every other poet, with the sole exception of Shakespeare, were in all the papers – with samples of his indescribable doggerel. Ludicrous incidents were invented – like his attempted interview with Queen Victoria at Balmoral; and most of his alleged sayings and poems (certainly all of these which show the slightest wit or advance his claims in a super-Shavian fashion) were invented by his baiters.

The way in which McGonagall's effusions were thrown off in penny broadsides makes anything like a collection of authentic examples at this time of day impossible. But the genuine McGonagall article is fairly easily distinguishable from the far too farcically funny efforts fathered upon him. There is nothing superficially funny about his authentic productions at all – they are all dead serious.

Through it all McGonagall remained a perfect Micawber,

always looking for something to turn up, and believing that at any moment he would be translated to his rightful place in the enjoyment of world-wide fame. The only little tokens he ever got which he could construe as the smallest advance instalments of the meed of praise that was his due were the formal acknowledgements he got from various distinguished people to whom (as is the custom of Scottish poetasters) he sent copies of his productions. These acknowledgements enabled him to have an elaborate headpiece set at the top of his broadsides – with the Royal Arms, the Lion and Unicorn, and V.R. in heavy type; extracts from the letters flanking the poem which occupied the centre of the page; and, under his own name beneath the title of the latest effort, the magical phrases 'Patronised by Their Majesties, Lord Wolseley of Cairo, H.R.H. the Duke of Cambridge, the Right Hon. W. E. Gladstone, and General Graham, etc.'

As one of his editors, Lowden Macartney, says:

> He was a strange, weird, drab figure, and suggested more than anything else a broken-down actor. He wore his hair long and sheltered it with a wide-brimmed hat. His clothes were always shabby, and even in summer he refused to discard his overcoat. Dignity and long skirts are considered inseparable, and a poet is ruined if he is not dignified. He had a solemn, sallow face, with heavy features and eyes of the sort termed fish-like.

Nothing in the history of modern Scotland is more discreditable than the treatment accorded – and allowed by the authorities to be accorded – to McGonagall. It is without a single redeeming feature. Certainly the type of 'humour' it gave rise to does nothing to redeem the brutal baiting to which he was subjected; it is more deplorable than McGonagall's poems in every way and has been one of the most widespread and powerful influences operating in Scotland, for upwards of a century, amongst all classes of the population. It is wholly vicious and unintelligent facetiousness – the flower of which is the 'Scotch coamic' and the typical 'Scotch joke'. It is displayed at its very worst, perhaps, in the bogus autobiography of McGonagall, entitled *The Book of the Lamentations of the Poet McGonagall*, and sold at a shilling a copy. This is now exceedingly rare, although it was published as recently as 1905 – of course, in Dundee. Its only really valuable feature is its magnificent frontispiece photograph of McGonagall, an appalling portrait, a fish-belly face, as of something half-human struggling out of the aboriginal slime. All the incurable illiteracy, the unaccessibility to the least enlightenment, and the unquenchable hope of the man are to be seen in the eyes. It is, indeed, a face to make one despair of humanity. What passes almost universally for wit in Scotland is splashed all over these unspeakably nauseating pages. The book is 'Dedicated to Himself, knowing none Greater'. The chapters are headed by fake quotations, like this, from the *Delhi Thug*:

> Rejoice, Edina, shout and sing,
> And bless your lucky fates;
> McGonagall, the lyric king,
> Was born within your gates.

We are given harrowing pictures of the ill-used bard 'cleansing my garments from rotten eggs, ostensibly administered as an antidote to rotten egotism'. Writing of the Grass-market in Edinburgh, we find him quoting Mark Twain's statement about a city in Italy: 'The streets are narrow and the smells are abominable, yet, on reflection, I am glad to say they are narrow – if they had been wider they would have held more smell, and killed all the people'. An alleged gift to be sent to the famous poet by the King of Burmah leads McGonagall's wife to complain of the idea of sending 'an elephant to a man that couldna feed a canary'; and there is any amount of this sort of thing (an alleged dialogue between McGonagall and one of his patrons, following a misunderstanding) – ' "I am prepared to apologise, poet," he frankly rejoined; "when I called you by that dreadful name, believe me, I meant the opposite of the reverse". "Thank you," I replied, "I can see now that it was only the want of ignorance on my part, and I am fully satisfied with your apology" ' – and he holds out his hand, only to get a copper tack rammed into it. These are the excruciatingly amusing things which delighted McGonagall's baiters.

'Look here, poet,' a shopkeeper in Perth is reported saying to him, 'I do not wish to flatter any man to his face, it is against my creed; but common honesty and a sense of fair play compels me to say that your poems are unique. In Scott, Byron, or Burns, for instance, if you omit a line, ten to one you lose the sense. With you it is totally different. I have read a whole production of yours, omitting each alternate line, and getting quite as much sense and literary power out of it as ever. Nay, more, if you read the fourth line first, and work back, the effect is quite wonderful. The other night my wife pointed out to me that, in experimenting with a recent issue, she managed to derive even more benefit from it by reading the last line first, the first line next, the penultimate line third, the second line fourth, and so on till its natural conclusion by exhaustion. With this one I have bought just now we are trying another experiment tonight. We mean to clip each word separately, shake them all up in a bag, and paste them together on a clean sheet of paper as they come, and will let you know the result. If it is as I anticipate, I would strongly advise you to take out a patent, and float it in £1 shares –"The Patent Reversible Poetry Company Ltd" – in which I would be glad to invest as a shareholder.'

'I thanked the gentleman cordially,' McGonagall is given as replying, 'but told him that such commercial enterprises were not at all in my line, but that I would gladly supply the raw material and sell him the patent rights for a consideration if the result of his next trial justified his anticipations. At our next interview he told me that "the test was too severe even for my effusions, so that meantime at least the matter would go no further". At the same time he answered me that both he and his good lady fully agreed that the individual words were fully up to the Shakespearean standard, the only difference discernible in the completed article consisting merely in the matter of their arrangement.'

A few pages further on, the autobiographer recurs to the matter: 'And now, gentle reader, I will give you an object lesson regarding the peculiarities of my poetry, so eloquently referred to in a previous part of this chapter by my Perth shopkeeper friend and his lady. I refer, of course, to the reversible, interchangeable, double-breasted, universal-jointed nature of my composition. This is the distinguishing mark of my work, to copy which is moral felony. Like the rock we used to buy at the fairs, break it where you will, the hallmark of excellence stares you in the face. Read the lines in any order you like; begin at the top, middle, or bottom, and continue in any direction you choose, and you receive the same benefit.'

The song given in the spurious autobiography, 'I'm the rattling boy from Dublin town,' with its catchy refrain

> Wack fal the dooral, ooral, ido,
> Wack fal the dooral, ooral, aà,
> Wack fal the dooral, ooral, ido,
> Wack fal the dooral, ooral, aà,

is not an authentic McGonagall item. He worked in a different vein altogether. His true sort is to be found in the verses on 'The Attempted Assasination of the Queen':

> God prosper long our noble Queen,
> And long may she reign.
> Maclean he tried to shoot her,
> But it was all in vain.
>
> For God he turned the ball aside,
> Maclean aimed at her head,
> And he felt very angry
> Because he didn't shoot her dead.
>
> Maclean must be a madman,
> Which is obvious to be seen,
> Or else he wouldn't have tried to shoot
> Our most beloved Queen;

or, again, in his 'Address to the New Tay Bridge':

> Beautiful new railway bridge of the silvery Tay,
> With your strong brick piers and buttresses in so grand array,
> And your thirteen central girders, which seem to my eye
> Strong enough all windy storms to defy.
> And as I gaze upon thee my heart feels gay,
> Because thou art the greatest railway bridge of the present day,
> And can be seen for miles away,
> From north, south, east, or west, of the Tay;

or, once more, in his 'Descriptive Jottings of London':

> As I stood upon London Bridge and viewed the mighty throng
> Of thousands of people in cabs and buses rapidly whirling along,
> All furiously driving to and fro,
> Up one street and down another as quick as they could go,
> Then I was struck with the discordant sounds of human voices there
> Which seemed to me like wild geese cackling in the air;
> And the River Thames is a most beautiful sight,
> To see the steamers sailing upon it by day and by night.

All these are typical McGonagallese. As Mr Macartney remarks:

> One of the things that go to make a man great is uniqueness. He must in some way be totally unlike anybody else in the world. McGonagall did most certainly possess this qualification. Not only did he excel in the peculiar form of writing with which he clothed his ideas when offering them for the edification of an astonished, if somewhat irreverent, public, but while others might write a little like him, no one has ever succeeded in successfully copying his style. In that respect he remained the master, unapproached and unapproachable. Another individual can thrust aside any rule or regulation calculated to hamper his movements; and here McGonagall excelled every other singer of sweet song. Literary composition is an art, and like other arts, is governed by certain rules and limitations – we might even say conventions. So great indeed was our 'poet' that he deigned to observe only a few – and that the simplest of these. In rhymed verse a certain amount of harmony is considered necessary. It is one of the elements totally lacking in the writings of this wonderful man. Rhythm and measure, also, have been considered from time immemorial as essential to the making of good verse, but rhythm and measure were cast aside when our bard took up his pen . . . In the words of his own favourite poet, we may say
>
> > Take him for all in all,
> > We shall not look upon his like again.

In view of certain developments in Scotland it is interesting to note that McGonagall was opposed to Home Rule. He sang:

The man that gets drunk is little else than a fool
And is in the habit, not doubt, of advocating Home Rule.
But the best of Home Rule for him, as far as I can understand,
Is the abolition of strong drink from the land.

And the men that get drunk, in general, wants Home Rule,
But such men, I think, should keep their heads cool,
And try to learn more sense, I most earnestly do pray,
And help to get strong drink abolished without delay.

William Power in his book *My Scotland* tells how he attended one of McGonagall's performances in the Albion Halls in Glasgow many years ago.

> He was an old man, but, with his athletic though slightly stooping figure and his dark hair, he did not look more than forty-five; and he appeared to have been shaved the night before. He wore a Highland dress of Rob Roy tartan and boy's size. After reciting some of his own poems, to an accompaniment of whistles and cat-calls, the Bard armed himself with a most dangerous-looking broadsword, and strode up and down the platform, declaiming 'Clarence's Dream' and 'Give me another horse – Bind up my wounds'. His voice rose to a howl. He thrust and slashed at imaginary foes. A shower of apples and oranges fell on the platform. Almost before they touched it, they were met by the fell edge of McGonagall's claymore and cut to pieces. The Bard was beaded with perspiration and orange juice. The audience yelled with delight; McGonagall yelled louder still, with a fury which I fancy was not wholly feigned. It was like a squalid travesty of the wildest scenes of *Don Quixote* and *Orlando Furioso*. I left the hall early, saddened and disgusted.

'The mental condition of the Melancholy Dane', Power concluded,

> is not more debatable than that of McGonagall. Was his madness real or feigned? I imagine that at first it had been no more than harmless conceit; that it was a rather deliberate pose for a time, when the poet found it paid; and that finally

he became, like the 'Sobieski Stuarts', the victim of his own inventions. He was a decent-living old man, with a kindly dignity that, while it need not have forbidden the genial raillery that his pretensions and compositions provoked, ought to have prevented the cruel baiting to which he was subjected by coarse ignoramuses. McGonagall deserved well of his day and generation, and Time has dealt handsomely with him. He added to the gaiety of at least one nation, and, as the Ossian of the ineffably absurd, he has entered upon immortality.

20   Scottish Arts and Letters: the Present Position and Post-War Prospects

This essay was published in the middle of the Second World War, in *The New Scotland: 17 Chapters on Scottish Re-construction, Highland and Industrial* (Glasgow: The London Scots Self-Government Committee, Civic Press, 1942). This symposium of essays included work on legal reform, trade unions, rural reconstruction, industrial planning and proposed new local and national structures of government. MacDiarmid's essay followed on from the introduction he provided for *The Golden Treasury of Scottish Poetry* (London: Macmillan, 1940). In the *Golden Treasury*, MacDiarmid had included translations from Scottish Latin and Gaelic poets, in an attempt to present an 'all-in view'. He also claimed as Celtic the Scandinavian Eddic poetry of the sagas, and the erstwhile English poetry of *Pearl* and *Gawaine and the Green Knight*, and would have included them, were it not 'for considerations of space'. However, most of MacDiarmid's introduction involves a passionate argument with Edwin Muir's thesis, adumbrated in his book *Scott and Scotland* (1936), that the presentation and development of distinctive Scottish traditions was useless, and that Scottish writers should surrender themselves to the English literary tradition. MacDiarmid's vehement opposition to Muir in this regard was exacerbated by his enthusiasm for the work of the Gaelic poets George Campbell Hay and Sorley MacLean. MacLean had helped him translate the Gaelic poems included in the *Golden Treasury*. Hay, MacLean, and a host of 'younger' Scottish poets – the 'second wave' of the Scottish Renaissance – are welcomed in this essay, and strategically placed in the front-line of opposition to Muir's Anglocentrism.

THIS does not purport to be a full and balanced account of recent Scottish literature. Space is not available here for such an undertaking – all that I propose to attempt is to bring the introductory essay to my *Golden Treasury of Scottish Poetry* (Macmillan, 1940) up-to-date. It must be stated uncompromisingly at the outset that my findings are based on an acceptance of two remarks of Plekhanov's, 'the quality of a work of art is, in the final analysis, determined by the "specific gravity", as it were, of its content,' and 'when a work of art is based on a fallacious idea, inherent contradictions inevitably cause a degeneration of its aesthetic quality.' The touchstone, then, which I apply to determine whether a writer is or is not of any significance may be appreciated in the light of the following quotation:

> We are living in such a grave, such a dark, such a dangerous epoch, and the artist who is not willing to participate in its course, i.e., as a leader of men, seems to me to be feelingless and senseless, and I cannot acknowledge his talent, unless as a formal talent, such as we acknowledge in a good vocalist who can sing well the songs created by a composer some two or three centuries ago.

'War,' wrote a film commentator recently, 'is a good thing for the documentaries.[1] Nowadays a field of corn in the Carse or a sheep-shearing in the Lothians is worth any Hollywood epic. That is what patriotism does. We are having our sense of values restored.' One certainly hopes so. There is great need. But it is a tragedy that it takes such a terrible upheaval to turn people's minds to matters like these. So the old routine of plough horses against the sky-line, fishermen tatting their nets, steel workers flexing their muscles, and Clyde shipyards at work is deployed to give a rich, rounded impression of our own country, but one wonders just what proportion of the cinema patrons really feel terribly ashamed of the furtive relief with which they turned, in the pre-war days, from earnest long-shorts on silage and such to Joan Crawford's eye-lashes.

That healthy change in the direction and quality of Scottish national attention is certainly what all that was worth-while in Scottish literature and art and nationalist cultural and political propaganda and the few vital stirrings in the dead waters of Scottish education was directed towards, earnestly and enthusiastically, in the period of 1918–1939. It had a certain small amount of success. That is the basis upon which Scottish literature and the other arts must build after the war – the process they must carry to complete success. The kulturkampf this implies is described in one of my poems, 'Art and the Workers' in which I say:

> I come away with a heavy heart
> From these fellow-workers' homes. My sadness can be

---

[1] And we ought to remember that the documentary was practically invented by one of the most brilliant of contemporary Scots, John Grierson.

Best illustrated, I think, by the fact
That each of these houses has two or three
Framed pictures of the grocer's calendar type
— The antithesis, the foe, of all art.

I wonder how men like these
With a knowledge of the dynamics of pitch
In propellor blades, say, or the distribution
Of forces in a ball-bearing, which
Enables them to share imaginatively
In the action of mechanical functions
Can endure such monstrosities.

I want no pictures of the King or Queen,
General Haig, or Christ, or the Madonna,
Shaggy cattle knee-deep in a mountain tarn,
Or pretty rural scene. Photography is the art
Of super-reality, essentially mechanical, essentially human,
But the converse of humanistic. Then give me
Good photographs of a line of high pressure
Oil switches in a grid station, of turning
An insulator base to size, and the like —
Religion, exploitation, Kings and Queens, Nature
Are unthinkable anachronisms – museum pieces – here;
Reinforcing tungsten steel with chocolate,
Eking out arc lamps with 'the inner light'.

Fancy engineers with stuff on their walls,
In their minds, as if they were yokels,
Or old women, or ministers! Ugh!

The switch over from the old to the new in Scottish life and literature and the other arts, which has been proceeding slowly and against immense difficulties – in the teeth of the opposition of the whole Anglo-Scottish educational machine, the press, the Churches, and all the other bulwarks of English Finance, Imperialism and black reaction, can hardly be better illustrated than just by the insistence of this poem upon the difference today between most professional painters and the photographers. The camera men show far more enterprise and true originality. They are far more closely in touch with the ramifications of modern life. Light and shade mean everything to the photographer. He must have an infinite capacity to wait hours, and days if need be, for the right moment. This would exhaust the patience of most painters. The artists think too much of themselves, take the phenomena of the outer world too much for granted, concentrate on self-expression – and have nothing to express! Happy practitioners of a younger and newer craft, the photographers still look out on the world with eyes of enquiry and wonder: they escape from the environment of their own petty personalities, lose themselves in the fascination of all the marvels light reveals to a zealous observer, and in losing themselves find themselves. So may science liberate all men yet!

'Remember the Bristol merchants,' a character in one of Margaret Irwin's historical novels would say when told that Englishmen would not stand this or that – 'it strikes me that Englishmen will stand anything as long as they can pretend that it's legal.'

M. André Maurois, in his life of Disraeli, tells how, at one of the theatres, Gladstone was represented receiving an embassy from China come to demand Scotland from him. 'The Prime Minister reflected, then discovered that three replies were possible; to yield Scotland at once, to wait a little and end by yielding it, or to name an arbitrator. The public found the likeness a close one.'

Verily the artist in Scotland in such circumstances must be like the buffalo, of whom the Abyssinians say that 'when he has his head set, nothing can stop him but death.'

Few of our writers or other artists are yet in that condition or realize the imperative need to be so – or, in fact, have the heads for it; and the kind of knowledge of Scotland needed is still extremely rare. Our schools and universities supply anything but! And even in the ranks of the Socialists there are few who remember Lenin's words: 'Now, for the first time, we have the possibility of learning. I do not know how long this possibility will last. I do not know how long the Capitalist Powers will give us the opportunity of learning in peace and quietude. But we must utilize every moment in which we are free from war that we may learn, and *learn from the bottom up.* . . .'

THE INSPIRATION OF JOHN MACLEAN

The hope of Scotland lies in the fact that all the younger Scottish writers of any significance have glimpsed that great truth, are possessed with a furious need to make up for the waste of their school and university years and learn Scotland in that way – Scottish history, Scottish literature, and all the ins and outs of Scottish life, the physical Scotland, and the Scotland of all its international contacts, ramifications, and affiliations, the Scotland whose circumference is that of the whole world. And because all these younger Scottish writers and politicians recognize as their leader a great, murdered, and hitherto most cruelly misprized and neglected Scotsman, the late John Maclean (1879–1923), and because it is under the slogan of Maclean's name and animated by the example of his incredible energy and equipped, thanks to him, with the necessary knowledge of Dialectical Materialism, that the whole movement is at last developing something like the requisite knowledge, determination, and dynamic power, when I have been reproached at times for a propaganda that could only succeed if there were a sudden and profound change in the psychology of the majority of my compatriots, I have replied that it would be by no means the first time that that happened – *and that it must be made to happen again now!*

In the latter part of the 16th century and nearly the whole of the 17th century, Scotland was engrossed in questions of theology and politics and war. Then came a sudden change in the direction of the national aspirations – the desire to become colonists, instead of soldiers; to become traders instead of theologians.

When discussing this question, Fletcher of Saltoun, writing in 1698, says that by an 'unforeseen and unexpected change of the genius of the nation, all their thoughts and inclinations, as if united and directed by a Higher Power, seemed to have turned upon trade, and to conspire together for its advancement.' An unidentified pamphleteer, writing in 1696, comments on this change in the Scottish attitude, for, he says,

> the bias of their people seems generally to be another way – yet that is merely the effect of custom and not of nature, and as it would not have been difficult at any time heretofore to have diverted and turned their inclinations and humours from soldiering to commerce, so it is not to be doubted but that upon their being once brought to apply unto it, they would be found as ingenious and brilliant in trade as they have had the character

to be skilful and brave in war.

I have, therefore, ample grounds for believing it to be far from impossible that the Scottish national genius may yet be turned to Literature and the Arts, and certainly it is urgently in need today of such an application to adult education and to scientific thought and research as have been brought about in a single generation both in Russia and Turkey, and I still hope and believe that my life-time may see such a concentration of Scottish national purpose as is long overdue and most badly needed in these neglected fields. Scotland's sudden switch-over to Trade has in the intervening centuries more than abundantly justified the unknown pamphleteer's prophecy. I have no doubt whatever that if a like switch-over to philosophy and the arts could be effected it would justify itself as completely in its revelation of the national aptitude in departments in which it has hitherto been content to play second fiddle to many other European countries really incapable of competing with it at all were it once effectively roused to apply itself in these connections.

'WHA' DAUR MEDDLE WI' ME'

That is for the future. But if, among our corrupted people, there is still no more than a tiny minority audience for the truly Scottish, a still-better parable for the present state of arts and affairs in Scotland occurs to me. The 'Dundee bap' – a 3¼ oz. roll that is a famed production of Dundee and East of Scotland bakers might have disappeared from breakfast and tea-tables a few months ago, along with various other tea-time favourites, if Scottish bakers had been able to understand a new Bread Order scheduled by the Ministry of Food. The Order was made to save labour and waste in the bakeries of Britain by abolishing various fancy loaves and restricting bakers to only four standardized types of loaf. It also laid down that rolls must not exceed 2 oz. in weight – a provision that would have banished the 'Dundee bap' among other forms of rolls. But Scottish bakers continued to make bread and 'baps' as usual, because they were completely confused by the terms of the Bread Order. They did not know what it meant. A leading baker said: – 'We appealed to the Ministry of Food to state in plain language the meaning of the Order, and the reply was that we should merely carry on as we have been accustomed to do.'

The bakers themselves agreed that there were too many types of loaf, and wanted to co-operate in the economy move to reduce the range. But their confusion, they declared, was due to the fact that the Order had been framed by English minds to suit English trade conditions. It defined a 'Scottish loaf' as a 'tin loaf of 1 lb. 12 ozs.' – which is an accurate description of the 'pan loaf', a product that represents only one-tenth of the bread output from Scottish bakeries. Ninety per cent of Scotland's bread, however, is made in the form of the ordinary square of batch loaf. So the bakers, unable to understand what the Ministry of Food wanted them to do, have simply carried on with 'business as usual'.

This subterranean persistence of unchanged Scottishness under official Anglification and apparent acquiescence in assimilation to English standards occasionally rises to the surface in more significant forms than 'legislation by appendix' makes inevitable every now and again in every practical connection; and I believe that the whole hidden Scotland will soon break through the crust of Englishry. In this sense, the whole Scottish Movement might define its purpose in the lines of Matthew Arnold (himself half a Celt – his mother was a Cornishwoman):

> To see if we will poise our life at last,
> To see if we will now at last be true
> To our own only true, deep-buried selves,
> Being one with which we are one with the whole world.

THE LAD O' PAIRTS TRADITION

The curse of Scottish life, and literature and the other arts, has been (and, save for the group of writers who constitute the spearhead of the Scottish Workers' Republican Movement today, remains) an appalling infantilism. A splendid case in point was provided by the late Lord Tweedsmuir (John Buchan) of whom one obituarist told the exact truth when he wrote:

> John Buchan wrote some of the best thrillers ever published in English and some of the best popular historical biographies. Some of his books sold by the hundred thousand, but, like some greater men, he always hankered after success in spheres not suited to his talents. Just as Cicero wanted to write poetry,

so John Buchan wanted to be a statesman. He was obsessed with the idea of greatness. Those who knew him will tell that he had no political gifts of any kind. As a result his achievements were mainly ceremonial. When he was Lord High Commissioner of the General Assembly of the Church of Scotland he wore splendid robes and was radiantly happy in their magnificence. The House of Commons led him not to Cabinet office, but to the Governor-Generalship of Canada. Here was the perfect honorific post. If one cannot achieve real political success, to be the King's representative is surely the best possible substitute.

Scottish Notes and Comment (Arthur Donaldson's roneo'd monthly which contains more significant and valuable Scottish fact, and the only Scottish journalistic comment that is not at once childish and base, and every issue of which will be worth more to the future historians of Scotland than all the files of the *Glasgow Herald*, the *Scotsman*, the *Aberdeen Press and Journal*, and all the other Anglo-Scottish capitalist papers put together) summed up Lord Tweedsmuir – and all his kind – very well when it said that he was the typical Anglo-Scot, the 'heid of the depairtment' type, who does very well for himself – and nothing at all for Scotland.

KNOWING SCOTLAND

The way in which Scotland must be seen can hardly be better expressed than it is in that great Aberdeenshire Doric classic 'Johnny Gibb o' Gushetneuk', when Johnny says to his wife:

'The Apos'le speaks o' the life o' man as a "vawpour that appeareth for a little, and then vanisheth awa"; an' seerly there couldna be a mair nait'ral resem'lance. Fan we begood the pilget here the gither, wi' three stirks an' a bran'it coo't cam wi' your providin', the tae side o' the place was ta'en up wi' breem busses an' heather knaps half doon the faul'ies, and the tither was feckly a quaakin' bog, growin' little but sprots and rashes. It luiks like yesterday fan we had the new hooses biggit, an' the grun' a' oon'er the pleuch, though that's a gweed therty year syne. I min' as bricht's a pentet pictur' fat like ilka knablich an' ilka sheugh an' en'rig was.'

That is how we must learn to see and know Scotland again. The War has made it clear that our choice is either that – or starve. And Sir John Boyd Orr and others have made it clear that Scotland is potentially a rich country, well able to feed our population, if proper use is made of our land which, under the present dispensation, has been abominably wasted and converted to an appalling extent into derelict areas reserved for plutocratic sports. As Sir John Orr has said: 'Scotland is one of the finest agricultural countries in Europe. It is a rich country. The Clyde Valley has terrific powers of production *which are lying half idle.*' This is true of many other great areas of Scotland. And along with that return to an intimate first-hand practical knowledge of every inch of our terrain, there will be a return to the languages (Scots and Gaelic) which are the proper media for the expression and extension of that knowledge – a purpose for which English is worse than useless.

SCOTS STILL THE LANGUAGE OF THE PEOPLE

It is in keeping with the whole present position – what Mr William Power has called 'the mystery of Scotland's self-suppression' – that the defeatist writings against a return to Scots have been by Anglo-Scottish authors. As I have shown in the introduction and notes to my *Golden Treasury*, Mr Edwin Muir in his *Scott and Scotland*, and Mr John Spiers in his *The Scots Literary Tradition*, have not a leg to stand on in their contentions that Scots has lapsed so greatly that its resuscitation is now out of the question. The facts (a great mass of which I adduce in the introduction and notes in question) are all the other way. All over Scotland – in the 'Black Belt' as well as in the rural areas – Scots is still the native speech of the great majority of the people; and the real objection to it is a class objection – for Scots is the language of the working class.

An Inspector of Schools who said he could not see the argument nearly so clearly in regard to words, told me he must admit the national cleavage (between Scotland and England) was most marked and most important (important practically, i.e., in relation to teaching singing in schools, etc.) in regard to music. In this respect, as in all others, the real life of Scotland is being denied. He gave me many striking instances from his own experience of experiments with children in senior classes when pseudo-Scottish work by very competent English or Anglo-Scottish composers was at once spotted by the children as 'not the real thing', and, in one case, though the children could not explain just what was wrong, a setting of Reid's poem 'Kirkbride' was tried on them in which the first two lines were set in the Scottish folk-song tradition, and the next in an English medium. They felt at once, however, that there was something very queer and not in keeping about this setting – as well they might, since it switched back and forward from one country to another, from one tradition to another radically different one. *Which* tradition made all the difference in the world to the whole-hearted responsiveness of the children – their ability to reach to what, in Jeeve's phrase, is really 'of the essence' – and this difference was *not* in favour of teaching English songs in Scottish schools. The children could not enter into the spirit of the former and sing them with any authentic effect. This must be taken as an analogue of what has happened, and is still happening, in all directions in Anglicized Scotland, and a convincing index to the immeasurable loss sustained. Our national life has been reduced to a shadow of its former self, and what little vitality still remains is being continually sapped by the English connection.

But under the English Ascendancy the Scots are so subjugated and befooled, so deceived and self-deceiving, that they persist in singing even their great national song, 'Scots Wha Ha'e', expressing Bruce's address to the Scottish army before the Battle of Bannockburn, to a hopelessly inappropriate dirge-like German setting, despite the fact that the only national composer worth a rap, Francis George Scott, we have ever had, has supplied a magnificent re-setting in thorough keeping with the spirit of the poem. The poor creatures are so tradition-bound, so spiritless, that they dare not substitute the new for the old setting, although the latter is a lugubrious idiocy in conjunction with the verses in question, and the other dramatic and dauntless in perfect keeping with Burns's immortal words. This is an exact parallel to the plight of the Scottish people – the superficial Anglicization, and, hidden underneath it, and still visible now and again in a man like F. G. Scott true Scotland's *raucle* spirit. They have gelded Burns – Burns of all men! It is only the more innocuous pieces, the silly love-songs, they are concerned with him in Burns; they have no desire to remember that 'Auld Scotland has a raucle tongue.'

They know that if they give *that* a chance it will be turned against *them* with devastating power.

In a recent memorandum, pleading for the more serious treatment of the Scottish Vernacular in our schools, put forward to the Scottish Education Department by a deputation representative of the Burns' Federation, the St Andrew's Societies of Edinburgh and Glasgow, the Scottish National Dictionary Association, and the Ballad Society, it was rightly declared that 'in spite of some decay in the towns the Vernacular is still the speech of those who do the work of Scotland in field, mine, workshop, or fishing-boat.' But the campaign of these bodies for the revival of the Vernacular makes no headway. It has not the people behind it. These bourgeois agencies cannot reach the hearts of the workers; they do not trust them and will not follow them. The Vernacular to these people is only a fad, a hobby, a lovable whimsicality of well-to-do business men, their pleasure in occasionally sitting in shirtsleeves and hobnobbing with their betters. The last thing these 'well-to-do business men' want to do is to 'go too far' in the matter – to arouse the genius of the Scots language, and, with it, of the Scots working class. So they have no sympathy with recent creative work in the Scots medium – any attempt to use Scots for serious modern purposes and bring it abreast of contemporary requirements. Theirs is entirely a conservative manoeuvre; they think of Scots entirely in terms of the past, and of the worst elements of its past at that. All they want, or want the people to want is 'the songs my mither used to sing', the toast of 'Gentlemen, the King!' before proposing 'The Immortal Memory', and 'God Save the King' sung as a wind-up to a concert of Scottish songs. Scots culture must be taken out of the hands of these people altogether.

Cut off from their real life, the Scottish workers cannot be appealed to in a fundamental way by the Tories, the Liberals, the Socialists, or any such agency as the Burns' Clubs or other Scottish societies. They can only be dynamically reached – stirred to the very depths of their beings – through the Scots Vernacular, applied to modern purposes, and expressly directed to their vital needs. This is the dynamic angle – the only way to get right into the hearts of the Scottish people and rouse them. A mighty force will be generated as soon as that is done. It is worth concentrating all our energies on; it will burst the existing system in Scotland into smithereens. This is why the English and Anglo-Scots have sought by every means to restrict it to the past, and to unreal romantic subjects, and to bourgeoisify and emasculate the Burns' Cult, until, today, they have made it, and the whole range of Scottish sentiment, describable only in the well-known phrase of Professor Hanover, of the Chair of Greek in Aberdeen University – 'isn't that perfectly obscene – perfectly obscene!' So obscene that our Anglo-Scottish press is constantly filled with the philippics of men like Professor J. L. Morrison of Durham University, who trounced the young intellectuals of the Scottish Movement for the delectation of probably the fittest audience he ever had – to wit, a lot of Greenock grocers and pettifogging lawyers and assorted 'nyaufs' constituting the Burns' Club there – secure in the sense that he was in his proper element at last, and that none of the young intellectuals in question was present to expose (as any of them could easily have done) his (Professor Morrison's) total lack of capacity to discuss the subject at all.

THE CAUSE OF THE SCOTS LITERARY MOVEMENT
IS THE CAUSE OF THE SCOTTISH PEOPLE

In a word, Scottish poets have regained for themselves – and seek to regain for their misled and maltreated country as a whole – that lost tradition of Scotland to which Louis Pasteur paid tribute (albeit he associated it with names to which it is impossible now to concede any respect, and impossible to believe that the homage once given was ever in any degree really due) when, on the occasion of the tercentenary of Edinburgh University in 1884 he said, in a speech to a gathering of students: 'A French writer, one who had carried abroad the philosophy of Robert Reid and Dugald Stewart, addressing young men in one of his prefaces, has exclaimed: "Whatever career you may embrace, look up to an exalted goal; worship great men and great things." Edinburgh students have recently seen such men as are there mentioned, and in Scotland their memories are accorded rightful recognition'; and, again, at the tercentenary banquet, Pasteur said:

> The city of Edinburgh is now presenting a spectacle of which she may well be proud. All the great scientific organizations, assembling here, seem an immense gathering of hopes and mutual encouragement. The honour reflected by this international concourse rightly belongs to you, for centuries

ago the fortunes of Scotland were joined with those of the human mind. She was one of the earliest nations to realize that intellect rules the world. And the world of intellect, gladly responding to your call, places a well-deserved homage at your feet. Yesterday, when the renowned Professor Robert Flint, in his address to the Edinburgh University from the pulpit of St Giles', uttered the words, 'Remember the past and look to the future', all the delegates, sitting like judges at a great tribunal, called forth a vision of bygone centuries and united in a unanimous desire for a still more glorious future.

THE CUILLIN

All this is, for example, splendidly exemplified in Somhairle Mac Gill Eathain's long poem (in Gaelic – the English into which the passages I quote are put, gives little or no idea of the fire and fury of the original) 'The Cuillin',[2] with its conjuring up of the whole pageant of Hebridean landscape history, literature and music, and its constant references to Mary Macpherson, the poetess of the Land League (1820–95), the great pibrochs of the MacCrimmons and others, like Patrick Caogach's 'Flame of Anger' and the melody of piercing 'Maol Donn', adaptations and parodies of poems by Iain Lom and other Gaelic singers and of anonymous folk-songs, the beginning of the crofter struggle in Braes in 1882, Neil Macleod, the Skye poet (d. 1913), the Skye Slave Ship of 1739, the *Annie Jane*, ship of Skye emigrants, drowned off Vatersay, *c.* 1820, the end of a rhymed list of place-names alleged to have been spoken by a kidnapped girl of the Slave Ship, and a thousand other names and events, and literary, musical and political allusions. The Stallion, the magnificent sea-cliff at Waterstein, is used as an effective symbol of a heroic conception of Skye and Scotland, while Mararaulin, a marsh in the north of the Cuillin, is equated with the bourgeois-capitalist bog

> . . . streaming and rising,
> Drowning in your great flood of falsehood
> All that is hospitable, generous and straight,
> You shaking bog of every land. . . .

[2] The Gaelic title is *An Cuilthionn*. It is published in Gaelic with a translation by the author in *O Choille gu Bearradh/From Wood to Ridge*, Sorley MacLean's collected poems in Gaelic and English (Manchester, Carcanet, 1989) – Ed.

'The Cuillin' is a great anti-Imperialist and Marxist poem, inspired by the thought that

> Even in the ugly bog
> I saw the shadow of loveliness;
> I saw youth, music and laughter,
> I saw valour, wisdom, honour;
> I saw generosity of heart,
> Heroism and unattained spiritedness;
> I saw every flower that grew,
> Even the wounded, tortured side;
> But in one was never seen there
> The intellect of Lenin and the red side of Christ.
> These two may not be seen together
> Despite the spaciousness of the morass.
> They are not seen in one place
> Except on the bare top of the high mountains.

Again and again the poet inveighs against 'the scum and the bog':

> Has it not overcome the world
> Overflowing on all sides?
> Has it not made a Dachau of the world?

Yet he affirms of his great muse that

> On heights beyond thought in the mountains
> She spoke to me saying:
> There is no doubt that hope and expectation
> Will be seen in their truth,
> Joy's head and desire of the poets
> . . . the ultimate course of the spirit's way.
> Arising from poverty and hunger,
> From suffering and wounds,
> The great red standard of the spirit
> That will not be cast down after rising.

> Blood and sweat of toilers,
> The scarlet that will give freedom,
> Brain's blood of poor and sage
> That will overcome oblique wealth.

Mac Gill'Eathain's poem sees the wild peaks of the Cuillin in terms of the endless struggles of mankind and is not only a magnificent evocation of the Hebridean landscape but of the whole tumult of history and human hope, for the poet sees not only the superficies of the scene, and not only the local history of which these Skye hills have been the theatre, but the entire perspective of human history of which they provide such a tortured and towering symbol,

> . . . the high mountain bluffs
> Surging in proud crags
> Like the mother-breasts of the world
> Erect with the universe's concupiscence.

And always there is the keen political realization:

> I turned and, behind
> Minginish was in the sweep of my eye
> And green Bracadale
> And Duirinish and Trotternish beyond;
> There arose the glory of the excellent island,
> Arose – but came another thought;
> What to the Skyeman the significance of my desire
> When he rises bourgeois-ward?

He relates the storied landscape of Skye to the whole range of world affairs today.

> . . . Scotland a porridge of filth,
> England and France together
> A dung-heap of bourgeois capitalism,
> Great Germany a delirium of falsehood,
> And Spain a cemetery where valour lies.

and asks

> What will avail our island,
> Another Festubert or Loos,
> When there are more names than enough

> On the Stone of Portree under the lion's arse?[3]
> It is devilish little that came to our enjoyment
> Though you took Beaumont Hamel.[4]
> And if you survive this you will see
> Other rotters with the O.B.E.
> And wealthy old women in Sligachan[5]
> Guzzling and viewing the Cuillin.

He is constantly concerned in the midst of all the beauties of Nature with:

> The love and grief of the peasants of the land
> Scattered for exploiters' wealth . . .
> The hardship and poverty of the thousands
> Of the peasantry and lowly of the land,
> My kin and my people;
> And though their fate did not make
> The sore world-cry of Spain
> And though their dispensation did not make
> A mantle of blood on the face of the firmament
> As Marlowe saw the blood of Christ
> And Leonhardt the blood of Liebknecht
> And though no news came
> Of their destruction's night
> To rival the world-agony of grief,
> The fall of the Asturians in glory,
> Their lot was the lot of peasant and poor,
> Hardship, want, and injury,
> Ever since the masses of the lands
> Were deceived by the ruling class, State and civil law,
> By priests, ministers, and prostitutes
> Who sold their souls for the price
> Which the bitches of the world have earned
> Since the ruling class piled capital.
> I'd see them in one drowning-sack,
> Ruling class and lawyers,

---

[3] The Portree War Memorial has a lion on top.
[4] The 4th Cameronians took Beaumont Hamel.
[5] Big holiday hotel in Skye.

> Thrown over the Stallion[6]
> Through the middle depth of the surging sea
> Down to the hell of gentry.

But the poem is no mere savage flyting, no mere diatribe, but a positive achievement and great affirmation, full of lines that stir the long-winding fibres of memory, enriching the future with a most precious past.

> In rocky Cuillin
> I heard the great pipe booming,
> Roaring of mankind answering,
> Brain and heart in harmony.
>
> I heard the cry on the mountains,
> The liberty-shout of the people rising.

And again

> The balance of the mountains weighing together
> The brain of Einstein and the live-red spirit,
> Understanding of a universe and the changing of a world
> Meeting on the bareness of the mountains.

The eyes of these younger Scottish poets are indeed set on the

> Summit wall
> Of man's spirit,
> Dangerous rocks
> For the élan of desires.
> Skye of the people
> Taking the torrent stream
> Over ancient barenesses
> Of the torn mountains.
>
> The vessel of a great nation
> Tacking windward
> Over ocean rocks
> Of the blue roaring waves.

---

[6]Great sea-cliff of Waterstein in north-west Skye.

The great ship of newness
And her rudder stream
Raising billows
Above the black rock of a mountain.

The ship of the world,
Without deviation or surrender,
Without veering or obliquity,
Before the great wind of heroism. . . .

Beyond poverty, consumption, fever, agony,
Beyond hardship, wrong, violence, distress,
Beyond misery, despair, hatred, treachery,
Beyond guilt and defilement, watchfully,
Heroically, is seen the Cuillin
Rising on the other side of sorrow.

THE NEW SCOTTISH POETS

I have only had space here to give some account of Mac-Gill'Eathain's work, but the fact is that on the eve of the war a more impressive phalanx of young poets began to emerge in Scotland than our country has ever had at one time and despite all the war-time difficulties[7] (including the fact that many of them were conscripted for military service, under conditions which forced most of them to pour out protests against conscription and English Imperialism and bitter complaints against the cruelly unfair treatment meted out to Scotland, as well as, in many cases, poems expressing solidarity with Soviet Russia, and with autonomist and other 'rebel' movements among

---

[7] Scottish culture has had serious losses too, like that of Prof. James Carmichael Watson, lost at sea, a young scholar who had already done magnificent work in Scottish Gaelic studies which, it was widely hoped, was but the earnest of what he would live to achieve for our Gaelic language and literature. Tribute must be paid here, too, to the magnificent courage and noble utterances of many of the conscientious objectors who, as independent Scots, objected to English military service and who, as a consequence, had to endure long terms of imprisonment in Barlinnie and elsewhere. The true voice of Scotland was heard in these trial speeches as it had scarcely been heard since the incomparable phrases which constitute the Arbroath Declaration of Independence were put together over six centuries ago, phrases which have such a strong family likeness to these later ones as to constitute a most remarkable example of the continuity of our national spirit changeless throughout the centuries in its call for Freedom.

the subject peoples of the British Empire) this group has continued to grow in performance and promise. All I can do here is to list some of these poets – all united by a sense of the Scottish Literary Tradition (Scots and Gaelic) as opposed to the English, by a comprehensive knowledge of Scotland's past, a thorough acquaintance with the Scottish present, and a passionate concern with our particular problems and potentialities and their relationship to the crucial issues of the world at large. I name, then, as brilliantly exemplifying this general development – and as each, though young, and, in most cases, unpublished as yet, at any rate in volume form, having to his credit poems in English, Scots, or Gaelic which ought to be included in any good representative anthology of the work of Scottish poets during this period and which, indeed, strike a level equal to all but the very highest yet attained by any Scottish poet in the past – George Campbell Hay, Douglas Young, Sydney Smith (whose first volume, *Skail Wind*, 1941, at once established him as a master of synthetic Scots and one of the few good poets we have had in our vernacular since the death of Burns), J. F. Hendry, Nicholas Moore, G. S. Fraser and Norman MacCaig (a group of Scottish poets influenced by the Surrealist Movement and associated with such group-publications as 'The New Apocalypse' and 'The White Horseman') W. S. Graham (a young Glasgow poet whose work in many ways resembles, and at its best is not inferior to, that of Dylan Thomas), John Hannah and Alex. Galloway, two other promising poets in Scots. In addition to these poets, there is the poet whom Mr Cyril Connolly recently called 'the mysterious Adam Drinan, with his Highland nostalgia, his indignation over the fate of the Highlands, his strong Socialism merged into his Western melancholy, his sense of ancient wrong' and of whom another reviewer has justly said that his work is especially interesting 'for combining the literary traditions of England and Scotland'. Drinan is the author of *Men of the Rocks*, 1942, a verse-drama of the type of *Maud*, and he is also one of the poets represented in John Lehmann's *Poets of To-morrow*, 1942. There is Norman Cameron, one of the three poets responsible for *Work in Hand*, 1942. There is Francis Scarfe, the young lecturer in French at Glasgow University, a sensitive and intelligent poet and good translator of Mallarmé and Rimbaud. And along with these poets we have in the other fields of the arts men of such outstanding promise (and already remarkable achievement) as the art-critic Robert Melville, the Scots dramatist and short-story writer Robert MacLellan, the brilliant publicists Oliver Brown and Thomas Burns whose pamphlets on Scottish issues have had sales running into the scores of thousands, one of the most powerful and original artists (and art-teachers) in Britain today in William Johnstone, a splendid playwright in Paul Carroll. Scotland, in fact, has never before in one generation had such a remarkable showing; it gives every reason to hope that there is about to be such an effervescence of high and varied talent, running through all the departments of Scottish arts and affairs, in the age-groups of the late 'teens and early twenties among us, as characterized (and constituted) the conditions in Ireland at and after Easter 1916 – such a general effervescence of ability in our younger people as is perhaps a requisite and guarantee of that real Scottish National awakening of which there were in the decade preceding the outbreak of this Second World War so many hopeful, if hardly quite convincing signs, and the need for which – the objective conditions necessitating which – have grown steadily so much more compulsive as to seem to ensure that it could not be much longer delayed. The war may thus have acted as a forcing-bed, bringing to somewhat speedier development what was already securely rooted in the circumstances of our nation; and in this sense it may, perhaps, be said later that: *The Scottish renaissance was conceived in the First World War, and leapt into lusty life in the Second World War.*

Part Two: 1945–1978

21 On Modern Scottish Drama

> This is the 'Introduction' to Ewan MacColl's play *Uranium 235* (Glasgow: William MacLellan, 1948), the most compelling dramatic presentation of the morality of nuclear power in Scottish literature until Troy Kennedy Martin's television series *Edge of Darkness*, screened in 1985. The essay effectively summarizes MacDiarmid's thoughts on the potential for theatrical developments in post-war Scotland, and picks up where his early comments on Scottish drama (Item 3) left off. The significance of *Theatre Workshop* and the activities of Ewan MacColl and Joan Littlewood in the growth of working-class drama are well known. MacDiarmid's association with and support of that movement are less familiar, but they effectively highlight his interest in that area of modern theatre whose principal theorist and practitioner is Brecht.

'IF we may judge by Sir David Lindsay's *Satire of the Thrie Estaitis*, no nation could have shown a fairer promise (than Scotland) of playing a worthy part in the dramatic recital which is the glory of English literature at the end of the sixteenth and the beginning of the seventeenth century. But *dis aliter visum*; that promise was irretrievably blasted.' So wrote J.H. Millar in his *Literary History of Scotland*, and went on to show what forces had prevented the development of drama in Scotland. Earlier he had remarked: 'There is scarcely a country on the continent of Europe today where the systematic publication of such diatribes as he indulged in against the existing order in Church and State would not expose their author to the pains and penalties of the law. Even in England the public performance of a drama in the least degree resembling the *Satire* in tone or aim would be absolutely out of the question.' Mr Millar also noted that Sir David Lindsay 'never made a secret of the fact that he wrote for the commonalty; and we can picture to ourselves the enthusiasm and delight with which the most telling scenes and speeches in the *Satire* would be received by an audience drawn from the ranks of a people never averse from subjecting their rulers to the wholesome test of ridicule.'

A many-sided movement to create a Scottish National Drama and to provide Scotland with an adequate theatrical service has been making headway during the past few years. It is fitting that the *Satire* – albeit only in abridged, bowdlerized, and modernized form – is to be put on at the second Edinburgh International Festival of Music and Drama. Unless it is shortened and 'purified' out of all resemblance to the original, that will serve in some sort as a test to show whether Scotland stands where it did in open contempt of the Powers-That-Be, whether the commonalty today will respond as their predecessors did upwards of four centuries ago, and whether anything like the same freedom is accorded to the arts in Scotland today as was enjoyed then. It will not be anything like a complete test; none of these issues will be clearly and challengingly joined in this revival of Lindsay's *Satire*. That is welcome enough in itself. There can have been precious few, if any, productions of it in Scotland (and none anywhere else, of course!) since its first performances at Cupar, Linlithgow and Edinburgh round about 1540. Though we have dramatists in Scotland today of the calibre of 'James Bridie', Paul Vincent Carroll, Gordon Daviot, William Douglas Home, and best of all, Robert MacLellan, none of them are dealing with 'dynamite' – the authorities are not likely to fall foul of them, or their audiences to riot in protest against them; in so far as they deal with live issues, these are of a minor order. This applies to all of them, except the author of the present play. In so far as we have one, he is the Sir David Lindsay *de nos jours*; Lindsay would have been a greater dramatist (and the whole history of Scottish drama very different) if he had been also the Ewan MacColl of the sixteenth century.

MacColl's work is radically different from everything to which modern Scottish theatre-goers have been accustomed – and modern English theatre-goers, too, for the matter of that. It deals fearlessly and dynamically with the crucial problems of our own day and generation. It is forward-looking, and for its effective production demands the utilization of all the most advanced theatrical means. It is the work of one fully aware of, and working for, *l'avant garde* in the theatre the world over – and, therefore, it is also, like Sir David

Lindsay's, written for the commonalty and certain to appeal to them tremendously whenever they get such a chance in this fourth decade of the twentieth century. MacColl has suffered from political victimization. The way has been made hard for him in every connection by the stooges of the *status quo*, despite the tributes his work has evoked from George Bernard Shaw and Sean O'Casey. Arthur Rimbaud spat contemptuously on almost the whole succession of preceding French poets. MacColl has expectorated in like fashion against contemporary English (and Scottish) playwrights; and, worse still, against London West-End standards, and the whole confraternity of authors, managers, producers, and actors of our theatredom of today. He did not think it worthwhile to appeal to any ready-made public; with his friends of *Theatre Workshop* he took his plays to places that had never had a theatre before, and played to audiences that had never seen any theatrical production before – and carried them by storm. The enthusiasm of these working-class audiences, uncontaminated by any previous acquaintance with the commercial theatre, little read in bourgeois literature, and mercifully devoid of all but a minimum of our so-called 'popular education', was an eye-opener. It 'blew the gaff' with a vengeance on all other play-writing and producing in Great Britain today – and for an incredibly long time back. To couple MacColl's name with Sir David Lindsay's is not absurd. That coupling is the accurate measure of the distance Ewan MacColl and his colleagues had to travel back to reconnect with the true tradition of the theatre. It was hard going, and plenty of enemies were encountered to see that everything possible was done to aggravate, and nothing to mitigate, the hardships of the enterprise. Nevertheless, *Theatre Workshop* played almost without a break for nearly two years to audiences in Lancashire, Yorkshire, Northumberland, Cumberland, Westmorland, and, later, Scotland and in Germany. Most of these engagements were in halls and small theatres which were, in general, unsuited to their purpose. Yet they got their audiences, and laid the foundation of a whole new system of acting and production.

To have an experimental theatre of his own in this way has been an immense advantage to MacColl – just as, *per contra*, MacColl's work was the staple of the company's activities. Mrs Winifred Bannister was right when, stressing these mutual advantages, she said:

> If an experimental theatre – and this [*Theatre Workshop*] is the only theatre in this country advancing the theory of drama through a revolutionary technique – can keep its head above water without subsidy for a year, it must be said to have unique qualities, especially when such a theatre has devoted most of its time to playing in industrial centres to dramatically uneducated audiences. The vital methods of *Theatre Workshop* make the average production look like Victorian charades. This young company has worked hard and made many sacrifices to hew out a new technique of presentation and production which has the stamp of contemporary life. The lively methods of this company reflect the determination of the young to pull up the dead wood; to grow from the seed instead of pruning plants which are better dead.

Ewan MacColl's principal plays to date – and he is still a young man – are *Johnny Noble*, *Rogue's Gallery*, *Blitz Song*, *Uranium 235*, and *Operation Olive Branch* – a tale of progressive achievement which establishes him (apart altogether from his great mission as a revivalist of true theatrical values and destroyer of false standards – and apart, too, from the related matter of his literary value, since plays can be effective in production though their purely literary value may be small) as by far the most important and promising young dramatist writing in English, or any dialect of English, at the present time.

Of the production of *Johnny Noble* the more perceptive critics had no hesitation in saying that it was a perfect example of team work and it was doubtful if groupings had ever been more naturally achieved (or seemingly so). 'Some of the mass movement here is really beautiful and effective, and the whole play is extremely moving.' Again, of the present play, *Uranium 235*, the *Glasgow Herald* said:

> It is described on a publicity sheet as 'a vivid portrayal of

the history of atomic research and the problems raised by the atom bomb.' That does less than justice to this moving and beautiful modern morality. That there is great drama in the discovery of the atom bomb and all it implies is obvious, but many dramatists would have been equally obvious in their treatment of such a theme, in which, no doubt, secret agents and dictators would have been prominent. Not so, MacColl, to whom the spiritual values are the realities. The result is an absorbing play, although 'play' is hardly the right description. Rather is it an absorbing experience to watch and listen to his ideas on the stage, expressed by speech, mime, dances, and song. Using this method, peculiarly suitable to the ideas he has to express, the playwright tells the story of mankind through the past 2,500 years, his struggle against stupidity and ignorance, his misuse of science – 'We searchers after knowledge, we hunted men,' says one of the characters – and his undying spirit. A noble conception, the work of a man with something to say. *Uranium 235* has never a hint of pretentiousness or preciousness, a trap waiting for so many who use mime and dance in a work of this kind, There is too, real poetry in the dialogues and monologues.

From this documentary play dealing with the problems raised by the recent discovery of methods for utilizing atomic energy, and tracing the history of thought into the fundamental nature of things from Democritus to the present, held together by dramatization of contemporary events relevant to the theme, back to the documentary ballad-opera of *Johnny Noble*, Ewan MacColl has already covered an immense field in pursuit of his unchanging purpose, and mainly justified the claim of Ian Mhor writing in *Reynolds* that 'the little Perthshire town of Auchterarder has produced a truly great dramatist.' I entirely agree with him, and, privy as I am to some of MacColl's more recent work and plans for future development, I have no hesitation in believing that, if health and harness hold, Ewan MacColl will substantiate that claim during the next few years by completing a body of work in the field of drama beyond comparison greater alike in quality and quantity than that of any other playwright

Scotland has yet produced. I have no doubt of his first-rate significance for the whole future of drama, or of his great creative potentialities (apart from stage production altogether) as a writer and political and aesthetic thinker. This is the first of his plays to be published. It is an honour to have been asked to write these few words of introduction, inadequate as they are, to the vitally important work of my compatriot and friend, and to express the confident hope that the publication of *Uranium 235* will be the forerunner of the appearance of the whole notable sequence and progressive development of a creative enterprise of which Scotland has been singularly destitute for four long centuries and is perhaps too dazed by this sudden unheralded resumption to assess at its true worth, which is unquestionably very great.

22 Knoydart Land Seizures

Land-raids had been a successful tactic of the 1880s in the crofters' movement against the landlords, organised around the Highland Land League, and had continued into the 1920s. The policy of land-raiding was simply for crofters to trespass on arable land and begin to cultivate it. This is what seven men did in Knoydart in 1948. Each man staked out sixty-five acres of arable land. Knoydart had been a populous district until the 1850s but by the 1940s it was literally a waste land. Lord Brocket, the owner, who also owned estates in England and Ireland and was vice-president of the Anglo-German Fellowship, an association of 'well-wishers of Hitler', took legal action. The land-raiders, rather than carry their action through and be incarcerated, let the matter fall into the lawyers' hands, and MacDiarmid, who reported on the whole course of events, wrote the following article for *The National Weekly*: 'The Weekly Review of National and Local Affairs' (vol. 1, no. 10, 20 November 1948), where it appeared on the front page. The publicity which followed the land-raid was considerable and it is commemorated in Hamish Henderson's folk-song, the 'Ballad of the Seven Men of Knoydart'. The reference MacDiarmid makes to the 'The Clann Albainn Society' giving advice to the raiders' spokesman, the Roman Catholic Priest at Inverie, Father Macpherson, suggests a tantalizing link with the 'Clan Albainn' secret society discussed in the early 1930s (see Item 9).

THERE was widespread disappointment throughout Scotland, and in Scottish communities abroad when it was announced on Friday, that following the receipt of formal notices from Edinburgh notifying them of the interim interdict granted against them in the Court of Session, Edinburgh, six of the men involved had quietly left the farmlands of Kilchoan, near Inverie, which they had seized a few days earlier. After the solemn assurances given earlier in the week that the men would submit to arrest for their continued occupancy of the land, this unexpected development was in the nature of an anti-climax.

It is not too much to say that a real fight at long last had been widely anticipated. As soon as the seizure of the land was made public, expressions of support and eagerness to help, financially and otherwise, flowed in from far and near. The Clann Albainn Society suggested to Father Colin Macpherson, the Roman Catholic Priest at Inverie who has supported the men's claims, that a meeting of all organizations in favour of the men's demands be convened immediately to decide on further action. A students' organization in Edinburgh forwarded a sum of money to help to meet the men's expenses. The Scottish National Party set up a fund for the purpose of supporting the men, and it was stated that contributions to the fund which had been opened 'in response to a widespread demand' were being received by the Party Treasurer at 59 Elmbank Street, Glasgow. It was also stated that the Party had sent a letter to the Secretary of State for Scotland, Mr Arthur Woodburn, on the subject of Knoydart. The men themselves had sent telegrams from Knoydart to four Crofter Unions in the Highlands and Islands, and also to the Fort William branch of the British Legion, asking for support in representations to the Secretary of State for Scotland and members of Parliament.

There were accordingly good grounds for hoping that a big fight would eventuate. Such a fight on a national scale – and involving also the big Scottish populations overseas – is, of course, long overdue, and it seemed likely that it could not be initiated under better auspices. The Knoydart land wastage is a particularly flagrant one. The type of landlord involved made the case a peculiarly likely one for bringing to a head at last all the subterranean anger at the way in which vast areas of Scotland have been depopulated and turned into private preserves by alien owners. Sooner or later the whole issue must be forced into the arena of practical politics. Why not now? It was assumed also that the men involved were likely to be the best type to fight the issue. They were all ex-Servicemen and family men, of mature age and experience.

Hope centred in particular on the type of landlord concerned. A neighbouring landlord puts the matter very mildly in saying, 'I am afraid Lord Brocket is very unpopular. He does not seem to understand our people at all.'

Perhaps, on the other hand, the trouble is that our people understand Lord Brocket only too well – and have no use for him. It is impossible to regard the possession of this 52,000 acre estate by the millionaire Lord Brocket as other than a peculiarly ugly example of the way in which great tracts of Scottish land were acquired by all manner of foreigners while our own men were fighting overseas. It is appalling that a man of Lord Brocket's type should have been permitted to purchase land in Scotland at a time when all our resources were mobilized against an ideology with which he was actually to some extent identified as a member of the notorious 'Link' and the German Fellowship. It is not clear how Brocket secured admission to Inverie at that time, since it was a confined area; but once there, he seems not to have been allowed out. It will be remembered that the late Mr Neville Chamberlain of unhallowed memory holidayed at Knoydart while Prime Minister. It is intolerable that a person of this description, using Knoydart as a funk-hole during the war, should be in a position to deny the means of livelihood now to ex-servicemen who are natives of the area in question. Certainly it is in the public interest that the utmost light should be concentrated on the personality and motives of such a man as Lord Brocket – and that enquiry should not stop short of ruthlessly illuminating the reasons for his ennoblement. There are far too many of these 'business peers' swanking about, who are not worth a lance-corporal's stripe let alone a peerage – and far too many of them seem to have acquired vast Scottish estates in recent years. They ought to be expropriated and deported as soon as possible.

What has happened on the Knoydart estate is, of course, only too similar to what has happened elsewhere in Scotland where estates have come under the control of English or other foreign landlords. These people seem to have an urgent need for the utmost privacy. Until 1946, Mr MacLellan of the Marine Hotel, Mallaig, ran ferry services to Armadale in Skye, and to Loch Nevis and Loch Hourn. But in 1946 Lord Brocket took over the Inverie run. Up till then the ferry had carried passengers, freight, and mails, but under the new regime passengers were, of course, discouraged. When the landlady of the hotel at the head of the jetty at Inverie died,

Lord Brocket acquired it, discontinued it as an hotel, and put his factor into it instead. It is so placed that it had the further 'advantage' that no one can pass it unnoticed, which is very convenient as, of course, it is now the policy to discourage any visitors.

As a consequence of the policy that has been pursued in recent years, Inverie has now lost its entire population of young people. There is no livelihood for them under present circumstances. This is the inevitable consequence of the decline in agriculture and forestry. Yet it is not necessary at all, but deliberately contrived. One of the men involved in the present land seizure, Jack MacHardy, spoke of developing market-gardening to supply the Mallaig hotels and ships. MacHardy's plan is entirely practicable. Vegetables and such fruit as strawberries and raspberries are already grown locally. A flourishing trade could be built up if the overriding policy permitted it. That, however, is the last thing it is prepared to do.

Another of the men involved, Sandy MacPhee, forester and land worker, was right when he said: 'It's bad husbandry that has caused this state of affairs. In living memory the present Knoydart estate carried 15,000 sheep. There's fewer than 5,000 now and it was lower during the war. The oats on two farms this year were not harvested, not even for silage in the three silos Lord Brocket has built. There isn't a cartload in any of them. Last year the potatoes were not lifted until winter and were dumped in the sea.'

Sandy MacPhee added that all his life he had longed for a good croft of his own. So had his father before him. They are tired of fair promises from the Department of Agriculture – and no fulfilment. Why should such splendid Scots be denied the land they need and deserve at the instance of creatures like Lord Brocket, who is not fit to clean the shoes of any of these men, and whose presence amongst them is a complete negation of all our men fought for in the two World Wars?

In addition to Knoydart Estate, Lord Brocket has also acquired land south of Loch Nevis, round to Swordlands on Loch Morar.

It must be remembered when considering the Inverie case, that the only way out of Inverie is by sea to Mallaig.

As a further instance of Lord Brocket's unpopularity, it is alleged that when he refurnished part of Inverie House, the old furniture was taken out and dumped in the sea. Some of it floated back, and the local men went out in boats and took back some more of it, and put it into their houses. Whereupon Lady Brocket and the factor made a tour of the houses and reclaimed it all, and had it taken down to the foreshore and burned.

The interim interdict notices provided for the lodgement of answers to Lord Brocket's petition within fourteen days, so there is still some time to go, and it may be hoped that this matter will be carried further. It is time it was and that an end was put alike to the alienation from the rightful population of great areas of Scottish land bought over by Englishmen, Americans and assorted riff-raff of all sorts, and to the deliberate withholding from profitable development of the estates in question. The matter is a national one, bound up with the whole question of the future of Scotland and the Scottish people, and it is intolerable that the private interests of a person like Lord Brocket should weigh in the balance at all. It is not in the public interest that he should be allowed to remain in Scotland at all, let alone own territory here. The right to own Scottish land should be confined to Scots, living in Scotland, and continued title to it should be dependent upon proof that it is being used to the best advantage in the public interest.

As we go to press, hope that the fight at Knoydart has not been abandoned are revived by the news that on Tuesday Mr John M. Shaw, solicitor, Edinburgh, interviewed at Inverie all the claimants for land on Lord Brocket's Knoydart estate. The interviews took place in the home of Mr Alexander MacPhee, the men's leader.

23 The Coronation Stone

The Stone in the chair upon which the kings and queens of Britain sit at the time of their coronation was brought to Scotland from Ireland around 500 AD by Fergus Mor mac Erc when he established the dynasty of Dalriada. Kenneth MacAlpin, the first King of Scotland, moved it to Scone for his coronation in 843 AD. In 1296 it was stolen by Edward I and taken to Westminster Abbey, where it has remained. Its removal from Westminster Abbey was understood to be an insult to the constitution, as well as a criminal offence. MacDiarmid had planned to lift the Stone of Destiny from Westminster Abbey in 1930's and on a visit to London in 1934 he enlisted the help of two rugby forwards from Edinburgh and had hopes of getting them to heft the Stone out of the Abbey and into a fast car bound for Scotland. Once there, he had the beautiful hope that it might be dropped into a Border stream and look like any other boulder until the time came to restore it to Scone. This plan came to nothing, but when a group of young Scots removed the Stone to Scotland in 1950, MacDiarmid wrote the following front-page leader for *The National Weekly* (vol. 3, no. 119, 30 December 1950), and came out with the idea once again. The Stone had been taken from Westminster Abbey on Christmas morning, and was later deposited in Scotland, in Arbroath Abbey. The authorities then took it back to London. The story is told by Ian Robertson Hamilton, who helped organize the removal, in *No Stone Unturned* (London: Gollancz, 1952).

WHOEVER has succeeded at last in removing the Coronation Stone from Westminster Abbey is to be heartily congratulated. In certain quarters, of course, there is talk of 'sacrilege' having been committed. That is nonsense. The real sacrilege lies in Westminster Abbey having for the past six and a half centuries been made a depository for stolen goods. It is satisfactory to find various leaders of Scottish opinion like John MacCormick and Oliver Brown stressing the fact that this is not a case of theft but of recovery from the consequences of theft when all other means had failed to induce those responsible to return the stolen article.

If those who have taken the Stone are discovered in the

course of the nation-wide police search, it will be an admirable test of Scottish national feeling to see if the English authorities are permitted to punish this patriotic and long overdue action. Even more important will be the test if the Stone itself is recovered. It must not be allowed to go back to Westminster. If the Scottish people allow it to be taken back there and those who have removed it to be punished, they will cover themselves with an ignominy that will more than counterbalance the services to Scottish Independence of Wallace, Bruce, and our other national heroes. To allow anything of the sort will be a final voluntary liquidation of Scottish Nationality. No doubt all the toadies of the English Ascendancy, all the pro-English Quislings in our midst, will be willing enough to do that. But the two million signatories of the Covenant and all other Scots worth the name must take every action, no matter at what cost, to ensure the immunity from any punishment whatever of those who have removed the Stone, and to resist any attempt to replace it under Hanoverian bottoms.

I said *IF* the perpetrators are discovered and *IF* the Stone is found again. Neither of these things may happen. There have in recent years been many threats, and several attempts, to remove the Stone and bring it back to Scotland. Many interested in the matter had deemed it impossible – not because of the way it was guarded, but because of its *locus* in the Abbey. The position had been from time to time carefully reconnoitred, and the general opinion reached was that the weight of the Stone and the difficulty of manoeuvring it down the steps put the matter out of the range of the practicable unless a considerable number of individuals took part in its removal. The reason for this was that it was believed that if only two or four people took part the difficulty of getting the Stone down the steps would result in angling it into a top-heavy position which would prove unnegotiable. However it seems that these opinions were wrong. The thing has been done. All that remains now is to ensure that it is not undone but that all the efforts of the authorities are set at naught.

I also said '*IF* the Stone is recovered'. That may never happen. If those responsible for its removal have acted in accordance with previous ideas on the subject – and simply lie doggo and say nothing – the authorities can have no means of ever finding it again. The ideas in question were simply that once it was out of the Abbey and into a waiting motorcar, the latter should be driven out of London and towards the North – and that a halt should be made in some lonely spot beside a river and the Stone placed in the running water there. In such a position it would be quite unidentifiable, and could be left until all the hue and cry ceased. If the river should be on the Scottish side of the Border all the better. Even if there is little ground for over-estimating the patriotic courage and determination of the population of Scotland today, it is surely inconceivable that they are so cowardly and servile in spirit as ever to allow one of their greatest historic treasures to be transported back to London and re-installed in a church foreign to them and obnoxious to their whole tradition. That would indeed make Scotland not a laughing stock but an object of just contempt for the rest of the civilized world. *It must not go back. And its takers must not be punished by an alien Government but rewarded by their own people.*

24   The Key to World Literature

On 3 November 1952, the journalist and broadcaster Moray MacLaren wrote a deliberately provocative piece for the *Scottish Journal*, a Glasgow-based magazine published by William MacLellan. In a chatty article entitled 'A Coat Trailed before Chris Grieve', MacLaren referred to a statement MacDiarmid had made in the previous issue regarding Communist poets 'in other lands': 'So far as poetry is concerned, the Communist poets Paul Eluard of France, Nazim Hikmet of Turkey and Eugenio Montale of Italy compare favourably with any non-Communist poets in the world today.' MacLaren's question was, 'How can he possibly know?' Doubting MacDiarmid's knowledge of French, Turkish and Italian, MacLaren suggested that any appraisal of a poet's work made by someone unfamiliar with that poet's language was rather questionable. In the Christmas 1952 edition of the *Scottish Journal*, MacDiarmid replied with the following essay, 'The Key to World Literature'.

I AM sure the long friendship between Moray MacLaren and myself is not likely to be broken by the way either of us express any of our differences of opinion, great as these are, on cultural or other matters. But I confess it had not occurred to me before – though I am not surprised at the discovery now – that our differences in regard to poetry are so abysmal. Phrases in Moray's article like 'inward quality of true poetry' make me shudder. They manifest not only an attitude to and choice of poetry diametrically opposed to my own, but one which, thanks to the over-influence of English literature in our midst, is horribly general in Britain today, and against which I have been warring with all my might for the past thirty to forty years.

Sir Maurice Bowra has pointed out that the kind of poetry so favoured is almost exclusively English (i.e. an aspect of English insularity, shown also by the very small proportion of the best European literature available in English translation), and has little or no counterpart in the poetry of other European countries, and Professor Curtius of Marburg has attributed to this deplorable verbalism the fact that English poetry has practically no influence in European countries. There is only a one-way traffic. From the nineties onwards English poets have been greatly influenced by French and German poets in particular. One thinks of Baudelaire, Rimbaud, Laforgue, Corbière and others in this connection, and more recently of the vogue of Rilke. But there has been no reciprocity. This is one of the reasons why I agree with those who contend that English poetry took the wrong turning centuries ago, and agree too with Ezra Pound that it badly needs what he calls 'desuetization'. It all comes back, I suppose, to the fact that Moray is still under the influence of the Romantics, whereas I hold that poetry is an affair of the practical reason.

In any case, as a Marxist, I am interested in the history of the matter, and aware that the kind of poetry he champions is relatively a very recent phenomenon, confined to a few countries, and appealing only to an extremely limited public. Moray defeats his own argument when he says: 'Poetry above all demands an absolute and intimate knowledge of the medium in which it is composed.' Who possesses such a knowledge of any language? Has it ever been possessed? Any language is a living thing, constantly and unpredictably changing and developing in all sorts of ways. I do not know Turkish – but neither do I know English! – as well as I know Scots.

Since it is the sort of thing that will strike every fathead in Scotland as 'plain commonsense' and consequently comes under suspicion of 'playing to the gallery' and getting an easy – and worthless – horse-laugh at my expense (like everything worth bothering about, my position certainly lends itself to that brainless facetiousness which is Scotland's greatest curse!), I find it astonishing that Moray should on *a priori* grounds attack my statement (or rather my entitlement to make the statement) that 'so far as poetry is concerned, the Communist poets, Paul Eluard of France, Nazim Hikmet of Turkey, and Eugenio Montale of Italy compare favourably with any non-Communist poets in the world today.'

The proof of the pudding is in the preeing of it. I could justify myself by quotations from these poets. Moray does not attempt however to make any comparisons between their work and that of any contemporary non-Communist poets.

If he cares to investigate he will find that a consensus of the best writers on contemporary poetry throughout the world agree with me. The work of these three poets has been widely written about in literary periodicals in every European country and in the United States and elsewhere during the past few years. There are tests other than a thorough, or even any, knowledge of the language of the originals one is entitled (and even, if one is a reasonable person, bound) to accept. I have not, for example, such a low view of the value of translations as Moray has. I cannot read Russian but I have no difficulty whatever in believing that Dostoievsky and Tolstoy are among the world's very greatest novelists.

Despite his many errors in translation I do not think C. K. Scott-Moncrieff's rendering of Proust fails to provide English readers with a perfectly adequate means of estimating the genius of that writer. Contrary to general opinion I think prose more difficult to translate than poetry. I could even cite many cases in which translations of poems are better than the originals, and certainly Sir Maurice Bowra's essays on Pasternak and Alberti and others will give most English readers a far better understanding of their work than they could ever reach themselves through no matter how good a knowledge of Russian or Spanish. In practice my attitude is generally adopted. Most English readers find no difficulty in declaring that Shakespeare is one of the world's greatest poets. How can they know if they do not know all the others? How can any statement be made as to the rank of any writer without that impossibly extensive knowledge?

So I challenge Moray in turn. I determined long ago not to learn every language, but to acquire such a body of knowledge and understanding that I could see the poetical output of mankind as a whole and know what every sizeable poet 'stood for' and 'amounted to' in relation thereto, no matter in what language. There can be no absolute agreement on these things, since tastes differ, but what I proposed to myself was that with regard to any such poet in any language I should be able at any moment to show (1) that I have a good appreciation of his (or her) achievement, i.e. know which of the six classes of writer as defined in Pound's *How To Read* he or she falls into and precisely why, and (2) that I have, if not a consensus, at least an important and defensible body of critical opinion with me in regard thereto.

In regard to the sentence Moray challenges, however, I must go further and point out that I read French as easily as I read English, and have read a great deal of the work of all the leading French poets of today, including Eluard, and deplore that they are so little known in Scotland where they could be far more profitably read than the English poets who virtually have the field to themselves. I read Italian too, and was acting as Italian Secretary of a Fabian Research Committee on Syndicalism over forty years ago. Besides, I know Montale personally and have had the privilege of discussing his poetry, and the problems of poetry generally, with him. The same applies to Hikmet. Few poets depend less than Hikmet does on those untranslatable imponderables of language to which Moray refers. Hikmet's work is, on the contrary, readily translatable without appreciable loss into other languages. I have read a great deal of it in both English and French.

Finally, on the general issue, I think perhaps Moray will agree that in approaching foreign poetry and divining its quality I have one great advantage over those who only know the language – that of being a poet myself! – since knowledge of a language is no guarantee of any ability to appreciate the poetry in it, and, indeed, as Professor I. A. Richards and others have shown, British university students taking honours courses cannot be trusted in the vast majority of cases to understand passages of poetry by poets generally accepted as among England's greatest even when the passages in question present no difficulties of vocabulary or syntax whatever.

So I agree with Dr David Daiches that 'linguistic barriers are the most trivial of barriers that separate *literate* peoples. Language is never a serious barrier to those who really wish to understand each other.' Probably that is why my Scots poetry has been so much better appreciated by French, German, American, and other foreign critics than by their English and Anglo-Scottish contemporaries.

25   The Dour Drinkers of Glasgow

> This was subtitled 'A Letter from Scotland' when it appeared in Kenneth Buthlay's selection of MacDiarmid's prose, *The Uncanny Scot* (1968). It appears to have been written in the form of just such a bulletin (in the manner of Alistair Cooke's 'Letters from America') for its original periodical publication in *The American Mercury*, in March 1952.

GLASGOW! 'This savage, wild, ridiculous city', as the playwright 'James Bridie' called it, in a speech in which he very properly praised 'the right kind of lunatic, daft, Scottish panache', an attribute most easily encountered in the pubs, but difficult to find elsewhere except (by accident) in the course of a battle, a political meeting, a love affair, a theological wrangle, or a literary controversy.

I have never been able, despite repeated efforts, to understand the periodicity of those complaints against the Scottish pub which have been made during the past half century. Made, I suspect, when not by women or clergymen, either by English visitors or by Scots who, as Sir Walter Scott said, 'unScotched make damned bad Englishmen'. They are usually accompanied by envious comparisons with the amenities of English inns, which we are told are far more sociable and cater to family parties in a way Scottish pubs do not. For, in the latter, at their most typical, the rule is 'men only' and 'no sitting' – you stand at the counter with your toes in that narrow sawdust-filled trough which serves as a comprehensive combined ash-tray, litter-bin, and cuspidor. So it was when I first began to drink nearly fifty years ago; so it still is for the most part. Certainly nowadays, in addition to the common bars and to the jug (or family) departments to which women, mostly of a shawled, slatternly, and extremely subfusc order, still repair with all the ancient furtiveness, there are bright chromium-fitted saloon bars, cocktail bars, and other modern accessories in the more pretentious places. And even in most of the ordinary bars there is now a fair sprinkling of women not only of the 'lower orders' or elderly at that, but gay young things, merry widows, and courtesans. Men (if you can call them that) even take their wives and daughters along with them to these meretricious, deScotticized resorts.

Now, I am not a misogynist by any means. I simply believe there is a time and place for everything – yes, literally, *everything*. And like a high proportion of my country's regular and purposive drinkers I greatly prefer a complete absence of women on occasions of libation. I also prefer a complete absence of music and very little illumination. I am therefore a strong supporter of the lower – or lowest – type of 'dive' where drinking is the principal purpose and no one wants to be distracted from that absorbing business by music, women, glaring lights, chromium fittings, too many mirrors unless sufficiently fly-spotted and mildewed, or least of all, any fiddling trivialities of *l'art nouveau*. If there are still plenty of pubs in Glasgow which conform to these requirements and remain frowsy and fusty enough to suit my taste and that of my boon companions, in another respect the old order has changed sadly and I fear irreversibly. Our Scottish climate – not to speak of the soot-laden, catarrh-producing atmosphere of Glasgow in particular – makes us traditionally great spirit-drinkers. That has changed. Most of us cannot afford – or at any rate cannot get – much whisky or, for the matter of that, any other spirit. There are, of course, desperate characters who drink methylated spirits. I have known – and still know – resolute souls partial to a mixture of boot-blacking and 'meth', and I remember when I was in the Merchant Service during the recent War a few hardy characters who went to the trouble of stealing old compasses off the boats at Greenock (where we had the largest small-boat pool in Europe) in order to extract from them the few drops of spirit (well mixed with crude-oil and verdigris) they contained. But in Glasgow pubs today at least ninety per cent of the drinking is of beer – and mere 'swipes' at that; 'beer' that never saw a hop. I can remember the time when it was the other way about. What beer was consumed was used simply as a 'chaser' to the whisky in precisely the same way as a 'boilermaker' in New York. For of course you get drunk quicker on whisky plus water than on neat whisky, and whisky and soda is an English monstrosity no true Scot can countenance at all.

There are other sorry changes in even the lowest-down pubs which in general hold to the grim old tradition of the true Scottish 'boozer'. The question of hours, for example. In London one can still drink legally twenty-three hours out of twenty-four. That is because London is a congeries of different boroughs which have different 'permitted hours' so that by switching from one borough at closing time it is easy to find another where 'they' will still be open for an hour or two longer. In Glasgow, moreover, unlike London, there are few facilities for drinking outside the permitted hours. For most people, that is. It will hardly be thought that I am pleading for decreased consumption, but I believe that the same amount of strong drink taken in a leisurely way over a fair number of hours is less harmful than the rush to squeeze in the desired number of drinks in the short time the law allows. Our national poet, Robert Burns, was right when he said: 'Freedom and whisky gang thegither.' What he meant is precisely what my own motto means: 'They do not love liberty who fear licence.' I speak for that large body of my compatriots who uphold this great principle and regard respectability and affectations of any kind as our deadliest enemy. There are, of course, clubs and hotels, but *hoi polloi* have nothing to do with either of these.

Only a few years ago there were also Burns Clubs which took advantage of a loophole in the law and did a roaring trade especially on Sundays. You did not require to be introduced. You simply paid half-a-crown at the door and automatically became a member for the day. The difficulty – especially for the thirsty stranger within the gates, and indeed for the bulk of the citizens themselves – was to find these places. One heard about them. One heard, indeed, fantastic tales of the alcoholic excess which went on there. But they were exceedingly difficult to find. You had to be 'in the know'. Suddenly they disappeared entirely. I have never been able to discover why. There was nothing in the press – and I could learn nothing over my private grapevine either – about police action having been taken. They must have been very profitable to those who ran them, and a substantial source of revenue to the 'liquor trade' generally. They served a very useful purpose since no one not resident in a hotel and not a member of a club could otherwise get a drink in Glasgow on Sundays. (It was – and is still – jolly difficult to get a meal even.)

During these two wars there were all kinds of interferences with the incidence and duration of the 'permitted hours'. Quite a proportion of licence-holders got it into their heads that they could close earlier than the decreed closing-time – and even take a weekly half-holiday and in some cases shut shop and go off for a week's holiday in the summer time. They still do, and act arbitrarily in many other ways. All that is, of course, quite illegal, although the magistracy and police authorities turned a blind eye at these irregularities and even welcomed them. The fact is, of course, as the very term 'public house' shows, that the condition of the licence obliges the licence-holder to have his place at the disposal of citizens at all times – not necessarily for drinking at all; a citizen is entitled to have the use of these places whenever he wants if only to use the lavatory or shelter from the weather, or read his newspaper, or meet a friend. It would, in practice, be virtually impossible to fight this and other corrupt practices the authorities have winked at. Recognizing this, some of us tried to organize a 'Consumers' Union', since the consumers are the only unorganized and helpless factor in the liquor situation. It proved impossible; the consumers won't combine. They are far too individualistic. Though such a Consumers' Union might have been very useful in certain connections *vis-à-vis* the Liquor Trade, the Municipal, State, and Police Authorities and every variety of blue-nosed snooper, I am on many other counts enough of an 'unregenerate sinner' not to regret that the effort failed. Yet at times I like to toy with the idea that if it had been possible to organize even a high proportion of pub-users (leaving out consumers who consume elsewhere) the result would have been one of the strongest organizations in the world. No Trade Union, or combination of Trade Unions, would have been a patch on it.

I trust I have made myself clear. The majority of Glasgow pubs are for connoisseurs of the morose, for those who relish the element of degradation in all boozing and do not wish to have it eliminated by the introduction of music, modernistic fitments, arty effects, or other extraneous devices whatsoever. It is the old story of those who prefer hard-centre chocolates to soft, storm to sunshine, sour to sweet. True Scots always prefer the former of these opposites. That is one of our principle differences from the English. We do not like the confiding, the intimate, the ingratiating, the hail-fellow-well-met, but prefer the unapproachable, the hard-bitten, the recalcitrant, the sinister, the malignant, the saturnine, the cross-grained and the cankered, and the howling wilderness to the amenities of civilization, the irascible to the affable, the prickly to the smooth. We have no damned fellow-feeling at all, and look at ourselves and others with the eye of a Toulouse Lautrec appraising an obscene old toe-rag doing the double-split. In short, we are all poets (all true Scots – that is, all Scots not encased in a carapace of conventionality a mile thick) of *l'humour noir* and, as William Blake said, 'All poets are of the devil's party'.

There is a well-known story about Carlyle and Emerson spending several hours together without exchanging a word. Carlyle declared it was one of the best nights he ever spent with anybody. A lot of us spend many nights in Scottish pubs in the same way and we agree with Carlyle. Scotland produces a type of man who can dispense more completely than any with what James Joyce called 'the atrocities of human intercourse'.

There is nothing less exportable than a national sense of humour. The Scottish temper I am writing about is little known abroad. Our internationally famous comedians purvey a very different account of us. The sorry joke is that so many Scots believe the latter and model themselves all too successfully on it. Yet what I am trying to express is well-enough known about us in other connections. It is this that for centuries has made the Scottish soldier famous as a bayonet-fighter. A similar preference for naked steel runs through every phase of our life. It is summed up in the old Gaelic proverb: 'Fingal's sword never needs to cut twice.' Burns says in one of his poems that you need not be 'nice' with him. No one need be 'nice' with any true Scotsman – in fact, he will not allow it at all. The only kind of friendships one makes – or wishes to make or could tolerate at all – in such pubs was well described by my Irish friend, the late W. B. Yeats, when he wrote:

> I called him a knave and a fool –
> But friendship never dies!

In other words, the injunction which is as one with the very marrow of our bones is 'Woe to him of whom all men speak well.' We have no use for emotions, let alone sentiments, but are solely concerned with passions.

One of the best essayists on aspects of Scottish literature, Mr J. D. Scott, has pointed out how deep in Scottish life are the roots of this 'slow and vicious enjoyment', this 'formidable and ferocious scorn'. It is the tremendous animating principle of three of the greatest modern Scottish novels – George Douglas Brown's *House With the Green Shutters*, R. L. Stevenson's unfinished *Weir of Hermiston*, and Sydney Goodsir Smith's super-Rabelaisian story of Edinburgh today (doing for it what Joyce's *Ulysses* did for Dublin), *Carotid Cornucopius*. It is precisely this element, utterly different from English humour, that is the essence of any number of the most typical Scottish anecdotes. Like, for example, the story of the minister who told his congregation that in a dream he had seen them all in Hell suffering the tortures of the damned. 'Ye lifted up your eyes to the Almighty God and ye said to Him. "O Lord, we didna ken it would be like this", and the Lord God Almighty, (*slowly and unctuously*) in His infinite mercy and compassion, looked down upon ye and He said, "Weel, noo ye ken!" '

We (if I may speak for all of us) do not go to pubs for chit-chat, we do not wish them crossed with some sort of café or tea-party or concert or damned *conversazione*; we are fond enough of our women-folk, but there are times when we want away from them as no doubt there are times when they want to be away from us. The keynote of Glasgow life is still expressed in the song sung by Will Fyffe, the great Scottish comedian, which runs:

> I belong to Glasgow,
> Dear old Glasgow toon.
> But what's the matter wi' Glasgow?
> For it's going roon' and roon'.
> I'm only a common old working chap,
> As anyone here can see,

> But when I get a couple o' drinks on a Saturday,
> Glasgow belongs to me.

Our attitude is not inhuman. We are experienced men of the world. We like what we like to be a little grim – in keeping with the facts of life, and loathe facile emotions. We cherish no illusions, and consequently prefer a mutual taciturnity to any sort of social joy, standing shoulder to shoulder with other men we do not know from Adam and do not want to know. We feel no necessity whatever to indulge in any airs and graces, are not fond of promiscuous conversation, at least of any sustained sort, and if our risible faculties are moved at all by the human spectacle, that movement only adorns our face intermittently with some sort of *risus sardonicus* that in flickering across our features barely interrupts the emission of the dense smoke of the black tobacco going well in our clay pipes. It is, indeed, a sort of fleeting facial comment hardly distinguishable from the effect of that gagging which an unwarily deep swig at what passes for Scotch Whisky is apt to etch on the granitic features of even the most hardened soak.

Elsewhere I have summed up my regard for Glasgow in a brief poem, '*Placenta Previa*', which runs:

> It'll be no easy matter to keep the dirt in its place
> And get the Future out alive in *this* case.

On the last Hogmanay night (New Year's Eve), as on all its predecessors, no matter how dourly and darkly I take my pleasures, the same way some people keep snakes for pets, I once again, with a great upsurge of savage joy, recalled another verse of mine and practised what I preach, namely:

> O this is the item for all mankind
>   To rejoice without a doubt
>   ——And break the neck of the bottle
>   If the cork will not come out!

And that is precisely how Scots do bring in the New Year. They gather in the public squares of their cities and towns, and as the bells ring out the Old Year and ring in the New, they empty their bottles and smash them on the street. On this most recent Hogmanay I was one of a company of many uproarious hundreds doing this in George Square, Glasgow, undeterred by the fact that a day of gale and sleet was giving way to snow and ice and that hundreds of people in Glasgow alone had been rendered homeless by blown-down houses or injured in the streets by falling chimney-pots and torn-off slates.

A wild night, so our merriment had to be correspondingly wild to lift our hearts above its hazards. A typical incident was the ripping apart of a newly-built school. It was hurled by the gale towards a house occupied by a family of Kellys. One section of the steel-framed school was lifted in the air and wrapped round an electric standard at the Kelly's back fence. That standard saved the Kelly house. If it hadn't been there the school would have gone right through the house.

Hail Caledonia, stern and wild!

Scott Fitzgerald speaks of 'Jay Gatsby breaking up like glass against Tom Buchanan's hard malice.' I sometimes think all the shams and unveracities in the world will break up in the same way against the Scottish spirit of which I am writing. Scots of that particular mettle are the very salt of the earth. I am one of them and so I know. It would not pay anyone to dispute the point in any of the Glasgow pubs I frequent.

Let me finish this Scottish letter on a different note altogether. Otherwise it will not be true to Scotland, which is a country of sharp transitions and extraordinary variety, in its landscape, weather, people and everything else. Glasgow is only a part of it, and utterly unrepresentative of the rest. Well, I was talking to an Edinburgh man yesterday and I said something about the unexpectable character of Scottish scenery, and Scottish life. And he pulled me up at once. 'Nonsense,' he said, 'there is nothing inexplicable – nothing to account for which almost anybody cannot devise at once some reasonable hypothesis.' And he challenged me to give an example. I replied that I was walking across a moor in Rosshire one summer afternoon. There wasn't a soul in sight, hardly an animal, only a bird or two. It was almost twelve miles to the nearest village. Suddenly among the heather I spied a yellow glove. It was almost brand-new, did not look as if it had been worn at all. I picked it up and as I did so I heard a clicking noise

The Dour Drinkers of Glasgow

inside it. I took it by the tip of one of the fingers and shook it gently – and out fell four fingernails and a thumbnail, the complete set of nails from one hand. They were perfectly clean, like sea shells. However they had come off it had quite obviously neither been through any disease nor violence. It was impossible to conceive a man drawing off his glove and nails with it, tossing them into the heather, and walking on unaware, or, if aware, as if nothing has happened. I found it – and find it – impossible to imagine the state of mind of a man who a few miles further on discovered he had done just that. I have been haunted ever since by a sense of the horrible blunt feeling of nailless fingertips. I should have thought in such a case a man would have reported the matter to the police or discussed it with friends and that somehow or other news of such an extraordinary occurrence would have got round and out, and even into the papers. I made all sorts of inquiries and found that nothing was known or could be discovered about the matter. I enquired of medical friends and found that no known disease could account for it and that no similar case was cited in any medical or scientific book known to them.

I have never succeeded in solving the mystery or getting any light on it at all. But it can certainly serve as a parable of much that has happened in what has been called 'the self-suppression of the Scot' and the way he has sloughed off his literature, history, native languages, and much else in the past two and a half centuries. Another and equal mystery is the way in which he is today resuming them, just as if the nailless finger-ends were suddenly growing new nails. There is widespread agreement that a great Scottish National Reawakening is in progress. I'd know more about that if I could hit on any explanation of the preceding loss. As matters stand, I take it, in the Scots law phrase, to *avizandum*, i.e. defer for further consideration. And yet I am conscious of my inability to make up my mind to deal with the situation because there are no facts on which one *can* make up one's mind, and a pressing desire to seize on small clues, to build up something in order that one may do something – *anything* – knowing all the time that if one *did* do something it would probably be wrong because the basic facts are missing. Whether I am right or not in fancying that this is something that could only have happened in Scotland, I think it will be agreed that it is exceedingly unlikely ever to have happened anywhere before and highly improbable that it will ever happen again. Above all, I wonder how the hell I invented it at all. Apart from just being Scotch, of course – really Scotch.

26 The Politics and Poetry of Hugh MacDiarmid

> This essay appeared in *The National Weekly* (vol. 4, nos. 198, 199) in 1952, and was attributed to 'Arthur Leslie', which was one of a number of pseudonyms MacDiarmid used over the years. It was later published as a pamphlet in a limited edition and collected in Duncan Glen's *Selected Essays* (1969).

EVER since his boyhood 'Hugh MacDiarmid' [Christopher Murray Grieve] has been working towards, and in the service of, that 'first truly human culture', as Trotsky calls it in *Literature and Revolution*, which socialism is eventually to make possible; and his Scottish nationalism is simply his concentration on that task in his own immediate neighbourhood, leaving his comrades in all other countries to do likewise in their own particular spheres, confident that all these will become one – or rather at one – in the era of integrated communism. Like Trotsky too – as his autobiography, *Lucky Poet*, makes abundantly clear – he could have said truly of himself at any time after his early teens:

> The leaders of the Social Democracy used the same formulas that I did, but one had only to turn any of them five degrees around on their own axes to discover that we gave quite different meanings to the same concepts. Our agreement was a temporary one, superficial and unreal. The correspondence between Marx and Engels was for me not a theoretical but a psychological revelation. *Toutes proportions gardées*, I found proof on every page that I was bound to these two by a direct psychological affinity. Their attitude to men and ideas was mine. I guessed what they did not express, shared their sympathies, was indignant and hated as they did. Marx and Engels were revolutionaries through and through. But they had not the slightest trace of sectarianism or asceticism. Both of them and especially Engels, could at any time say of themselves that nothing human was strange to them. But their revolutionary

outlook lifted them always above the hazards of fate and the works of men. Pettiness was incompatible not only with their personalities but with their presences. Vulgarity could not stick even to the soles of their boots. Their appreciations, sympathies, jests – even when most commonplace – are always touched by the rarefied air of spiritual nobility. They may pass deadly criticism on a man, but they will never deal in tittle-tattle. They can be ruthless, but not treacherous. For outward glamour, titles or rank they have nothing but a cool contempt. What philistines and vulgarians considered aristocratic in them was only their revolutionary superiority. Its most important characteristic is a complete and ingrained independence of official public opinion at all times and under all conditions.

Almost all the writers who have appraised MacDiarmid's personality and poetry have realized that that quotation fits him like a glove. Norrie Fraser, for example, wrote twenty years ago in the *New English Weekly*:

'The most persistent and consistent critic of Scottish life in recent years.' The place is Hugh MacDiarmid's whose trouncings of hypocrites and sycophants are the only consistent bright spot in contemporary affairs, and who should play a major part in any realist Nationalist Party who are beyond thinking that a Parliament in Edinburgh, an increased percentage of bare knees in Scotland, and far more Gleneagles would mean anything in the face of a remaining British Imperialist Economics.

About the same time a writer in the Edinburgh University *Student* said:

No fresh idea has entered the nation's head since the Disruption – our Socialism is still Burnsite in spirit – MacDiarmid has splendidly pioneered here. His thought-poetry, besides its criticism of lingering opinions, is a veritable mine of the best European ideas expressed in their relation to our living problems at home. Heir of our Radicalism, he is always a left-wing man, possessed with the idea of Freedom. In thought as in attitude to language it is for the masses of us that he is working. His poetry is essentially popular. Our inner longings, our inmost resolves, so long inarticulate and half-conscious, find in MacDiarmid's the voice they have lacked since the time of Burns and the great Highland poets. One day his work will be allowed to get across to Scotland.

While so much is common ground to the great majority of those who have written about him, it is necessary (not to point out that his intense Scottish nationalism coexists in him with an almost unbelievably extensive and minutely detailed knowledge and appreciation of a great number of other literatures and languages – that is clear enough in all that he has written; if he is an extreme Scottish nationalist he is also one of the greatest internationalists even Scotland has ever produced) to stress here the way in which he has squared precept and practice in his life. He joined the I.L.P. when he was sixteen, and a little later, the Edinburgh University Fabian Society and took an active part in the formation of the University Socialist Federation. He began open-air speaking, too, in his teens, under the tutelage of 'Jimmy Buchanan', an Edinburgh Corporation scavenger who was one of the stalwarts and pioneers of socialism in Edinburgh. Before he was twenty he had served on a Fabian Research Committee on agriculture on whose behalf he surveyed the whole Scottish aspect of the matter and submitted a series of brilliant memoranda which formed part of the joint volume *The Rural Problem* [London: Constable, 1913] in which the findings of the committee were embodied. In the preface to that book, the chairman (Mr Henry Harben) paid special tribute to Mr MacDiarmid's work, coupling his name, in this connection, with that of Mr Sidney Webb (Lord Passfield). A little later, MacDiarmid ran a newspaper, *The Monmouthshire Labour News*, for the South Wales Miners' Federation. Living in Ebbw Vale he used to walk over to Merthyr Tydfil to see Keir Hardie and was a contributor to Hardie's paper, *The Merthyr-Pioneer*. Other friends of MacDiarmid's at that time included Vernon Hartshorn, Tom Mann, Victor Grayson, Frank Hodges, and Denis

Hird, first Principal of Ruskin College. Since then to the present time he has been continuously actively associated with the working-class movement and has served it as a Town Councillor, Parish Councillor, and Justice of the Peace and in many other capacities. He is a member of the Writers' Group of the Society for Cultural Relations with the USSR; a director of Theatre Workshop Ltd; President of the Dunedin Society for the encouragement of the arts in Scotland; a Vice-Chairman of the British Peace Committee; and his friendships with communist and near-communist politicians, writers and artists in many countries, are very numerous – amongst those who should be mentioned being Nancy Cunard, Valentine Acland, Sylvia Townsend Warner, Sean O'Casey, Josef Hermon, Norman MacLeod, Horace Gregory, Muriel Rukeyser, and Kenneth Patchen. He is one of the most incessant public speakers in Scotland and there are few places in the country in which his has not long been a 'ken-speckle' figure now.

★

Hugh MacDiarmid was born in 1892 in the little Dumfriesshire burgh of Langholm of working-class parents. Writing of his boyhood in *Lucky Poet* he says:

> The main thing about these early days, however – because of its bearing on my subsequent literary work and my later life generally – is that they made me a man naturally fitted for Communism – a man, moreover, who found ready and waiting in himself by the time he came to write poetry a sound relationship between the political thinker in him and the artist. I had not to adjust myself in either connexion: above all, I had not to scrap or transform any part of myself which by education was antagonistically *bourgeois*, because I had been on the alert from the very start and had never developed any such part. If I came in the end to Communism (that is, to membership of the Communist Party, instead of the Independent Labour Party, of which I had by then been over twenty years an active member) I also *grew* into it through a class-conscious upbringing

which conditioned but did not distort my view of life. My development owed a very great deal to my growing-up in a working-class family and being fed on out-and-out Radicalism and Republicanism when still a child. This was so intense that I was spared any out-growing of it by virtue of a *bourgeois* education and conversion to *bourgeois* manners – and remaining solid with the working-class throughout. Even if I had outgrown the early influence through education and so on, I would have recurred all right to the early standpoint; it was potent enough to have reclaimed me. But in point of fact this was not necessary in my case at all – I had never allowed myself to be drawn away from it; the working-class have always stood, and will always stand, in the relation to me not of 'they' but of 'we' – and so instead of having it recur to mind after the disillusioning lessons of the (First World) War, it only confirmed what from the beginning was my strongest tendency and completed the course I had been pursuing into actual Party membership – a decision that had been implicit in most of my previous reactions to experience. This book, therefore, is not (like the autobiographies of so many fellow-writers of my own generation or thereabouts) the story of a man who came belatedly to Communism, or came rebelling against his temperament, or came – in bitterness of spirit – to save his precious soul. My coming to Communist membership was not the resolution, as it were of a career; no conflict existed except on very minor points – the attitude of the Communist Party to Scottish Nationalism, for example, in regard to which, for a time, I was at variance, not with Communism, but with the unfortunate limitations of certain leading members of the Communist Party in Scotland, and with a deplorable 'twist' given in this connexion to the Communist Party of Great Britain by the circumstance of its inception. For it had never been my aim to rise above the class into which I was born – it had, indeed, been my vigilant determination to see that I allowed nothing to come between me and my class – and my regression to Scots (i.e. the Scots language, in which most of his best poetry is written, instead of English) was, in fact, the counter-process to the usual course; where others were concerned to rise, I, on the contrary, was determined to strengthen and develop my organic relationship to the Commons of Scotland by every means in my power, not to get back to the people – for I had never allowed myself to get away from them – but to get under the skin, to get deeper and deeper into their innermost promptings, their root motives. The tremendous proletarian virtue of the little town I knew as a boy saved me – despite the religiosity, the puritanism, of both my parents, and the ambitious gentility of my mother, and despite my own literary gifts – from the ordeal so many young writers and artists are going through today, of rising again to proletarian integrity, of becoming once more organically welded, to the working-class. From the beginning I took as my motto – and I have adhered all through to it in my literary work – Thomas Hardy's declaration: 'Literature is the written expression of revolt against accepted things.'

Today with over a dozen volumes of poetry to his credit – not to mention abut thirty prose works – MacDiarmid might say with the American poet, William Carlos Williams:

You see, as a writer I haven't even begun to do anything
Yet all I've been able to achieve so far has been survival.
My idea of myself as an artist is that of a man running as
Hard as he could put it from the wolves. I knew what it
Would be from the first and I was right. I made up my
Mind that I'd have to live to be very old, like Titian or the
Jap whose name I have forgotten, before I should be able to get
Into that peaceful country where I could sit down to the
Difficult task of composition. All I've accomplished so
Far is to build up a grand artist's constitution, to be so
Tough that I could take it on the chin from anybody at any
Time and be able to come back in the last round and knock
Them out of the ring.

MacDiarmid has carefully defined his communism in *Lucky Poet*. Here it will suffice to say that the keynote of his whole position is his agreement with the late Ford Madox Ford that:

The only human activity that has always been of extreme

importance to the world is imaginative literature. It is of supreme importance because it is the only means by which humanity can express at once emotions and ideas. To avoid controversy I am perfectly willing to concede that the other arts are of equal importance. But nothing that is not an art is of any lasting importance at all, the meanest novel being humanly more valuable than the most pompous of factual works, the most formidable of material achievements, or the most carefully thought out of legal codes.

Always anxious to find chapter and verse for his positions in the literature of his own country, MacDiarmid might well have taken as the best expression of his spirit that part of John Ruskin's *The Stones of Venice* in which he compares the three thrones set upon the sand: Tyre, of which only the memory remains; Venice, of which only the ruin; and England, which, if she forgets the example of the others, 'may come to less pitied destruction'. Thus, as Robert Furneaux Jordan has said,

> Ruskin took the step great artists have to take, from intrinsic beauty to social passion, ethics and political economy. It is superficial to regret it. The central work of Ruskin's life is that chapter in the second volume called 'The Nature of Gothic.' the true nature of gothic, it tells us, is the 'dependence of all human work for its beauty on the happy life of the workman . . . you must either make a tool of the creature, or a man of him. You cannot make both.' That was shattering – in that smug world of academics and patrons! William Morris said that it was 'one of the very few necessary and inevitable utterances of the century.'

And, again, the reason for his hatred of Anglo-Saxondom, and the essence of his hope for mankind, is clearly discernible in the following passage from the same writer:

> The little society in which D. H. Lawrence moved (i.e. 'all the young people were talking about Nietzche and Wagner and Leopardi and Flaubert and Karl Marx . . . and they would discuss the French Impressionists and the primitive Italians and play Chopin or Debussy on the piano . . . I

have never anywhere found so educated a society. These young people *knew* the things that my generation in the great English schools hardly even chattered about') was a microcosm of what the world must come to if it is to be permanent. Its existence foretold to me even then the disappearance of the ruling power of the middle-classes as they then were and even of the class that in England was called the ruling class. The disappearance of Eton as the educational home of the nation's legislators was there as plainly foreshadowed as the fact England's victories were never again to be won on Eton's playing fields. The one was to go down before the type of education that had produced Lawrence's small coterie and nourished the genius of Lawrence himself just as surely as the other was to disappear before wireless telegraphy, the aeroplane, motor traction and the other wonders of science. You cannot fight an atmosphere of poison gas with the rules of cricket any more than you can expect to rule cultured people – or any people – if you are unacquainted with the highest imaginative thought of the world of your day. This Anglo-Saxondom has never believed. That is why Anglo-Saxondom is crumbling as Rome did to its doom. Even in the Middle Ages they knew that. They used to say:

When lands are gone and money spent
Then learning is most excellent.

And the root of MacDiarmid's loathing of the British Empire is certainly to be found in the fact that

the population of the British Empire at that date [1916] was some 250,000,000. For the purpose of the hostilities in which we were engaged it could find seven million men and two or three million women – say one in twenty-five. For its intellectual front line that two hundred and fifty million could find 14,000 – one in 17,857. It is not much consolation to say that a large percentage of that 250,000,000 do not read English. If the greatest Empire the world has ever seen cannot induce its subject races to assimilate its highest form of culture its existence seems unjustified. And unjustifiable.

MacDiarmid has stated that his visit to the USSR in 1951 has powerfully strengthened all his ideas, since the development of local languages and cultures in the various republics represents just that 'diversity in unity' he has always desired and is the very antithesis of what has always obtained in the British Commonwealth of Nations. He is delighted too by the tremendous educational avidity throughout the Soviet Union and the splendid facilities available everywhere for cultural development. His meetings with leading Soviet writers, including Alexei Surkov, Pavlo Tychina, Konstantin Simonov, Samuel Marshak, and others – as, later, his meetings in the Soviet zone of Germany with Pablo Neruda, Nazim Hikmet, Johannes Becker, Anna Seghers, and other communist writers – have all confirmed his ideas in this connection.

MacDiarmid is tough all right, he has needed to be to survive in Scotland, and there is ample proof of it in the fact that in his fifties, during Hitler's war, being too old for military service, he qualified as a fitter and served two years in a Clydeside engineering works, becoming charge-hand in the copper shell-band department, and then did another year as an estuarial seaman on a Norwegian boat on admiralty service and has since, with an interval as a post-office sorter, had to endure the hardship and ignominy of being unemployed for, although he has had twenty years' experience as a journalist, is generally recognized as the leading living Scottish writer and, as Compton Mackenzie has put it, as 'the most powerful intellectually and emotionally fertilizing force Scotland has known since the death of Burns', and has held all his previous jobs, journalistic and otherwise, with the highest credit and possesses first-class testimonials, he is a 'dangerous man' and there is no job for him in Scotland today. Unemployed or not, however, he is pouring out articles and poems, broadcasting, addressing all sorts of meetings, perpetually engaged in violent controversies with all sorts of people from one end of the country to another, and somehow or other contriving to create an extraordinary impression of ubiquity and omnicompetence.

The present writer once drew MacDiarmid's attention to the following statements made in the *New Statesman and Nation* by

Mr Raymond Mortimer:

> What one may call the theologians of Communism profess some highly irrational doctrines derived ultimately from the ill-regulated imagination of Hegel. Look, however, for the most active principal of this faith, and you find, combined with patriotism of the most old-fashioned sort, 'a belief in man's ability to conquer nature, to solve the most difficult problems, and to make or create history.' This belief, which every Soviet artist is under an obligation to propagate, is one that has never in history succeeded in attracting any great poet, or indeed, any mind of the first order.

MacDiarmid expressed his contempt and contented himself with remarking that Mr Mortimer's contention was 'on all fours with the disbelief formerly so frequently expressed in this and other countries that the Russian Revolution was real and irreversible', or again, he said, 'it is just the same frame of mind as led so many people prior to August 1914 to imagine that a modern war could not possibly last more than a week or two. I may not be a great poet or a mind of the first order, but in so far as I am a poet and have a mind, I am certainly – and will continue to be – dependant upon the active principle of that faith which, like every Soviet artist, I certainly regard myself as under an obligation to propagate by every means in my power.'

*

His poetry has always been one of the weapons of his general political fight. It is a mistake to imagine that he came to political poetry late; his poetry was political from the outset, as the 'Ballad of the General Strike' in his *A Drunk Man Looks at the Thistle*, and many other poems there and in earlier books makes clear enough. Not only his work as a seaman and an engineer, but all his life has testified to his complete agreement with his old friend, the late Sir Patrick Geddes, who, addressing a company of distinguished Frenchmen of letters and noted philosophers from Germany and France at Montpelier in 1929, said:

I have the greatest respect for my friend Desjardins as an intellectual and for his colleagues too. But as gardeners they are complete failures. Neither I nor any peasant in the village can have respect for them as men able to do real work. Of course I can't offend my old friend but I say that not until men of learning and of letters can win the respect of peasant or workman *on his own level* will they ever escape from that isolated barrenness which threatens the cultured *élite* of every nation.

He has always been fond of quoting William Dean Howells's remark that 'those who rise above the necessity of work for daily bread are in great danger of losing their right relationship to other men.' MacDiarmid had put this most effectively perhaps in the lines which run:

Above all – though primarily a poet myself –
I know I need as large an area of brain
To control my hands as my vocal organs
And I am fully alive to the danger
Of only grasping so much of the scientific outlook
As is expressed in words or symbols
Rather than actions,
– The common mistake of regarding
The skilful manipulation of symbols
As an activity altogether more respectable
Than the skilful manipulation
Of material objects.
I am organically welded with the manual workers
As with no other class in the social system
Though superficially my interests may seem to be rather
With the so-called educated classes.

Again, in the words of Patrick Geddes, he might say of the spirit that has animated all his work: 'The great need: Intenser life for men and women! Thus in this period of intensest crises in all main lines of life and thought, social and individual alike, I have been seeking life more abundantly. Seeking life first for myself, then others; but now more fully for others, beyond my ageing self. Thinking and doing, seeking for others . . .

now and beyond . . .'

As he has said of himself he is a communist, but *in excelsis* a communist of the kind Lenin described when he said:

> Now, for the first time, we have the possibility of learning. I do not know how long this possibility will last. I do not know how long the Capitalist Powers will give us the opportunity of learning in peace and quietude. But we must utilize every moment in which we are free from war that we may learn, and *learn from the bottom up* . . . It would be a very serious mistake to suppose that one can become a Communist without making one's own the treasures of human knowledge. It would be mistaken to imagine that it is enough to adopt the Communist formulas and conclusions of Communist science without mastering the sum-total of different branches of knowledge whose final outcome is Communism . . . Communism becomes an empty phrase, a mere façade, and the Communist a mere bluffer, if he has not worked over in his consciousness the whole inheritance of human knowledge . . . made his own, and worked over anew, all that was of value in the more than two thousand years of development of human thought.

In his fight against ignorance and anti-intellectualism, and the incessant cry of stupid socialists and communists that nothing should be written save what is intelligible to the mass of the people, and that consequently there should be no learned allusions or high-brow difficulties in the work of writers, MacDiarmid has frequently quoted:

> Marx and Engels laid down almost no literary theory as such; profoundly cultivated men both, they merely presented an example of scholarship and cultivation, and trusted to the cultivation and good sense of their followers. Laying the groundwork for the greatest single event in human history as they saw it – the Socialist revolution that would eventually bring in a superperfect harmony and humanity amongst men – they automatically in sketching out the naturalistic and economic foundations of all human experience, subordinated literature and art

under the general heading of culture, and studied culture itself as a body of human activity grounded, as they thought all human activity to have been, in the material relations of production. But they did not believe that works of art come into being through mechanized causation, nor did they anticipate that in speaking of culture as the 'superstructure' above the main groundwork of economic relations – a trunk on the central tree – their imagery would be taken to mean that literature, for example, is nothing but a by-product of material activity. 'The economic factor is "not the sole determining factor",' Engels wrote in a letter towards the end of his life. 'The production and reproduction of real life constitutes in the last instance the determining factor in history.'

What this 'last instance' was to mean, Edmund Wilson has pointed out, was confusing enough since it could mean either the last in time or the last in the sense of being the fundamental motive of human behaviour and culture. But it has been confusing only because Engels and Marx took it for granted that their radical insistence on the material foundations of art and literature would not be seized on to confuse the social origins of art with its aesthetic values. Towards the end of his life Engels himself came to deplore the unthinking use so often made of historical materialism and wrote sharply to a correspondent: 'I must tell you from the very first that the materialist is converted into its direct opposite if, instead of being used as a guiding thread in historical research, it is made to serve as a ready-cut pattern on which to tailor historical facts.'

'Marx and I', Engels once wrote significantly to Franz Mehring, 'both placed and *had to place* the chief weight upon the derivation of political, legal, and other ideological notions from fundamental economic facts. In consequence we neglected the formal side – i.e. the way in which these ideas arose – for the sake of the content.'

For all their understanding of the social origins of art, Marxist critics – if they seek to be critics – begin at that point. What the Marxist critic particularly is faced with – since no field of criticism makes so many demands on the active imagination as the study of literature in its relations to society – is the obligation to show just what those relations are and just what values emerge from a study of them. Condemning the aesthete who seems to believe that art exists in a vacuum, he must yet show that art is something more than the 'ideological' representation of class forces in society. Patronizing the genteel impressionist who does not know to what extent works of art themselves have often acted as social forces, battlegrounds of ideas, he must yet show that the significance of any art work begins with its immediate success and fulfilment as art, its fulfilments of aesthetic need and pleasure. Fighting the reactionary ideologue, who holds that art is aristocratic and the property of a few exquisite sensibilities, he must yet admit (precisely because he is confident that it is only with the advent of socialism that human energy will be great enough, human fellowship broad enough, to make great works possible again) that without individual talent and humility and discipline, without its immediate origin in exceptional persons, no art is possible at all.

Emerson says that we 'descend to meet'. This is no doubt true of certain kinds of meeting, of the kind that takes place at an afternoon tea, let us say; and Emerson probably did not mean more than this. But the phrase may evidently have another, and, from the humanistic point of view, far more sinister meaning. Instead of disciplining himself to some sort of perfection set above his ordinary self, a man sinks down from the intellectual to the instinctive level, on the ground that he is thus widening his instinctive sympathies. A study of literature in its relation to society is not a feather-bed for minds seeking cosy formulas. It is presumably a rousing-up of the best intellectual energies, and a stimulus to the richest structural imagination that criticism affords.

MacDiarmid, who has quarrelled bitterly with the late Mr Ramsay MacDonald, Sir Hugh Roberton of Orpheus choir 'fame' and other Scottish socialists with petty cultural pretensions and no capacity for doing anything but darkening counsel and further confusing the issues, has said somewhere in condemning the infantilism of Scottish Socialist MPs and commenting on the extraordinary absence of socialist achievement in any of the arts in Scotland that it has been and still is in Scotland as it was in the United States of America when Granville Hicks and other American Marxist critics were rightly characterized as

> a race of young men, lost in the tides of change and vaguely hostile to traditional forms, who submitted to Marxism so hungrily that their ambition overreached itself in that spell of the absolute. They had found a new purpose for themselves in the light of the Marxist purpose; but in them one saw the working of the absolute on minds never supple or imaginative enough, never talented or sensitive enough, to write significant criticism. It was this conventionality, aroused and militant in Marxist battledress, a conventionality moving briskly but with metallic ardour through a period of confusion, that betrayed them; their painful limitations all arose from their efforts to apply their seriousness in judgment of sensibilities immeasurably subtler and deeper than their own. Their main gift is seriousness – a quality of moral intelligence – and as a result they fell into a shrewish moralism, a moralism that is conscious of aesthetic differences but has no talent for conveying the necessary discriminations between them.

It is probably socialists of that type, talking down to the people, playing to the gallery, and priding themselves upon just that minimum of culture necessary to differentiate them from the great mass, MacDiarmid has in mind when in one of his latest books (*A Kist of Whistles*) he says that the kind of poetry he wants is a poetry

> That like a wrestling bout on a village green
> Divides the people and wins only those
> Who are honest, strong and true
> – Those who admire the man
> Who has the faster mind,
> The faster, suppler, better-governed body –
> For there is not only a class war
> But a war in the working class itself
> Between decency and self-respect on the one hand

And a truckling spirit, seeking self-gain, on the other.

MacDiarmid wrote his 'First Hymn to Lenin' for a collection the late Mr Lascelles Abercrombie was editing for Mr Victor Gollancz. Abercrombie was delighted with it and wrote saying that MacDiarmid had done something that was urgently wanted, and had done it in an extremely effective way. Of the 'Second Hymn to Lenin', Dr F. R. Leavis said in *Scrutiny* that it was 'sufficiently a success to deserve inclusion in the ideal anthology (which would be a very small one) of contemporary poetry'. These communist poems of MacDiarmid's were also discussed and highly praised in C. Day Lewis's book on poetry in England, and Miss Babette Deutsch's survey of contemporary poetry in America. The late 'Lewis Grassic Gibbon' (James Leslie Mitchell) said: 'The "Hymns to Lenin" are among the world's most magnificent hymns to the high verities of life. MacDiarmid has shown the Scottish speech capable of dealing tremendously and vividly, with the utmost extremes of passion and pity. All good art is propaganda, and MacDiarmid, *ex officio*, is a splendid propagandist.'

Stephen Spender has commented on the extraordinary beauty of MacDiarmid's lyrics and his particular power of achieving great poetry in the exposition of Marxist ideas; Alec Comfort has complained of the difficulty of procuring copies of MacDiarmid's 'Hymns to Lenin', and remarking that these are not dull duty-pieces but great poems, refers to the great virtues of character which have enabled MacDiarmid to approach and reapproach this theme in poem after poem without merely repeating himself; and 'David Martin', the former literary editor of *Reynolds News*, has written that

> the magnificent 'Hymn to Lenin' – not published in its entirety even now – is certainly on a par, to say the least, with Mayakowsky's in poetic intensity. He was John Maclean's friend. But like his friend, MacDiarmid has had trouble with the Communist Party. He has had trouble with everybody. He is too big for the nationalists too. Too big. Where there are so many cranks it is easy for the bone lazy to denounce as cranks those who do not fit with a pattern. But in his writing there is nothing ill-

organized or haphazard; on the contrary; his works range from translations from the Spanish to topographical surveys of the north, from poetry which is as lyrical and simple as that of Walter von der Vogelweide to literary essays, the brilliance and range of which are certainly not inferior to the best that is written in Britain today. He is as prolific as an iceberg; his throw-offs populate the oceans. And he is as hard, as uncompromising. Yet he is very little known in England, in spite or because of it all. Could it have happened to Swift?

As Mr Cecil Day Lewis has said: 'The "First Hymn to Lenin" was followed by a rush of poetry sympathetic to Communism or influenced by it.' Mr John Lehmann has pointed out that MacDiarmid 'stands alone, completely outside the Auden-Spender-Day Lewis group and its particular pattern of ideas'; and says that 'First Hymn to Lenin' was 'a poem much more directly and profoundly communist than anything that the others had written. In a sense it was the prelude to the whole movement. Though Auden, for instance, had established the corner-stone of his creed with the publication of *Poems* in 1930, he does not show any open and clear Communist leanings until after the "Hymn to Lenin" had been published, nor do any of the others.' Day Lewis and Orage were among the few who recognized the extraordinary quality of 'The Seamless Garment', about which Miss Vivienne Koch and other American critics have since had a great deal to say, recognizing MacDiarmid as 'by all odds by far the best of the really revolutionary poets'. Mr W. B. Yeats included 'The Skeleton of the Future' in his *Oxford Book of Modern Verse* and it has already appeared in many other anthologies. Except for a small portion printed in *Lucky Poet*, the 'Third Hymn to Lenin' has not yet been published. Also unpublished in any volume is 'The Communist Discipline'. 'The Glass of Pure Water' and 'Lamh Dearg Aboo' have appeared in the first and second collections of *Poetry Scotland* respectively, but are not yet included in any of MacDiarmid's volumes. 'Auld Reekie' has only hitherto appeared in *Lucky Poet*; and 'Art and the Workers' in *The New Scotland*. [See Item 20 – Ed.]

Reading these poems and looking back over MacDiarmid's entire poetic production and his record of active citizenship and of service to the socialist and Scottish nationalist movements it is clear that he has always applied to himself what, in one of his essays, he describes as the touchstone he applied to determine whether any writer today is or is not of any significance, viz.: 'We are living in such a grave, such a dark, such a dangerous epoch and the artist who is not willing to participate in its course, i.e. as a leader of men, seems to me to be feelingless and senseless, and I cannot acknowledge his talent, unless as a formal talent, such as we acknowledge in a good vocalist who can sing well the songs created by a composer some two or three centuries ago.' MacDiarmid's best exposition of his ideas on communist poetry – the role of poetry in the period of transition, and, later, in the integrated communist society – is probably his preface to John Singer's poems *The Fury of the Living*.

As Miss Nan Shepherd has said of him in a critical essay in the *Aberdeen University Review*, the vision behind MacDiarmid's creed – that focuses everything he has written in a point of light –

> never changes. Always he sees man 'filled with lightness and exaltation', living to the full reach of his potentialities. In that clear world 'all that has been born deserved birth'. Man 'will flash with the immortal fire', will
>
> > rise
> > To the full height of the imaginative act
> > That wins to the reality in the fact.
>
> until all life flames in the vision of
>
> > the light that breaks
> > From the whole earth seen as a star again
> > In the general life of man.
>
> The actuality is different. Men are obtuse, dull, complacent, vulgar. They love the third-rate, live on the cheapest

terms with themselves, 'the engagement between man and being forsaken', their 'incredible variation nipped in the bud.' Their reading is 'novels and newspapers', their preoccupations 'fitba' and 'weemen', their thinking 'treadmills of rationalizing.' They have hardly issued yet,

> Up frae the slime, that a' but a handfu' o' men
> Are grey wi' still.

They refuse to explore the largeness of life. This refusal he sees as cowardice.

Like Geddes he holds that 'our greatest need today is to grasp life as a whole, to see its many sides in their proper relations. But we must have a practical as well as a philosophic interest in such an integrated view of life.'

In his book, *Sowing the Spring*, Professor James G. Southworth says:

> To all classes with their increasing awareness of social problems and their revision of their views of life as science has pushed back the boundaries of the universe, Mr MacDiarmid has much to say, and he says it with force. One may cavil at individual poems, may disagree violently with specific ideas; but when one lays aside the volumes of his work and thinks about his accomplishment one realizes he has been in the presence of a man of erudition steeped in the best thought of the past and the present; that he has been in the presence of a man who by sincerity of expression, by subtlety and keenness of intellect, and by indomitable energy has sought to fire his readers to an adequate perception of the universe, of our immediate world and its needs, and of their place therein.

27   In Memoriam James Joyce

> *In Memoriam James Joyce* (Glasgow: MacLellan, 1955) was published with an 'Author's Note' consisting mainly of acknowledged quotations from authors with whose diagnoses of the condition of the modern world MacDiarmid concurred. The following extracts give some idea of the context in which MacDiarmid hoped *In Memoriam James Joyce* might be read.

MY earlier poems were lyrics or lyric sequences in the Scots language, which not only won me a reputation as 'the greatest Scots poet since the death of Burns,' but were largely instrumental in creating the Scots Literary Movement of the past thirty years. But there came a time when, like many other poets, I had to make a violent break with the kind of work, no matter how highly esteemed, I had been doing up to then. I began to write very long poems, abounding in phrases from many foreign languages and packed with literary and scientific allusions of all kinds. A sympathetic critic of that later poetry, Dr David Daiches, in a long essay on my work which appeared in *Poetry* (Chicago) in July 1948 said of these poems (such of them as have yet been published have appeared only in my autobiography, *Lucky Poet*, published by Messrs Methuen in 1943):

> MacDiarmid's non-lyrical poetry is very different from his lyrics. His most characteristic longer poems are much more complicated: they represent an attempt to include in each phrase of the utterance every relevant phase of human experience, an attempt to thrust multiple ideas at the reader more quickly and forcefully than can be done in prose exposition . . . This argumentative, ratiocinative verse (quite different really from the impressionistic associations of Pound's *Cantos*) with its great range of allusions and references presents a cerebral pattern to the reader which is rarely obscure and often exciting. One may not define this kind of writing as poetry – that is a question of definitions

and terminology – but it certainly has power and value.

The present poem represents my furthest development so far along that new line.

In *Literature In My Time* Mr (now Sir) Compton Mackenzie said, apropos my earlier Scots poetry, 'I have no hesitation in calling Hugh MacDiarmid the most powerful intellectually and emotionally fertilizing force Scotland has known since the death of Burns.' If my friend Mackenzie has since appealed to me in vain to 'return single-heartedly to the Scottish Cause' and has – as a majority of my Scottish friends have done – regarded my later work as a betrayal of that movement, just as in the case of Hugo von Hofmannsthal's later work, when he deserted the highly-wrought mode of the early lyrics and chamber plays which made him famous, for a speech that, while eloquent and vibrant with passion, was fundamentally plain, it is true of me as of him that 'his highbrow friends threw up their hands in despair; critics foamed at the mouth at seeing their auguries thwarted.' There was a general hue and cry over Hofmannsthal's defection. He was the renegade, the lost leader; for the most ardent among his one-time worshippers – Stefan George and his group – something yet more sinister: a false Messiah. (At a more shallow level, it was a matter of *Literaturpolitik* as well: Hofmannsthal had disappointed the hopes of those who wanted a representative South German writer to put against men like Thomas Mann and Gerhart Hauptmann.) How a poet can betray his destiny – rather than the expectations of his admirers – it would be difficult to tell; yet everybody told it of this one, glibly, with insouciance, until the occasion of his death (1929) redressed the balance as quickly as, on that earlier occasion, it had been disturbed. [. . .]

The parallel with Hofmannsthal is very exact; certainly the cause of my new departure, the crisis which so completely altered the nature of my work, can hardly be better expressed than by Francis Golffing's passage regarding Hofmannsthal:

> What happened to the young Hofmannsthal – he was still this side of thirty – during the crisis so profoundly portrayed in the *Letter of Lord Chandos* will never be known in full, yet one thing is certain: that crisis was not one of style alone but involved his

whole affective and imaginative range, together with the possibilities of speech and knowledge. A crisis as complete, as desperate, as one is likely to find in the annals of poetry; and Hofmannsthal saved himself as best he could. To this writer, at least, he was saved in more ways than one. Not only did he rise whole from the vortex of unbeing, but the new path he now chose to pursue spelt his salvation as a poet.

Something similar may yet be said of me. Too much attention was paid to Compton Mackenzie's declaration which I quote above; far too little to another which appeared in the same book and which struck a profound response in me, viz:

> While it seems fairly certain to me that except *Ulysses* no major work of art has yet been produced by those who, aware of the transition from one kind of man to another, are trying to achieve that transition within their own lives, I am perfectly certain that no major work of art will ever be produced again by those who fail to achieve that transition . . . It seems indeed that, unless some catastrophe of war or pestilence on a scale immensely greater than anything the world has yet known by exacerbating the struggle for existence intervenes to prolong the way of human thought since Genesis, the second millennium of the Christian era will see humanity launched upon a way of thought a thousand times more different from our present ways of thought than our present ways of thought from the thought of neolithic man.

I certainly agree with Mr Emrys Humphreys that 'It is not too soon to say that Joyce saved us from being smothered in the spurious: without Joyce (without Eliot and Pound) the atmosphere of English literature today would be that of the bar of a suburban golf club. Honest, serious, sensitive communication would have become practically impossible.'

It seemed to me that I need say little more than, as Miss Mae West has said, 'Well, Shakespeare had his technique, and I have mine,' save perhaps as that wonderful man, Gurdjieff, has said in his book *All And Everything*:

In my early youth I preferred the Armenian tongue to all others I then spoke, even to my native language . . . But the change I have witnessed in that language during the last thirty or forty years has been such that, instead of an original independent language coming to us from the remote past, there has resulted and now exists one which though also original and independent, yet represents, as might be said, a 'kind of clownish potpourri of languages', the totality of the consonances of which, falling on the ear of a more or less conscious and understanding listener, sounds just like the 'tones' of Turkish, Persian, French, Kurd, and Russian words and still others, 'indigestible' and inarticulate noises. Almost the same might be said about my native language, Greek, which I spoke in childhood and, as might be said, the 'taste of the automatic associative power of which' I still retain . . . It could assuredly be said that even the best expert of modern Greek would understand simply nothing of what I should write in the native language I assimilated in childhood because my dear 'compatriots', as they might be called, being also inflamed with the wish at all cost to be like the representatives of contemporary civilization also in their conversation, have during these thirty or forty years treated my native language just as the Armenians, anxious to become Russian intelligentsia, have treated theirs. That Greek Language, the spirit and essence of which were transmitted to me by heredity, and the language now spoken by contemporary Greeks, are as much alike as, according to the expression of Mullah Nassr Eddin, 'a nail is like a requiem'.

But Mr Thornton Wilder in *Goethe and the Modern Age*[1] has provided me with a much fuller explanation of what I am trying to do, when he says:

When Goethe spoke of a world literature he did not mean, as we are likely to, the treasury of masterpieces of all tongues and all ages. He seems – on a number of occasions, at least

---

[1] Mr Wilder's essay was delivered as a lecture at the Goethe Convocation in Aspen, Colorado, in 1949.

– to have meant literature of all times and languages, the merely good as well as the great, in so far as it can be felt to illustrate the concept so dear to him of the unity of all mankind. This epoch of world literature which in 1827 Goethe felt to be at hand – how does it appear to us now, one hundred and twenty-two years later? . . . It is now during the second quarter of the twentieth century that we are aware of the appearance of a literature which assumes that the world is an indivisible unit. Its subject has become planetary life. Without attempting to make a comparison of these writers with their predecessors in respect to degrees of genius it is possible to make a comparison in respect of fields of reference. It is not as an expression of Alexandrian wit that T. S. Eliot juxtaposes a verse from Gérard de Nerval and a Sanskrit invocation, that he furnishes a sort of *cento* of quotations from a dozen literatures; the differences between languages and cultures begin to grow less marked to one who is accustomed to contemplating the unity of the human spirit. *Finnegans Wake* of James Joyce not only uses twenty languages as a sort of keyboard, but the characters coalesce with a multitude of persons of myth and history. The *Cantos* of Ezra Pound require our familiarity with the civilizations which Frobenius claims to have distinguished in African pre-history, as well as a close knowledge of Chinese history, the Italian Renaissance, and the economic problems of the American Revolution. Such material is not embedded in these poems as allusion, illustration, or as ornament; it is there as *ambience*, as the 'nation' had been in what Goethe called national literature. For better or worse, world literature is at hand. Our consciousness is beginning to be planetary. A new tension has been set us between the individual and the universe. It is not new because poets and entire literatures have been lacking in the sense of the vastness of Creation, but new in the response provoked in the writer in relation to his own language and his own environment. Where in literature do we find signs of one or other aspect of this planetary consciousness? For all its xenophobia, the Old Testament abounds in the consciousness of the human as multitude and of item as incommensurable. The *Iliad* precisely states its rosters in the thousands but conveys them in millions. I do not find this sense in the *Aeneid*. Reading the *Divine Comedy* the head reels and the heart shrinks before it. Over and over one has felt it before Dante himself exclaims: 'I had not known that death had undone so many' (a phrase which T. S. Eliot calls upon in *The Waste Land*; and emotion scarcely to be found elsewhere in all European literature, for all its Dances of Death, its *Oraisons Funèbres,* and its Urn-Burials). I find it in *Don Quixote,* on that road which seems to have no beginning and no end. I do not find it in Shakespeare – diversity of souls is not the same thing as multiplicity of souls. I do not find it in English literature. I do not find it in French literature, not even in Pascal. Occasionally Victor Hugo seems to be blowing himself up to achieve it, but the efforts end in rhetoric. All Oriental literature is filled with it; it is the predominant note in the Sanskrit. Though the consciousness of the multiplicity of souls is not the only ingredient in world literature, it is an essential one. It is often present without being accompanied by its temporal component: the realization of the deep abyss of time. Nor does the presence of these realizations in itself constitute a superiority. For the present all we can say is that once a mind is aware of it, it is not possible to *unknow* it. And it is the character of the modern mind that it knows this thing. The literature that it writes must express it: that every man and woman born is felt to be in a new relation to the whole.

All these ingredients of world literature so defined, all these elements of its *ambience,* are to be found in this poem. That is why so much of it is concerned with Oriental literatures and languages. That is why I say quite clearly

> For unlike you, Joyce, I am more concerned
> With the East than the West and the poetry I seek
> Must be the work of one who has always known
> That the Tarim Valley is of more importance
> Than Jordan or the Rhine in world history.

That, again, is why I am so critical of English Literature.

And why, too, towards the end of the poem, I am so concerned with the very phenomenon which Mr Wilder stresses so strongly – the consciousness of the millions of the dead, of the multiplicity of souls, of the profounds of Time [. . .]

Then there is the question of my abandonment of the accepted forms of poetry, even rhythm, so many people condemn my later work as 'not poetry at all, but only chopped-up prose'.

I did not always do so but it is long now since I ceased to share what the great Jewish poet, Chaim Bialik, whom I met in Vienna called 'the folly of differentiating between prose and poetry' and the character of the present work shows that I have now come fully to agree with Jacob Fichman who, in an essay in *Di Yiddische Velt* in May 1928, wrote:

> When both poetry and prose contain that spiritual emotion of *'all my bones shall speak of thee'* [the Jewish idea of prayer; hence the intense swaying of the body while praying], what difference can there be between them; on the other hand, where that emotion is lacking in either how could one tell the one from the other. Where man's spirit is involved and revealed, there it is not the outward form, but the measure of sincerity and inner conviction that matters. Not the visible shine but the innermost earnestness sanctifies things. The immense attraction of the Fifth Book of Moses (Deuteronomy) has always puzzled me. Essentially it is a book containing the main historic chronicles coupled with strictly defined Laws. What then is the secret that radiates from this book with such enchanting charm? Why do we read those pages of prose as if we were reading a wonderful poem? And this applies not only to the solemnity of an epos, but also to the driest everyday language of the *Laws and Judgments*. The secret lies in the rare quality of their inner rhythm, in their complete unity which stretches like a burning red thread from beginning to end. It is exaltation of the spirit which lends it its inner holiness. In the purple gleam of dusk, the mightiest tree and the tiniest blade of grass are glowing in the same glory. It is that rhythm which is deeper than music. It is that refined

spiritual atmosphere in which all things are seen in the same light. What is Spinoza's *Ethics*? Plato's *Dialogues*? Aurelius' moral Sentences? Are they prose or poetry? In the region of the pure spirit everything is resounding poetry – even the barest geometrical formulae.

Mr Marius Bewley, in *The Complex Fate*, says:

But if one offered a synthesis of the fields covered by the various disciplines, which of the disciplines could possibly be competent to evaluate it? Where each specialty gets it worth precisely by moving towards diversity, how could any specialty possibly deal with a project that offered a *unification* among the diversities? Or, otherwise put, if one were to write on the inter-relatedness among the specialties, one would be discussing something that lay outside the jurisdiction of them all.

Theology, Mr Bewley goes on to say, 'would seem to be the only ground in which the desired unification might occur.'

Any theology is quite unacceptable to me, however, since like Joyce and Pound I hold no supernatural faith, but I believe that this unification will be achieved ultimately 'in a society in which the participant aspect of action attains its maximum expression' – a society which I naturally visualize as Marxist.

My love of the East, and my Anglophobia, are both evident in this poem, and I may say with regard to them here, (1) that I agree with a friend who recently said:

As Western urbanism wins its materialistic and Pyrrhic victories, as more sound barriers are broken, more assembly lines conquered, more culture diluted and debased, a sensitive man, given some sense of history, must centre his last hope upon Asia . . . Today there is more reason than ever – with Western culture in ruins about us – to suppose that an art both democratic and vital can now only come from Asia.

That, I think, is true, although I do not believe that our Western chaos has anything to do with technical inventiveness or mass production as such, but rather with the hopeless contradictions within our culture and society themselves.

(2) As to my Anglophobia, I cherish the following passage quoted by F. O. Matthiessen in *The James Family* (p. 286): 'They (the English) are an intensely vulgar race, high and low . . . They are not worth studying. The prejudices one has about them, even when they are unjust, are scarcely worth correcting. They belong, all their good and evil, to the past humanity, to the infantile development of the mind.'

This poem as a whole ('jujitsu for the "educated" '), which might be dubbed in South Africa a *frikadel*, is designed as a contribution to the new orientation envisaged by a reviewer in *Nine* of Professor Kenneth Jackson's *A Celtic Miscellany*, who says:

> One cannot help thinking that perhaps one should study Irish and Welsh poetry rather than French or German, both literatures of a comparatively narrow range, and that a poetic imagination tempered by Irish, Welsh, Scots, Gaelic, Spanish, Italian, Greek, Latin, Russian, Persian, Arabic, Sanskrit and Chinese would be much more fertile than the modern *paideuma* formed of English, French, German, Italian, and the Classics. The notable exceptions to the cultured man's reading seem to be the Celtic, Persian, Chinese and Russian. New orientations occur from time to time, and perhaps this is a new pattern for the future.

I also agree wholeheartedly with another contemporary poet who has said: 'It is an understatement to say that I look with profound suspicion on anything which would make art easier. If it makes art easier, it seems to me to require no other condemnation. Why should the fences be lowered till even the donkeys can jump them?' And, if the general intention behind this work is to be indicated, I can hardly do that better than by saying it is designed to express my complete agreement with what Mr John Holloway said in a recent Third Programme talk on 'New Territory for the Critic,' viz., that the visual arts have been fertilized during the past century by exhibitions of past and present work of many nations, but this has hardly happened in the case of writing, and, while there are, of course, translations, books on the literature of other nations are few: and with the general argument of M. André Malraux in *The Voices of Silence*.

> Under the pseudonym 'Arthur Leslie', MacDiarmid published an essay entitled 'Jerqueing Every Idioticon: Some Notes on MacDiarmid's Joyce Poem' in his journal *The Voice of Scotland* (Vol. 6, no. 2, July 1955). These are extracts from that essay.

Unless human beings are going to experience the same deterioration (i.e. as occurs in modern business, organized to cheat the public, and therefore involving a progressive deterioration of everything we buy, from the gas in our meters to the socks on our feet), in the very tissues of which their bodies are composed, unless their skins are to lose their resilience, their warmth, and all the other qualities which make them so high-class a covering for a man to have; unless nature is to begin to trouble over our nails, our hair (that may disappear altogether), our wonderful shining eyes, which may become dull and myopic, so that spectacles must be provided for all from the cradle onwards – unless all this is to come about there will have to be some great revolution.

So says Wyndham Lewis in *The Demon of Progress in the Arts*; and this is one of the principal themes in Hugh MacDiarmid's huge poem, *In Memoriam James Joyce* (Maclellan, Glasgow). But it ends with a Ghurkhali sentence meaning 'Everything's O.K.', amplified in a footnote which says that that sentence is intended to express the author's concurrence with Werner von Bergengruen's belief, despite all that may seem to enforce the opposite conclusion, in 'the rightness of the world'.

From another, and more personal aspect (more personal that is to the author's opinion of Joyce) one of the dominant notes of the poem may be expressed in Burmese as *Oway* (i.e. cry of the peacock), since, at different stages, reference is made to Bernini's Circe and the Peacock, to Juno and the Peacock, and Joyce's death and translation into eternity is described as (though most people might characterize it as merely 'another queer bird gone') the flight not of the 'metaphysical buzzard' but of a peacock flying in through an open window with its eight-foot tail streaming out behind. This is the method upon which the whole poem is built – the method of images which recur in varying forms and are steadily developed until we reach passages in which all that has been so conveyed of Joyce's character and achievement is comprehensively established.

★

It is in keeping with Joyce's own main interest too that MacDiarmid's poem is so largely occupied with music – Schubert, Mozart, Schoenberg, Hindemith, and many others are expertly utilized.

Another reason for the reiterated employment of the Peacock figure (in addition to indicating Joyce's vanity, or his Lucifer complex perhaps) is that as one writer on the Indian jungle (in the Silent Valley Forest Block in the District of Malabar-Wynaad) says: 'In the whole forest no more alert watchman than the peacock can be found.' No doubt the Silent Valley came to MacDiarmid's mind too, since it is also in accordance with his method, much of the poem dealing with Silence, the beyond-which-not of human expression. There are innumerable instances of this kind of thing throughout the poem, and to trace all these references to their sources and appreciate all their interconnections would be the work of a lifetime. Their world-ranging nature underlines the fact that this poem is designed as a kind of verbal equivalent of the Scottish diaspora which has carried men and women of our nation into every corner of the Earth. In the same way MacDiarmid's astonishing final figure of a peacock flying in through the open window with its eight-foot tail streaming out behind may be a recollection of a peacock at the foot of the eastern slopes of the Nilgiri Mountains 'as it sailed away above my head, its flowing tail glinting a greenish-red in the rays of the setting sun.'

As to MacDiarmid's abandonment of metre, rhyme, stanza form, and all the other traditional differences between prose and poetry which he justifies in his preface by, *inter alia*, a long quotation from a Jewish essayist, all that amounts to

In Memoriam James Joyce

simply endorses Marianne Moore's lines in the 'The Past Is The Present':

> I think that I repeat
> His identical words. Hebrew poetry
> Is prose with a sort of heightened consciousness.

The same may be said of this book. MacDiarmid himself doesn't care whether it is called poetry or prose, so long as it is agreed to have (as Dr David Daiches says it has) 'power and value'. But MacDairmid does not take his reference to Hebrew poetry from Marianne Moore. He used it in *Lucky Poet* himself a dozen years ago.

Cross-references of this kind are innumerable, while there are direct references to half the languages and literatures of the world and to literally hundreds of individual writers. It is for this reason – and because, after all, the principal theme of the poem is 'the world of words' and the marshalling and assessment of all the means and possibilities of human expression, past, present, and future, that the phrase 'jerqueing every idioticon' best describes the whole poem. For the phrase means to subject every language and dialect and device of rhetoric to, as it were, a Customs examination. Professor I. A. Richards has said that 'the study of the modes of language becomes, as it attempts to be thorough, the most fundamental and extensive of all enquiries.' The thoroughness with which MacDiarmid has conducted his study cannot be shown here but may be suggested in the form of a short Quiz, each term of which refers to something in the poem viz.

1 Where are the following languages found – Vogule, Efik, Tagalog, Soghdian Xhosa, Kumyk, Avar, Lezghin, Lak, Dargan and Tabagaran?

2 What do you know of the following writers – Andra Lysohorsky, Gjerj Fishta, Avetik Isaakyan?

Hundreds of similar questions from all the arts and all the sciences, all periods of history and all parts of the world, could be framed out of references in this poem.

It may be asked has MacDiarmid abandoned Scotland

altogether? Not at all.

★

In fact he is constantly bringing his global poem back to Scottish instances and in doing so reminds us of, and praises, many Scots too little regarded today. These include Sir Patrick Geddes, Hon. Ruaraidh Erskine of Marr, John Hunter the surgeon, E. J. W. Gibb the Glasgow Orientalist who wrote the *History of Ottoman Poetry*, Alexander Murray the great linguist, and many others. Joyce said he wrote for those who would devote a lifetime to reading him. To comprehend all the allusions in this poem (not to mention the range of reading shown in the formidable apparatus of footnotes) would certainly take as long. But that they are all closely interwoven and mutually indispensable to the whole is clear enough throughout. MacDiarmid says of them 'References each close as a Cumnock hinge' but how many Scots today know what a Cumnock hinge is well enough to appreciate the accuracy of the figure? Ezra Pound says in one of his poems that

> the 'modern world'
> Needs such a rag-bag to stuff all its thought in.

MacDiarmid calls his poem (among many other things) just such a 'rag-bag', and in this poem his endeavour seems to have been, in Wallace Stevens' words,

> to drive away
> The shadow of his fellows from the skies,
> And, from their stale intelligence released,
> To make a new intelligence prevail.

The poem unlike most contemporary poetry outside the Soviet Union, China, and the Peoples' Democracies is an optimistic one. The end passages of the poem insist that while the complication and erudition of Joyce's work vastly outrun the present requirements of the majority of people, nevertheless just as the provisions for all the organs necessary to mature human physique are present in embryo in the foetus so are the need for, and capacity to utilize, such work present in what Joyce himself called 'the uncreated conscience of the race' and just as an Indian poet has said that since the various components of a bed do not exist for themselves alone but presuppose a being who will occupy the bed so does work like Joyce's presuppose a development of the human mind that will yet take possession of and enjoy it.

Many passages show a full awareness of the dangers and horrors of Fascism and contempt for Christianity and the 'civilization' of the 'free nations' of the West, together with a frank admission of the author's Marxism. But the emphasis everywhere is on the role of the intellect. This is, of course, in keeping with the Scottish Renaissance programme, which proclaimed the need to intellectualize Scottish poetry and rescue it from the post-Burnsian slough into which it has been plunged by its analphabetic practitioners, whose crass sentimentality and 'chortlin' wut' remain in fact the general level of the vast majority of the Scottish people. The Renaissance Movement proclaimed that the curse of modern Scotland had been the constant tendency to 'domesticate the issue.'

*

MacDiarmid owes a lot (as he acknowledges) to David Hume. He (or Joyce, for the matter of that) might as easily have said as Hume:

> Think on the Emptiness, and Rashness, and Futility of the common judgements of men: how little they are regulated by Reason in any Subject, much more in philosophical Subjects, which so far exceed the Comprehension of the Vulgar. *Non si quid improba Roma, Elevet, accedas examenque improbum in illa, Perpendas trutina, nec te quaesiveris extra.* A wise man's Kingdom is his own Breast: or, if he ever looks farther, it will only be to the Judgement of a select few, who are free from Prejudices, and capable of examining his Word. Nothing indeed can be a stronger Presumption

of Falsehood than the Approbation of the Multitude; and Phocion, you know, always suspected himself of some Blunder, when he was attended with the Applauses of the Populace.

MacDiarmid pays little attention to English literature, except satirically, in this poem. German, Russian, Spanish, and Italian are his main concern, and even linguistically the chief foreign elements are German, French, Greek, Chinese, Sanskrit, and Scottish and Irish Gaelic. But he gives full vent in many passages to his Anglophobia and, in fact, his attitude is almost identical with Hume's where the latter asked:

Why still exalt Old England for a model of government and laws; praises which it by no means deserves? and why still complain of the present times, which, in every respect, so far surpass all the past? I am only sorry to see that the great Decline, if we ought not rather to say the total Extinction of Literature in England, prognosticates a very short Duration of all our other Improvements, and threatens a new and sudden Inroad of Ignorance, Superstition, and Barbarism.

And MacDiarmid might well add to that, as Hume did; 'There cannot be a stronger Symptom of this miserable Degeneracy, than the Treatment which I have met with for telling them Truth in these particulars.'

One of the recurrent themes in the Joyce poem is the utmost limit of human expression [. . .] and MacDiarmid develops it with a wealth of instances, physiological, literary and musical – not, like Hemingway, concerned with the dumb emotions rather than the intellect, but with, as he says, that paraleipsis when creative the intellect, but with, as he says, that paraleipsis when creative genius comes up against the unutterable. His preoccupation with this problem shows how accurately R. P. Blackmur placed MacDiarmid in his book, *Language As Gesture*, when he said:

Prosody as reason is what the central school of the time has over and above our two anti-intelligence schools. This is the school of Donne with which the largest number of individual writers of good verse fall when shaken up and let settle. If we generalize them, they are difficult in style, violent in their constructed emotions, private with actual secrecy in meaning. There is in their work a wrestling towards statement, a struggle through paradox and irony (forms of arrogance and self-distrust), and the detritus of convictions . . . John Ransom and Allen Tate, for example, around the gaps of the unstateable tremendous, are models of the uncontrollable in pseudo-control. John Wheelwright had again and again, the frightening stroke of direct wit on the thing itself unsaid, just as Empson can press his metres on the unsayable until it almost bursts into being. Hugh MacDiarmid is another, who has the force of immanent statement.

In a subsequent issue of *The Voice of Scotland* (Vol. 7, no. 1, April 1956), MacDiarmid published a critical essay on *In Memoriam James Joyce* by David Craig. He then published his rejoinder in the same issue, immediately following Craig's piece. These extracts come from that 'Reply to Criticism'.

. . . No long poem is without its inequalities. These may at best be managed in such a way as to afford relief from a long-sustained passage, to give variety, or to emphasize (throw into high relief) – or suggest some criticism of or alternative to – other more obviously-organized passages. But there is another explanation. The poem as Mr Craig fails to notice is a 'Vision', and therefore while certain elements are prominent others are, inevitably in such an immense panorama, barely or fleetingly discerned, and these subsidiary or submerged effects (perhaps very temporary – any or all of the elements so inadequately discerned may at other times as the vision is deployed emerge as of outstanding consequence) are suggested by a relative imprecision of expression. Poetry, too, is a term to which most people (in Britain – it varies in other countries) attach a certain meaning, but that does not (as Mr Randall Jarrell effectively stresses in one of his essays) correspond at all with what the term was accepted to mean through long stretches of history and in divers countries any more than it corresponds to the 'kennings' of Iceland today. Catalogue poems in particular are apt to be ruled out from a too narrow conception of poetry, or while certain kinds of cataloguing – of flowers, perhaps, or birds – are accepted, other kinds – say a list of books or authors or theses-titles – may not be. (I have written so much that in this latest departure I am entitled to expect that competent readers will bring to it a knowledge of all my previous work – an extension, perhaps, of Professor Bateman's notion of 'contextualism' but I think not only a valid one but one indispensable in regard to much of the most important contemporary poetry.) In any case it is bad criticism to do other than determine just what a writer sought to do and the extent of his success or non-success in achieving it, and certainly to take a few lines out of the context of the whole poem is not a valid proceeding, especially if on the strength of these few lines it is suggested that the whole poem consists or largely consists of the same sort of thing, when, as a matter of fact, such utterly different paragraphs or sets of lines appear in such close proximity to the passage quoted as to make it certain that the author had a particular purpose for such a looser passage, alternating with more closely-woven passages.

*

. . . Mr Craig's essay would not lead anyone to realize that the poem contains many lyrics – and two obscene poems (to correspond with that element in Joyce, just as many passages do not express the author's own opinions but reflect elements of Joyce's very different personality). Some of these lyrics in their discrimination of the autumn colours of various types of trees repeat in that particular connection a structural element that is shown elsewhere as identical also with the perception or meaning of regional differences in Italian literature, in Spanish music, etc. In so far from being unassimilated and poorly ordered or without order, the fact of the matter is that a consistent argument is pursued from beginning to end of the poem and illustrated in very many ways – not without humour, satire, the expression of doubts as to its own validity at times and at other times with a countervailing absence of any doubt whatsoever. (This 'consistent argument' runs throughout not only this poem but all my work – a belief that men yet use only a small fraction of their powers and must be compelled to realize all their potentialities.

My work presses this all the more urgently since it is ablaze with the sense that we stand at one of the great turning-points of human history – and one different from any other, since today for the first time, a complete breakdown of civilization is possible and can only be averted if we can succeed in unifying mankind at a high level of culture and, bound up with this theme throughout the poem – the method of which is the little-understood and as Pound says 'the latest come and most tricky and undependable' one of phanopoeia – is the realisation that 'our literature, our history, and our religious reflection are losing too many opportunities unless we see that they are produced on the hither side of the great transition effected by the transformation that has taken place in the nature of science during the present century.' It is, in short, a plea for a unification of knowledge, a general synthesis, an attempt to take a stand on the further side of that great transition.) If Mr Craig does not appreciate the close intellectual workmanship throughout, and the thorough consistency of the argumentation, it is perhaps because of a bias that shows itself in such phrases as 'the pernicious ideas which his mind takes up – the exaltation of science, etc.', and in an over-seriousness determined to assess my work in terms of an abecedarian logicality (completely foreign to my mentality and purpose) which complains about 'contradictory positions' when often what interests me in both or more is simply the various individualities that go to form them, their 'taste', their 'flavour', their 'atmosphere', and mere consistency is of no consequence on that level.

Another pointer to the defect of Mr Craig's method is that it compels him to make comparisons between my work and Shakespeare's, Pope's, or Blake's, instead of with Ezra Pound's or David Jones's.

I understand only too well how much of the poem may be felt (given certain limitations in the reader) shallow or flat. The multiplicity of quotations, references, and allusions in my poem (which must be completely understood, since they constitute the *language* in which it is written) recalls Baudelaire's phrase, '*immense clavier des correspondances*' (first used, I think, in his article on the Exposition Universelle de 1855, in connection with his sense of the diversity of beauty – the adaptable critic having the 'divine grace of cosmopolitanism', the narrow pedantic judge being likened to a pianist whose fingers cannot move lightly over '*l'immense clavier*') but a keyboard, of course, *is* horizontal; and that may be all Mr Craig means.

28 My Election Contest with Sir Alec Douglas-Home

MacDiarmid (or rather, C.M. Grieve) was chosen as the Communist candidate to stand against the then Prime Minister of Great Britain, Sir Alec Douglas-Home, in the 1964 General Election in Douglas-Home's own constituency of Kinross and West Perthshire. An interview with two journalists, Jack McGill and Charles Graham, was printed in the *Scottish Daily Express* on 8 October 1964, and subsequently republished in *The Company I've Kept*, MacDiarmid's 'essays in autobiography' (London: Hutchinson, 1966). 'This,' MacDiarmid commented, 'should serve to settle any doubts as to my political position.'

Q. Dr Grieve, you are contesting this election as a Communist. What kind of Communist are you? A Marxist-Leninist theorist? Or is your Communism simply a protest against British bourgeois society?

A. I am a Marxist-Leninist theorist Communist. I am a member of the Communist Party of Great Britain. All sorts of people try to discriminate between various kinds of Communist. There is only one, a man is either a Communist or he's not a Communist. I'm a Communist.

Q. Some years ago you were a Scottish Nationalist?

A. I still am.

Q. You still are?

A. Very much so.

Q. Do you feel you will get more votes as a Communist in Kinross and West Perth than you got as a Nationalist in Kelvingrove in 1950?

A. I didn't expect many votes in Kelvingrove because I was standing on a very extreme ticket – as a Republican Scottish Nationalist with Communist overtones. In West Perthshire, of course, the Scottish Nationalist (Mr Arthur Donaldson) has stood before, while this is the first time a Communist has stood in the constituency.

Q. This must surely, though, be only a demonstration against the Prime Minister? You can't be hoping, as Communists in some other constituencies may, to come anywhere near the head of the poll? In Fife, for example.

A. Yes, I think they have a chance in Fife. I don't think we have a similar chance in this constituency, but you've got to begin somewhere, you know. I think it is high time that the thin end of the Marxist wedge was inserted firmly into this constituency.

Q. So you selected it because you think it is a stronghold of feudalism and not just because of the Prime Minister?

A. It was largely for both reasons. It was essential to oppose the Prime Minister, as a Communist and as a Scotsman.

Q. You attacked the Prime Minister recently as a big landowner. Do you direct the same sort of attack against the constituency generally? It has a good many landowners in it.

A. I direct the same sort of attack against millionaire landowners, land monopolists actually.

Q. By standing here you are splitting the anti-Government vote. Would it not have been better from your point of view to avoid splitting left-wing support? – And incidentally dividing the Nationalist vote.

A. I don't think either of these things will happen as a matter of fact.

Q. What do you think will happen, then? Where are you getting your support from?

A. We are getting a certain measure of support, though I am not guessing how little or how big it will be. We have been encouraged by our meetings so far and by personal contacts. I put it like this when I became Communist candidate. There are 32,000 voters in this constituency. The great majority are working-class people. It is only a minority who are big landlords or business men. So with the great majority there must be some common ground, and I am trying to find that. I think my campaign will bear fruit in the future, if not immediately.

Q. Had you no difficulty in getting signatories for your nomination papers?

A. None. Quite surprising. We got them very quickly and very easily.

Q. Were all the people who signed really Communists or did they just sympathize with your broad ideals?

A. I can't say. But I should think that most, if not all, of them were certainly Communists.

Q. Why did you break with the Scottish Nationalists? Some of the things you have been saying seem to accord very closely with Nationalist ideas and the National Party has been making some recent headway in Scotland.

A. I think the Scottish policy of the Communist Party is a very much better practical programme for securing the things we require in Scotland. At the same time when I broke away from the SNP its policy was that defence, foreign affairs, and finance would be reserved to the Imperial Parliament. They have modified this to some extent, but so far as I can see from recent statements they have issued the first clause in their constitution still pledges loyalty to the Throne. Then they go on to indicate that they believe that the presence of the Queen in Holyrood Palace for two or three months per annum would in some way relieve Scottish political and economic problems. I don't agree with that at all. I think it is perfectly inept.

Q. On the economy, I see from your manifesto that you are utterly against closures of any kind. Surely, in the coal industry, with some pits worked right out, it is inevitable that there should be some closures.

A. Well, there are some outworked seams, of course. What I am really protesting about is the idea, current for some time among writers on economic affairs, that we have too many eggs in the one basket, that there must be a greater diversification of Scottish industry. I think that is bad economic doctrine. If we allow our basic industries to be drawn away from us, or become extinct or less profitable, then we are going to have to depend more and more upon light industries. That is to say, upon the periphery of an economic situation. If we lose the substance of the economic situation and depend upon peripheral developments, I know of no country that has succeeded in having industrial prosperity along such lines.

Q. Do you then agree with Harold Wilson that cars, refrigerators, and that kind of thing can become frivolous?

A. I think that we in Scotland must move with the times and have new industries – electronics and other science-based industries. But the American practice of overproducing certain things and overselling them is a short-term policy that may give an appearance of prosperity but is bound in the long run to land us in greater and greater crises as has happened in America

Q. Do you think that, economically, Scotland is still a badly neglected nation?

A. Undoubtedly.

Q. In spite of the advances in new industries and projects like Hunterston?

A. All the advances you speak of have not made the slightest difference to Scotland's basic economic problem – unemployment. It is still double that of the worst hit areas in the South. Our emigration drain is unparalleled. Our rural depopulation is continuing. We have had big advances in the tourist industry and in winter sports, but the big landowners who own so much of Scotland are more and more hampering that development, introducing restrictions that hinder access to the land.

Q. Do you not agree that there is bound to be some kind of rationalization, in, for example, shipbuilding, as there has already been in coal-mining?

A. There may require to be a certain rationalization. The thing is, we are on the verge of new developments, new techniques. If we are not in a position to ensure that we shall get a fair share of these developments then we will lose out again. The real trouble with Scotland, since the Union, is that we have not had a say in policy-making. We have always been a small minority in the House of Commons. Even on purely Scottish issues, our views could be over-ridden by an English majority who had no knowledge of or interest in us – indeed, whose interests were often opposed to ours. I think that will continue.

Q. This plan you have for meetings of Scottish MPs in Edinburgh four times a year, what difference will it make, when the national Parliament will still have supreme control? What is the purpose of these meetings?

A. I think it serves a better purpose than the parliamentary committees dealing with Scottish Bills at the present time. They do not consist entirely of Scottish MPs. There is room for intervention by English MPs whose interests are opposed to the Bill in question. By bringing the Scottish members together to thrash out Scottish problems I think we make a real gain. There has been far too little research into Scottish problems and discussion of them.

Q. Do you feel the Scottish Grand Committee is a waste of time?

A. Very largely, I think.

Q. If you were returned to Parliament, what would be your role in the Commons? Primarily as an agitator?

A. Yes. I think it would be a live – a very different – House of Commons if a few Communist MPs got in, or even only one. I think Willie Gallacher, for example, was one of the finest MPs I have known in my lifetime.

Q. You complain in your manifesto about the lack of university places. We have the four old universities plus Dundee, Stirling, Strathclyde, and Heriot-Watt. Do you want more?

A. Yes. We had four universities in Scotland before England had any. You must remember that England has had more than thirty new universities. Furthermore we have a dual culture. I certainly think we should also have a largely Gaelic University, probably in Inverness.

Q. The Scottish Nationalists produced a Budget this week in which they claimed we were subsidizing the English to the extent of, I think, £143 million a year.

A. Yes. I saw that. That is money that goes direct to the Exchequer without coming back to Scotland in any way.

Q. Have you any view on how this anomaly, if it does exist, should be put right?

A. It can only be put right by the establishment of an independent Scottish Parliament.

Q. Which is not a part of your current platform?

A. No, we have not gone into that particular point.

Q. Are you yourself working within the Communist Party for strengthening of its policy on Scottish independence?

A. Oh, yes, undoubtedly.

Q. There are nine Communist candidates in Scotland. How do you rate their chances? What measure of success can they look for?

A. One man sure to gain a good place in the poll is the

West Fife candidate. There are others who may not do so well. I am not a prophet nor the son of a prophet, so I am not prepared to prophesy. We will simply do our best. But we are satisfied that the whole campaign in the nine constituencies is well worthwhile. It has its propaganda value, and we are making new friends and members for the Party.

Q. Would you like to predict your own chances?

A. No. This is a first shot, a first time of asking. In a constituency with this particular composition it is perhaps more difficult to make much headway at first than in a more industrialized constituency.

Q. Would you be satisfied to save your deposit?

A. It would be an undoubted achievement to save our deposit. But as you know one of our reasons for fighting this seat is on the issue of political broadcasts and telecasts. I think we've won our point there – for next time.

Q. Have you noticed that the Tory candidate in West Fife is an engine driver and strong trade unionist? Does this not convince you of Tory democracy?

A. I thought that Tory democracy and Tory democrats were as extinct as the coelacanth or the Loch Ness monster. I'm surprised to know that any still survive and occasionally surface.

Q. One final point. you have it in for the big landowners. How would you deal with them? Abolish them?

A. We are going to nationalize the land, except owner-occupied land.

Q. And compensation?

A. Well, that's a matter for consideration. Personally I would be against it.

The newspapers followed the event closely, with a front-page photograph and article in *The Observer* (27 September), and an article by Honor Arundel in the *Daily Worker* (29 September), which registered the support for MacDiarmid from agricultural workers, railwaymen, market-gardeners – constituents for whom MacDiarmid's standing represented the first real challenge to Tory rule. James Cameron, writing in *The Sun* on 14 October, considered that 'For Dr Grieve, this campaign is a lovely labour of loathing. He does not like the

Prime Minister. "If you ask: Do I have a personal antipathy to Sir Alec Home, I say yes I have. This campaign is a personal issue. After all, I have a personality, and Home doesn't." '

In the *Daily Worker* of 4 September, MacDiarmid had written of Douglas-Home: 'He is in fact a zombie, personifying the obsolescent traditions of an aristocratic and big landlord order, of which Thomas Carlyle said that no country had been oppressed by a worse gang of hyenas than Scotland.'

Alex Clark, the Communist Party election agent for MacDiarmid, received the following press notices in MacDiarmid's hand. The second piece appears to have formed the basis for the 'Message from the Candidate' on MacDiarmid's election pamphlet.

1/10/64

Speaking at Aberfoyle last night, Dr C.M. Grieve, Communist candidate in Kinross and West Perthshire, said that the Communist Policy for Scotland issued by the Scottish Committee of the CP, was far and away the best of the many proposals for dealing with the grave problems besetting Scotland that had been published in his lifetime. He had been intensively concerned with every aspect of Scottish arts and affairs for over forty years. The various Scottish Nationalist organizations during that time had gone in for a great deal of futile constitution-mongering, none of which had grappled with the great issues affecting the broad mass of the working class, but the Communist policy was clear and comprehensive and set out a series of concrete proposals covering the whole field in the most practical way. He thought it would 'ca' the feet' from the Scottish National party altogether.

Dealing with the Tory proposal to do away with a host of small burghs, Dr Grieve said this was only the last and most drastic stage of the Tory determination to eviscerate Scottish local government and vest its functions in a few bigger bodies whose overall policy would be wholly dictated by the gentlemen in Whitehall, and their stooges in St Andrew's House in Edinburgh, while the elected representatives of the local people would be more and more restricted to merely 'rubber-stamping' the London decisions. What was needed was precisely the opposite of this, namely to get down to 'grass-roots' and deal with the realities of local affairs as they vitally affected the workers.

Giving an interview on French television, Dr Grieve said of his principal opponent, Sir Alec Douglas-Home: 'Je le considére comme une nullitè, l'apotheose de la mediocrité personnifiée.' (I consider him a nullity, the apotheosis of mediocrity personified.)

★

Why is the Communist Party contesting Kinross and West Ross [sic]? Why are you personally opposing Sir Alec Douglas-Home? These are the two questions I am being asked on all hands. In both cases the answers are implicit in the questions. This is the first time the Red Flag has been flown in this constituency. It is high time it was. The electors here, as everywhere else, cannot be indifferent to the greatest force in the modern world, which already commands the suffrages and support of half the inhabitants of the globe. The trouble is that hitherto they have not had any opportunity up to now of hearing the Communist case. Just as the Communist Party is debarred from political broadcasts and telecasts by the BBC and ITV, so the press of this country, controlled by three or four newspaper tycoons, is rabidly anti-Communist and accords little or no space to Communism save in a distorted and quite untrue fashion. I think the electors of this constituency are as intelligent and fair-minded a body as anywhere else in the country. Like myself most of them belong to the working class. Also like myself most of them are Scotsmen and Scotswomen, whereas Sir Alec is a Scotsman by title only – his upbringing, education, and whole outlook are profoundly anti-Scottish. Although he served as Secretary of State for Scotland, he has never done anything for Scotland and the great problems in Scotland of an unprecedented emigration drain, the depopulation of great areas of our land, the sacrifice of Scottish interests all along the line, the inadequate time given to Scottish affairs in Parliament where Scottish representatives are in a permanent small minority, with the consequent misgovernment due to London control, are matters that have never engaged his interest. Why then should he represent a Scottish constituency? Worse still is the fact that he is a big Scottish landowner – one of a small class holding most of our country to ransom and opposing all change and development tooth and nail. It is futile for such a man to prate of democracy and modernization, both of which he is constitutionally incapable of understanding or sympathizing with in the least. Sir Alec talks of doing away with restrictive practices. He and his class are the greatest of all restrictive practices and hang like millstones round the neck of our people, preventing progress and social justice wherever they can.

I think the good people of Kinross and West Perthshire were woefully mistaken when they elected him. They took him at face value, forgetting that appearances are deceptive. In Parliament Sir Alec had a thoroughly undistinguished career and was generally regarded as a political nincompoop. It was a matter of amazement to most students of politics when he was made Prime Minister. On his record he had no qualifications whatever for the post. At this great turning point in human history, a time of vastly accelerated change and scientific developments capable of transforming the conditions of human life out of all recognition, it was strange indeed that such a man as Sir Alec, utterly unscientific in mentality, confessedly ignorant of economics, with little political stock in trade but ignorance, arrogance and unabashed puerility, should have come to such a great post as the result of nothing but some shameful horsetrading among a few top Tories. From the point of view of any serious concern with the problems and potentialities of contemporary life, Sir Alec's emergence was as unexpected and useless as the discovery that a coelacanth, which all the authorities believed had been extinct for hundreds of thousands of years, was still alive and swimming about in the waters off East Africa. The appointment of the Loch Ness monster would have been just as appropriate. Handsome is as handsome does. I am told the electors have fallen in love with Sir Alec. He is their blue-eyed boy. They are due to be completely disillusioned.

Sir Alec talks largely about expansion and increasing prosperity for all, but a proposal of Lanarkshire County Council to establish an industrial estate was recently turned down by the Secretary of State for Scotland on the specious ground that a covenant existed with the Forestry Commission about the 97½ acres in question. There can be no comparison in economic and human value between the two projects, but the real reason for refusal was not the covenant with the Forestry Commission, which could easily have been adjusted, but the fact that the industrial estate developments would have been visible from Sir Alec's nearby mansion of Castlemains. This illustrates the real nature of this gentleman, and such cases, and likewise of harsh and unconscionable treatment of his dependants, can be multiplied a thousand times over. If a true perspective is needed on his position, one has only to remember his declaration that the miners had been misled regarding the nationalization of the mines and would gladly have them restored to private ownership. Ask any miner at the pit which is within a stone's throw of Sir Alec's mansion and you will learn in no uncertain terms what the workers think of such unscrupulous political reaction – and of Sir Alec and all his kind. It would not be expressed in publishable terms, but would certainly be none the worse for that.

> At the General Election of 15 October, Labour beat the Conservatives by a narrow margin, but in Kinross and West Perthshire Sir Alec Douglas-Home polled 16,659 votes and MacDiarmid came bottom of the poll with 127 votes. A possibly apocryphal story has it that MacDiarmid demanded a recount. On being advised that a recount could not possibly change the result of the election, MacDiarmid replied, 'Oh, no, perhaps not. It's just that it's hard to believe that there *are* a hundred and twenty-seven good socialists in Kinross and West Perthshire!'
>
> On 30 September, *The Scotsman* had drawn attention to another aspect of the election contest: 'The Communist threat to test the validity of the election unless their candidate is given equal broadcasting and television time with his Unionist Opponent . . . has to be taken seriously.' It was on this issue that MacDiarmid went to court. The following item is extracted from *The Company I've Kept*.

I think it useful to set out here in full the evidence I gave in my action against Sir Alec Douglas-Home in the Scottish Election Court in Parliament House in Edinburgh on 21 December 1964. The raising of this action, and the proceedings before the Court, attracted world-wide attention, and although I lost the case the great majority of the press at home and abroad thought I ought to have won it, and in fact political broadcasting and telecasting time has now been granted to two of the smaller parties – the Scottish Nationalists and the Welsh Nationalists; but not, of course, to the Communists.[1]

Summing up the case for me that first day of the hearing, Mr A. J. Mackenzie Stuart, QC, said that a General Election was no more than a panoply of individual elections. The question was not whether any party political broadcasts were fair to the Conservative, Liberal, and Labour parties, but to all four men standing in the Kinross and West Perthshire constituency at the General Election. Dr Grieve was asking the Court to declare the election of Sir Alec Douglas-Home as MP for Kinross and West Perthshire void.

Before the first witness was called to give evidence before the two Court of Session judges, Lords Migdale and Kilbrandon, Mr Mackenzie Stuart submitted that at least at this stage the BBC and ITA, who were represented by counsel, had no office in the proceedings.

The Hon. H. S. Keith, QC, explained that Sir Hugh Carleton Green and Sir Robert Fraser were present on behalf of the BBC and ITA organizations which were indirectly being accused of a corrupt practice in the petition.

In the witness box Dr Grieve said that in August this year (1964) he was invited by the BBC to take part in a centenary programme on the subject of Charles Murray, the Aberdeenshire poet. He prepared a script which was approved by the features producer. On 7 September he received a letter from the features producer telling him that as he had been adopted as a Parliamentary candidate, his contribution had to be excluded from the programme because it would be

---

[1]Despite the Election Court's finding, it should be noted that time for political broadcasts and telecasts was given to the Scottish and Welsh and Communist Parties in connection with the General Election (1966).

broadcast in the period of the election. Dr Grieve said he replied stating: 'I did not know that a Parliamentary candidature affected a purely literary, non-political broadcast.'

Mr Mackenzie Stuart said it appeared while he was not allowed to broadcast on a non-controversial subject he was going to be paid for it.

Dr Grieve: Yes, but I have not been. (Laughter.)

On 23 September he was one of a delegation who met officials of the BBC in Glasgow. The purpose was to find out, if they could, under what rule or enactment the BBC restricted political broadcasts or telecasts to representatives of certain parties and denied the same facilities to others; also, the purpose of the delegation was to find out if that rule could be altered for this particular General Election to enable the smaller parties to have a certain amount of political broadcasts and telecasts.

In the course of the interview he challenged the legality of the attitude taken up by the BBC. Later he wrote to both the Director-General of the BBC and the Chairman of ITA on the subject of broadcasting facilities. From the BBC he received a reply stating: 'The agreed series of party election broadcasts in which Sir Alec Douglas-Home takes part as leader of the Conservative Party makes no provision for broadcasts other than those arranged with the main political parties, and no change is contemplated in the arrangements already announced for this series of broadcasts.'

He received a reply for Sir Robert Fraser of the ITA stating: 'This broadcast in which Sir Alec took part as the Leader of the Conservative Party was one of a series of party election broadcasts of which the arrangements were agreed some while ago. This series will not contain broadcasts other than those arranged with the main political parties.'

Cross-examined by Mr Keith, Dr Grieve said that over a period the Communist Party had been in touch with the BBC about broadcasts. Repeatedly he had tried to find out, and had found out, that there was nothing doing as far as the minor parties were concerned. 'I was not able to elicit any information about how that rule was come by.'

Mr Keith: Were you never told that a party that put up at

My Election Contest

least fifty candidates at the General Election would be given a broadcast?'

A. No. They seemed to vary that figure. He had never seen an official announcement to that effect. He did not consider that it was reasonable policy by the BBC to make provision for broadcasts by parties with a minimum number of fifty candidates.

Asked if he considered if every party should have a chance of broadcasting even though they only had one candidate, he replied: 'Why not?'

Mr Keith: Would you have had any complaint if the BBC had allowed any party with twenty candidates to broadcast?

A. No, for the time being.

Q. Would you have thought that that was all right?

A. Yes.

Dr Grieve said it was questionable whether he would have raised the petition if the BBC had set the figure at twenty, but there were other factors. In his petition he was complaining about five Conservative Party political broadcasts.

Mr Keith: Do you believe that the BBC put out these broadcasts with the intention of promoting Sir Alec's election at Kinross and West Perthshire?

Mr Mackenzie Stuart intervened to tell the witness not to answer the question, which was a matter for the court.

Lord Migdale said the court would allow the question, and Dr Grieve replied: 'I believe the BBC were cognisant of the fact that this would be the effect of permitting those broadcasts.'

Mr Keith: So you believe that putting out these broadcasts did promote Sir Alec's election.

A. Undoubtedly.

Q. Do you believe that if these broadcasts had not been put out he would not have been elected?

A. No. I don't say that.

Asked if he believed that the broadcasts made any difference about whether Sir Alec was going to be returned or not, Dr Grieve replied: 'They were a valuable asset to him. I think the opposition candidates might have had much bigger polls if they had had equal facilities.'

Mr Keith: Are you referring to the Labour candidate?

A. Not necessarily. I was rather thinking of myself. I think if I had been allowed to broadcast and put the Communist case I wold have got more votes.

Mr Keith: I take it you do not maintain that the BBC had any intention to display any partiality as regards the Election?

A. Yes, undoubtedly. The BBC is part of the Establishment and is keyed to the requirements of the Establishment.

Mr Keith: Do you believe that the BBC deliberately intended to hamper the activities and prospects of minor parties?

A. Yes. I think so.

Q. Do you not agree that there are limits in the amount to which the BBC should provide facilities for all minor parties?

A. Yes, there are limits.

Q. Do you accept there are limits by which the BBC can cater for all parties, however small?

A. Not all parties, however small. They are in favour of climbing down in regard to small parties, but not the Communist Party. Re-examined by Mr Mackenzie Stuart, Dr Grieve said it was correct to say that Sir Alec was allowed to broadcast in the interest of the party he led while he (Dr Grieve) was not allowed to broadcast on a literary matter.

As I have already said I lost the case, but I, and the Communist Party, were greatly comforted by the general expressions in the press and elsewhere that we ought to have won, and that the political broadcasts and telecasts arrangements would have to be altered in the way we wished. We were satisfied too with the enormous publicity throughout the world the matter received, and with our thus having been able to so effectively expose a piece of characteristic anti-Democratic trickery.

In my petition I accused Sir Alec or his agent of 'corrupt and illegal practices' under the Representation of the People Act, 1949.

I alleged that Sir Alec or the agent acting on his behalf and with his consent or connivance aided, abetted, counselled or procured the BBC and the Independent Television Authority to incur expense with a view to promoting or procuring his election on account of presenting to the electors Sir Alec or his views or the extent or nature of his backing or disparaging another candidate by party political broadcasts on television and radio on 24 September and 13 October 1964.

I also alleged expenses were incurred by similar broadcasts on 26 and 30 September and 6 and 9 October.

I also accused Sir Alec or his agent of procuring the television companies to refrain from making any return or declaration of such expenses, contrary to Section 63 of the Act. Alternatively Sir Alec, I alleged, had paid or ought to have paid a sum to the BBC and ITA for such expenses, and in my opinion any such expense, together with the sums permitted to be expended under the Act, would have exceeded the authorized sum.

I also claimed that in Sir Alec's return of election expenses no expenses were included as authorized or incurred by or on his account of television or radio programmes. Such expense ought to have been included in the return, and Sir Alec's declaration under the Act was accordingly false.

I therefore asked the court to determine that Sir Alec was not duly elected or returned and that the election was void. Mr Mackenzie Stuart, reading from a joint minute, said the combined cost to the BBC and ITA in connection with the five Conservative-Unionist broadcasts was not less than £4600. The maximum expenditure allowed by any candidate in Kinross was £724 8*s*. 6*d*. and Sir Alec's total expenses amounted to £717 4*s*. 1*d*.

29 Ezra Pound: 'The Return of the Long Poem'

MacDiarmid and Pound had both contributed to A.R. Orage's *The New Age* and they had corresponded in the 1930s. After they met, in Venice in 1970, MacDiarmid referred to Pound as the most lovable man he had ever met. His appraisal of Pound was intellectual and literary as well as personal, and in this essay, 'The Return of the Long Poem' published in *Ezra Pound: Perspectives: Essays in Honour of His Eightieth Birthday*, a collection edited by Noel Stock (Chicago: Regnery, 1965), MacDiarmid usefully summarizes the points about Pound's work which he held in highest regard. In approving Pound's achievement in the *Cantos*, MacDiarmid is also implicitly setting out his beliefs regarding his own achievement in the genre of the long poem.

EZRA Pound is undoubtedly the greatest living poet writing in any form of the English language. T. S. Eliot was right when he called him 'il miglior fabbro'. Where in the course of his output Eliot contracted, Pound has expanded. There is no need here to consider the way he has always been in the forefront of technical developments, or his seminal influence on other important writers, or the brilliance of his work as a translator (or adaptor, if you like – I am not concerned with pedantic considerations of the extent of his knowledge of the languages with which he has intromitted) – my interest concentrates on the major character of the first of all these aspects of his creative activity, namely the *Cantos*. Many of those who are ready to recognize his importance in other respects jib when it comes to the *Cantos*, and find that in these all his other gifts have run irremediably into the sand. On the contrary I think it can be shown that they constitute the consummation and crowning of all the various powers exemplified in his previous writings.

For what is meant by great poet? What combination of qualities constitutes supreme poetic art? It has been said – and I accept the definition – that these qualities are three: (1) robustness of thought; (2) felicity of expression; (3) comprehensiveness of view. Many poets possess all of these qualities in *large* measure, many more possess one or other of them in *full* measure, but exceedingly few possess all three in full measure. The purely lyric poet, by the very character of his muse, is incapable of excelling in the first quality – robustness of thought. English poetry today consists almost entirely of short lyrics. These are quite incapable of measuring up to the requirements of our age with its great scientific discoveries and unprecedented acceleration of change. The best of these lyric poets may be recommended to read the late Professor Laura Richthofer's *Heine*, in which she shows in the most convincing way how Heine, after the great success of his early lyrics, found he must cease to write in that way altogether and needed to break up the unity of the lyric, create a new form that would accommodate shifting tonalities and levels so that he could introduce, and grapple with all manner of diverse subject matter and feelings. That crisis lasted for years before Heine solved his problem in his later work, which for that very reason has been either largely ignored or underestimated in comparison with the earlier lyrics he had found it necessary to abandon. It was obviously just as necessary for Pound to sheer away altogether from his earlier work with its *fin-de-siècle* characteristics and derivation from the nineties, and strike out in a different direction altogether. He did so. Heaven only knows at what cost – for such remaking of oneself is always a terrible undertaking – and plunged far ahead of the point at which Heine's difficulties found their resolution.

Writing of contemporary English poetry forty years ago, Mr H. P. Collins said that he had gone scrupulously through the whole of a widely acclaimed volume of Georgian poetry, not without pleasure, and afterward reflected with consternation that never for an instant had he the sensation of being in contact with the serious creative intelligence of a great modern nation.

That only brought up to the time it was written just what Matthew Arnold said in the first *Essays on Criticism*:

> It has long seemed to me that the burst of creative activity in our literature, through the first quarter of this century, had about it in fact something premature; and that from this cause its productions are doomed, most of them, in

spite of our sanguine hopes which accompanied and do still accompany them, to prove hardly more lasting than the productions of far less splendid epochs. And this prematureness comes from its having proceeded without having its proper data, without sufficient material to work with. In other words, the English poetry of the first quarter of this century with plenty of energy, plenty of creative force, did not know enough. This makes Byron so empty of matter, Shelley so incoherent, Wordsworth even, profound as he is, yet so wanting in completeness and variety.

I do not think it can be contended that any subsequent poet in English, till we come to Eliot and Pound, has 'known enough': most English readers so far as poetry is concerned are still living on the kind of poetry, or some weaker derivative of it, Arnold was exposing as inadequate and transient. If that bad influence ever disappears Pound will have been the main cause.

'The sovereign poet,' said Shelley, 'must be not only a singer, but a sage; to passion and music he must add large ideas and abundant knowledge; he must extend in width as well as in height; but besides this he must be no dreamer or fanatic; he must be as firmly rooted in the hard earth as he spreads widely and mounts freely towards the sky.'

The present writer has said elsewhere,

> The poetry of the past can only be properly appreciated when it is seen in its proper historical setting. The whole position of poetry has been menaced by the insistence in schools and elsewhere on the poetry of the past, divorced from vital current interests, which is as if children were compelled to learn Sanskrit or Anglo-Saxon before they learned English; and by our insistence that the general public must have things made as simple as possible for them. This, to my mind, is simply not true, and only a 'superior' bourgeois assumption, flattering to themselves and convenient to their interests as lecturers, teachers, reviewers, journalists and so forth. There is no divergence between the interests of the masses and the real highbrows. On the contrary, what menaces the deepest interests of the masses is all that would 'keep them in their place,'

spoon-feed them, pretend that certain things are beyond them and that they must be restricted to the conventional, the familiar, the easy. In the last resort, this makes for their stabilization – as the masses – in contradistinction to the classes; and finally it makes for the short-circuiting of consciousness, whereas all that is experimental, creative, repudiative of facile simplifications and established modes (incompatible, that is, with Pound's great slogan, 'Make It New') moves in the opposite direction.

Ezra Pound shows in the *Cantos* that he has never allowed himself to be (in Sean O'Casey's phrase) drawn away from 'the sensitive extension of the world'. There are few poets of whom this can be said, and Pound towers head and shoulders over them all.

It is the complicated which seems to be Nature's climax of rightness. The simple is at a discount. Poetry has nothing to do with religious mysticism but is entirely an affair of the practical reason. Our mind is part and parcel of terrestrial Nature, in which it is immersed, and there and only there can it meet with requitals and fulfilments. We are living in a time of unprecedented and ever-accelerating change. The insistent demand everywhere is for higher and higher skills, and as automation increases this will intensify. Hence it is good to see that in his latest work Pound is on the plane of what Teilhard de Chardin calls the *noösphere*. Much has been written recently of the need to bridge the gulf between the arts and the sciences. The call is for synthesis. Stress is laid on the fact that we are living in a great quantitative rather than qualitative age and that the only form adequate to the classless society is the epic – not like epics of the past, except in scale, but embodying a knowledge of the modern world and all its potentialities, not in bits and pieces, but in the round.

The reason Eliot is so inferior to Pound is simply that he never realized (moved indeed always further away from the realization) that what poetry (English poetry especially) needs above all is to break out of confinement to a more earthly endaemonism with Christian nuances – that pseudo-religious mental climate which keeps our harmonies and solutions on so contemptibly shallower a level than the conflicts and tragedies which encompass our lives.

Most English readers are automatically alienated from Pound's later work by the absence of that pseudo-religiosity they have been taught is synonymous with poetry.

The opinion of most people has been so conditioned – that omnipresent brainwashing of our society so effective – that few people nourished on Palgrave's *Golden Treasury*, the English Association's *Poems of Today* and perhaps the several volumes of *Georgian Poetry* cannot believe it is true that, as D. G. James says in *Scepticism and Poetry*:

> When we consider the tradition of English poetry since the Reformation, it is obvious that it is not a Christian poetic tradition. None of the major poets, with the exception of Milton, have written as Christians. The case of Wordsworth is of enormous interest and importance to us. During the years of his greatest poetic output he wrote as a man of passionately religious imagination, but not as a Christian. After his acceptance of Christianity he wrote indeed much fine poetry, but the fact of a decline of his poetic power is undeniable. Keats and Shakespeare sought to evolve their own mythologies; Wordsworth satisfied his imagination in the contemplation of Christian dogma, which considered as a mythology is absolute, where those of Shakespeare and Keats are halting and inexpressive . . . In Wordsworth, the non-Christian tradition in English poetry once more adopted Christianity; but to its detriment. Wordsworth's later poetry is therefore the most perfect comment we have upon the present state of mind of our civilization; for Wordsworth, who, when all is said and done, possessed one of the most powerful imaginations of our time, sought out Christianity and made it his own, only to impair, though by no means to destroy, the sources of his poetry. And we choose before the dogmatic poetry of the later Wordsworth the poetic failures of Keats and of Shakespeare.

Pound in the *Cantos* has led the way to the return of the long poem and to the implementation of Mr D. G. James's ungainsayable finding that

> as in science the formulation of a theorem must lead to further enquiry and research, so in poetry the enjoyment of poetic experience of any part of the world is fraught with the necessity of discovering a wider and more inclusive imaginative apprehension, in which more and more elements in experience are caught up and incorporated. The imagination of the great poet at least never rests from the momentous labour which endeavours to encompass the whole of life, and to achieve a comprehensive unity of imaginative pattern. In many minds, though by no means in all, such a labour, issuing in a failure to achieve such a harmony, leads on to an imaginative apprehension of life in which the world or our experience is seen as only fragmentary, and as a part of a wider reality which in its totality is susceptible only of the dimmest apprehension. Only in the light of that wider reality is this world seen as bodying forth a unity, a unity which in itself it does not possess. For some minds such an imagination of life comes to have a compulsive and controlling reality; an 'unknown and no more' takes on an overwhelming significance for the whole of life. The imagination in its passion for unity and harmony is driven to the indulgence of this 'dream', which, whether in reality it be 'dream' or not, is 'a presence which is not to be put by', and which conditions the whole of life. In other words, it is precisely the encompassment of the world by the imagination which is seen to be impossible; the essential labour of the imagination, its passion for unity and order, is defeated by experience; and whatsoever of unity and order life is seen to possess hangs on the sense of that which baffles the imagination . . . As Mr Eliot has said, religion is never wholly freed of scepticism: but it needs to be added, what is equally true, that scepticism can never wholly liberate itself from faith. Faith is 'somehow integrated' into faith. In these matters it is not given to us integrate' into faith. In these matters it is not given to us to *know*. The 'denial' into which some scepticism issues cannot be absolute. As Kant said, religion is an affair of

the *practical* reason; and for this reason explicit assertion or denial is superficial in its implications. Thus, it is in effect impossible to draw a line of division between what we call faith and what we call scepticism, for each is, whether it realizes it or not, 'integrated' into the other. If this is so, the poetry of mysticism exhibits something latent in all imaginative apprehension of the world which seeks to be comprehensive.

Apart from T. S. Eliot's *Four Quartets* and Pound's *Cantos* we must look elsewhere than to English literature for the best examples of the return of the long poem. We are apt to think that the poetic production of the socialist countries is confined, on the one hand, to short poems on a simple folk song basis, or, on the other, commonplace pieces of propagandist doggerel. That is not the case.

The character of the times, the tremendous revolutions through which we are passing have enforced the realization that what is needed now are giant syntheses – not only in prose but also in poetry. Mayakovsky's poems *Vladimir Ilyitch Lenin* and *Harasho* (*The Poem of October*) render in an impressive and lyrical synthesis the history of the preparation and carrying out of the first socialist revolution in the world.

The Chilean Pablo Neruda celebrates the fight for national liberation waged by the peoples of Latin America in monumental cycles of poems, such as the well-known *Canto General* or the more recent *Cancion de gesta*, devoted to revolutionary Cuba – not unlike the huge mural frescoes painted by Mexican painters.

The Turkish poet Nazim Hikmet worked out a colossal poetical edifice planned in nine volumes, with more than three thousand heroes, suggestively called *Human Panorama* or *History of the Twentieth Century*. After the 'epic' *The Desert and Spring* Vladimir Lugovski wrote, in fourteen years, the great work of his life, *The Middle of the Century*, a book of poems which he called *The Century's Autobiography*, the result of profound lyrical and philosophical meditations on man, mankind, happiness and politics.

These poems represent the growing end of poetry today, corresponding to the vast complexity of the modern world and the unparalleled perspectives opening out before mankind as a result of the tremendous developments of the sciences in our time. But by far the greatest of these is Pound's *Cantos*, since the others are comparatively plantigrade, lacking altogether 'the rise, the carol, the creation', as Pound never does, since in the *Cantos* 'the visions shimmer, float, harden, melt, spin, reflect, disperse, shoot away in vistas and expand in atmospheric sweeps, and then contract their focus on a bird or a plant or a face.'

Of the main objections I have found to the *Cantos*, the first is to its materialism. But, contrary to general belief, in actual aesthetic products materialist and sceptical writers have considerably surpassed religious ones. This is hardly true of ancient Greece, where the greatest poets, Homer, Sappho, Aeschylus, Sophocles and Pindar, preceded the age of unbelief. One must remember, however, that it was far easier to be an aesthetic pagan than it is to be an aesthetic Christian. Apollo, Hermes and Aphrodite were really aesthetic beings, but one must have a marvellous eye for beauty to discover it in the Three Persons of the Godhead. Every Latin poet without exception was a materialist or sceptic. Catullus spoke for all when he said:

> Soles occidere et redire possunt;
> Nobis cum semel occidit brevis lux
> Nox est perpetua una dormienda.

In Italy, Dante was religious; but Petrarch, Politian, Ariosto, Machiavelli, Aretino and all the Renaissance poets were sceptical. Tasso lived under the counter-Reformation, and was one of the first pupils of the Jesuits; so he may be called religious. That applies to Spain too. Cervantes, Calderon and Lope da Vega were not merely orthodox, but greatly approved the burning of heretics! In Germany, Schiller may have had a touch of religion, but Goethe was on the whole sceptical, and Lessing and Heine were the boldest of mockers. In France, nearly all the writers since Voltaire, whether in prose or verse, have been sceptics. I give my possible opponent Verlaine, however, unless he objects to taking him. In England, during the last couple of centuries, Shelley, Fitzgerald and Swinburne were sceptical enough, and where are there three religious poets to match them in aesthetic power? Tennyson alone can be named. It is a good deal to admit that the author of 'In Memoriam' was a believer, but I can afford to be generous.

In truth, it is ridiculous to call even the nominally believing poets religious men. 'The Blessed Damozel' is a poem about Heaven, but it is the very antithesis of a religious poem. The fact is that there has been unbroken enmity between religion and art. The Greeks in their best days were an exception, but even in Greece Plato at least appeared with his purer religion, and desired to expel poets and musicians from his republic. In Rome the fight of religion against the theatre lasted almost till the end of the republic. To this day there are no bells in Muhammadan churches because Muhammad thought music wicked. In Italy beauty was worshipped by the bad popes, but abhorred by the good ones, In the fifteenth century the Good Pope Paul II tortured and imprisoned poets, and next century the good popes of the Counter-Reformation waged implacable war against poetry and art. In England the theatres were closed for many years, fiddlers were put in the stocks and poets had a narrow escape. In France Molière could hardly get buried, and Lully was refused absolution till he burned an opera he had just composed. Even in the eighteenth century, the actress Lecouvreur was refused Christian burial, and had to be buried in a field for cattle. There is practically no form of art – neither music nor poetry nor dancing nor the drama nor the novel – which has not been persecuted for ages by every religion.

The second objection to the *Cantos* I have encountered is to the usury theme. It is suggested that this is a quite inadequate springboard for great poetry, and the importance he attaches to it shows a very serious flaw in Pound's scale of values. But those of us who, like Pound, have long been interested in the Money Question are familiar with the psychological barrier most people have in this respect. They are unable to contemplate the fact that we are potbound in an arbitrary an artificial money system which has no correspondence to reality at all. After all, as Pound has said, an earlier Scotsman had anticipated the realization that lies at the root of Major C. H. Douglas's system. It is expressed in the phrase I italicize in the passage in which Pound says: 'The Bank of England, a felonious combination, or, more precisely, a gang of usurers taking sixty per cent interest, was founded in 1694. Paterson, the founder of the Bank, clearly stated the advantages of his scheme: the bank hath the benefit of the interest on all moneys *which it creates out of nothing.*' It was on this basis that Major Douglas erected his charge that the issue and withdrawal of credit by the banking system does not reflect the physical realities of production and consumption, and that the theory of money so applied effects a continual and increasing indebtedness of the community to the banks. One debt cannot be liquidated without incurring a greater one. That is the lever of the Monopoly of Credit. The 'Douglas Theorem' is that, owing to credit being treated as the property of the banks, a loan repayable on demand, instead of being administered as the money of the community held as a right, purchasing power is withdrawn from the public at a faster rate than it ceases to figure in the prices which the public has to meet if all its production is to be sold. That is to say, there enters into the costs of final products a fictitious element due entirely to the property conception of credit, an element which is fictitious in the sense that it does not represent the money equivalent of wealth consumed in making that product. In fact, the amount of credit withheld from the community in this way is approximately the money value of the net difference between its total production (capital and ultimate goods) and its consumption (final products bought and depreciation of real capital). This, it is claimed, is the irreducible cause of the inability to distribute the whole volume of consumable production which increases as the proportion of power equipment to labour increases. Hence the defeat by Money Monopoly of any benefit which would accrue to humanity by the replacement of human energy by natural power in production. As the products of one set of processes cannot be sold by the purchasing power distributed in respect of those processes, industrialism has only survived at all because the unsaleable product of one period could be partly carried off by the credit distributed for inaugurating further production. So we are confronted with the logical but insane financial advice that the cure for an unsalable surplus is more production or economy. This is the very crux of the Money Monopoly. However successful man is in supplying his wants and saving his limbs, he must enjoy no relaxation of economic activity. In Major Douglas's words, as a mechanism for making work the financial system is as near perfect as possible, but as a means of distributing the products of what is now predominantly a natural power productive plant, it fails completely. In fact, that is not its objective.

Major Douglas was not, however, prepared to accept this 'philosophy' of economic activity as the chief end of man, and consequently – desiring *the economic independence and complete freedom of the individual* – made proposals for the return of credit to the people and the issue of national dividends as each citizen's share in the benefit of natural-power production. Major Douglas's proposals were in fact designed to answer the question which, with all their talk of freedom this and liberation that, the BBC and all the press and politicians ignore, namely: *And the liberty of not getting into debt – how about that?* A nation that will not get itself into debt drives the usurers to fury.

Listen to what Douglas himself said in a passage that strikes the very keynote of his philosophy (and incidentally aligns him with all that is best in Scottish thought from the Declaration of Arbroath to the present day):

> There probably never was a time in which disinterested legislation was so rare, just as there probably never was a device which was so effective in silencing criticism of interested legislation as this idea that self-interest on a worldly plane must necessarily be wicked. I would therefore make the suggestion in order to add to the gaiety of nations by creating a riot at once, that the first requisite of a satisfactory governmental system is that it shall divest itself of the idea that it has a mission to improve the morals or direct the philosophy of any of its constituent citizens. Sir Walter Fletcher said: 'We can find safety and progress only in proportion as we bring our methods of statecraft under the guidance of biological Truth.' I think that this is one of those remarks which illuminate a subject much as the

sky-line is illuminated on a dark night by a flash of summer lightning. *We know little about ourselves, and less about our neighbours, and almost nothing at all about the nature of a healthy Society. Nor do we display any particular anxiety to increase our knowledge in these directions.* Yet there is nowadays none so poor that he is not prepared to produce at short notice the plans which will put every human being in his place within the space of a few short weeks. . . . The physical scientist who wishes to obtain a sure foundation for the formulation of laws begins by standardizing his re-agents. Temperature would be meaningless if we had not something we call 'zero'. But in regard to biology we are in a difficulty. We do not even know how unhealthy we are, though we have a strong suspicion that we are very sick indeed. To those, then, who are anxious to make a definite contribution to the saving of a sick world, it may not be impertinent to suggest that the natural creative forces of the universe might plausibly be expected to produce at least as good results if left alone to work themselves out through the agency of the individual, as may be expected from planning which is undertaken without any conception of the relation of the plan to the constitution and temperament of those who are affected. If all history and all observation has not been misread, there is implanted in the individual *a primary desire for freedom and security, which rightly considered are forms of the same thing.* There is no such thing as a freedom which is held upon terms, whether these terms are dictated by the State, by a banking system, or by a World Government. Until it can be shown that, with the resources which science has placed at his disposal, the individual is incapable of making freedom and security for himself, this multiplication of organisations whose interference we cannot avoid will only make a world catastrophe the more certain.

The values to be safeguarded in the Douglas Commonwealth are Liberty, Leisure and Culture. The will-to-plenty of the individual is to be given satisfaction, and the whole business and industrial life of society relegated to a subordinate place, somehow as in the economy of the human body many biological processes proceed automatically or semi-automatically, leaving the psychology of the human being free to develop its interests.

Systems were made for men, not men for systems (declared Major Douglas in the first chapter of his first book), and the interest of man, which is self-development, takes precedence over all systems, economic, political or theological. A ringing statement to come from an economist!

No wonder the newspapers gave him less obituary space than they accord to any footballer, film star or crooner. Douglas himself would not have been surprised at all. His entire propaganda was founded on the centuries-old recognition of the fact that *nescis, mi fili, quantilla prudentia mundus regatur* (You know, my son, with what a small stock of wisdom the world is governed). And he might have explained at any time during the twenty-odd years of our friendship, as another friend of mine did, viz., 'God knows what gets into all governments at certain stages of their existence. It's easy to understand why Arab princes surround themselves with incompetents, eunuchs, dolts and degenerates, for Arab princes consider themselves infallible: whatever they do must of necessity be right. Consequently they elevate childhood friends or toadying relatives to the most important posts in their kingdoms. But only God knows why such things happen perpetually in countries regarded as politically enlightened, like England, France, America, supposedly governed by patriotic men. Yet they always have happened, and with horrifying frequency; the pages of history are sprinkled with dolts, idiots, drunkards maintained in the highest offices – mediocrities whose stubbornness has sacrificed armies, whose blindness has destroyed navies, whose bad judgment has ruined their countries' prestige, starved helpless people by the million, wrecked cities, toppled arts, civilization, learning and understanding in the dust – and most of these fools' names hold unsullied places in the lying annals of their respective nations.'

If Douglas would not have been surprised at the scanty obituaries accorded him, there need be no surprise that Pound has not been given anything like his due and that the *Cantos* are condemned as incomprehensible patchworks. The reason is the same in both cases. So it is inevitable that a recent critic should be compelled to say

> Over forty years ago, two Americans and an Irishman attempted to put English poetry back into the mainstream of European culture. The effect of these generations who have succeeded to the heritage of Eliot, Pound and Yeats has been largely to squander the awareness these three gave us of our place in world literature, and to retreat into a self-congratulatory parochialism. . . . Instead of the conscious formulation of a position, one has a provincial laziness of mind adopted as a public attitude and as the framework for an equally provincial verse. Against such a background poetic culture in Britain would seem to be living on an overdraft, the overdraft being the work of the writers of the older generation who are still with us.

It is true, as Emrys Humphreys said in a broadcast:

> It is not too soon to say that Joyce saved us from being smothered in the spurious; without Joyce, Eliot and Pound, the atmosphere of English literature today would be that of the bar of a suburban golf club. Honest, serious, sensitive communication would have become practically impossible. . . . The conditions of our time are fiercely inimical to the practice of the arts. Art: the very word invokes derision, contempt, suspicion, impatience.

Or as another recent writer (this time an American) puts it:

> The great surge of 'modern' poetry in the English language in the second and third decades of this century was, except for Yeats, and Eliot since his transference of citizenship to England, largely American in its most forceful and influential aspects. Housman, Kipling, AE, Monro, Sassoon, Stephens, Aldington, de la Mare, Graves, the Sitwells – these names have loomed large at one time and have their places; a few have a distinguished place indeed. But the main drift has passed these writers by.

Precisely. Pound *is* the main drift.

30   Growing Up in Langholm

This item was collected in a symposium of essays edited by Karl Miller, *Memoirs of a Modern Scotland* (London: Faber and Faber, 1970). It is an adaptation of an article entitled 'My Native Place' from the *Scots Observer* of 2 October 1930, to which has been added material from MacDiarmid's autobiography, *Lucky Poet* (1943) and his monograph on the composer *Francis George Scott* (1955). Tonally, the essay recalls the dedicatory verses of MacDiarmid's 1934 volume of poetry, *Stony Limits*, addressed to his wife Valda and son James Michael:

> I had the fortune to live as a boy
> In a world a' columbe and colour-de-roy
> As gin I'd had Mars for the land o' my birth
>   Instead o' the earth.
>
> Nae maitter hoo faur I've travelled sinsyne
> The cast o' Dumfriesshire's aye in me like wine;
> And my sangs are gleids o' the candent spirit
>   Its sons inherit.

The essay was assembled by Duncan Glen as a broadcast for MacDiarmid's seventy-fifth birthday and was later published in Alan Bold's anthology, *The Thistle Rises* (1984).

AFTER journeying over most of Scotland, England and central, southern and eastern Europe, as well as America, Siberia and China, I am of the opinion that 'my native place' – the Muckle Toon of Langholm, in Dumfriesshire – is the bonniest place I know: by virtue not of the little burgh in itself (though that has its treasurable aspects, and on nights when, as boys, we used to thread its dim streets playing 'Jock, Shine the Light', and race over the one bridge, past the factory, and over the other, with the lamp reflections wriggling like eels at intervals in the racing water, had an indubitable magic of its own), but by virtue of the wonderful variety and quality of the scenery in which it is set. The delights of sledging on the Lamb Hill or Murtholm

Brae; of gathering hines in the Langfall; of going through the fields of Baggara hedged in honeysuckle and wild roses, through knee-deep meadow-sweet to the Scrog Nut Wood and gathering the nuts or crab-apples there; of blaeberrying on Warblaw or the Castle Hill; of dookin' and guddlin' or making islands in the Esk or Ewes or Wauchope and lighting stick fires on them and cooking potatoes in tin cans – these are only a few of the joys I knew, in addition to the general ones of hill-climbing and penetrating the five glens which (each with its distinct character) converge upon or encircle the town – Eskdale, Wauchopedale, Tarrasdale, Ewesdale and, below the town Carlislewards, the Dean Banks.

As we grew up, too, we learned to savour the particular qualities and rites of Langholm in comparison with other Border burghs: the joys of Langholm Common Riding compared with those at Selkirk or Hawick, for example; the peculiar shibboleths of local pronunciation; the historical associations of our corner of the 'Ballad-land' rife with its tales of raidings and reivings and with the remnants of peels; the wealth of local 'characters' who were still about.

As I grew into my early teens I ranged further afield, and soon all the Borders were within my ken. Many places had their special beauties or points of interest and advantage; but none had the variety of beauty centred round Langholm itself – none seemed so complete a microcosm of the entire Borderland. I knew where to find not only the common delights of hill and forest and waterside (and chiefest of all these to me were the chestnut trees at the sawmill – even now it thrills me to remember the beautiful chestnuts, large and luxurious as horses' eyes, which so surprisingly displayed themselves when we cracked open the prickly green shells, and I remember many huge strops of them I strung and many a fierce competition at Conquerors), but also the various kinds of orchises, and butterwort, sundew, and the like; the various nests – including Terrona crags where ravens nested; how to deal with adders and smoke out wasps' 'bikes', and much other lore of that sort. In short, a boyhood full of country sights and sounds – healthy and happy and able to satisfy its hunger with juicy slices of a big yellow neep stolen from an adjoining field.

I never made any conscious decision that I should be a

writer. That was a foregone conclusion from my very early life. I don't know if it originated with myself. When I was nine or ten my teachers seemed to realize that writing was going to be my destiny and I may have absorbed the idea from them. Certainly from a very early age I had begun to try to write for the local paper at Langholm, where my father was the local postman. We lived in the Post Office buildings. The library, the nucleus of which had been left by Thomas Telford, the famous engineer, was upstairs. I had access to it, and used to fill a big washing-basket with books and bring it downstairs as often as I wanted to. There were upwards of 12,000 books in the library, and a fair number of new books, chiefly novels, was constantly bought. Before I left home (when I was fourteen) I could go up into that library in the dark and find any book I wanted. I read almost every one of them.

My grandfather, John Grieve, was a power-loom tuner in a Langholm tweed mill. I only remember seeing him once – shortly before he died, when I was about four years old. An alert 'jokey' little man, I remember he wore a transparent, butter-coloured waistcoat or linen jacket; and on the occasion I recall I caught him in the act of taking some medicine of a vivid red colour, and somehow or other got it into my childish head that he was drinking blood, and thought of him with horror – not unmixed with envy – for years afterwards. I resemble him physically (in point of leanness and agility, though I am considerably taller) and facially (a big brow and all the features squeezed into the lower half of my face); but when I was a lad the older folk used to tell me I took after him in another respect: 'Just like your grandfather,' they used to say, 'aye amang the lassies.' As boys my brother and I wore the Graham tartan. Our mother was Elizabeth Graham. If my father's people were mill-workers in the little Border burghs, my mother's people were agricultural workers. My alignment from as early as I can remember was almost wholly on the side of the industrial workers and not the rural people. I have never had anything but hatred and opposition for deproletarianizing and back-to-the-land schemes; my faith has always been in the industrial workers and the growth of the third factor between man and nature – the machine. But even as a boy, from the steadings and cottages of my mother's folk and their neighbours in Wauchope and Eskdalemuir and Middlebie and Dalbeattie and Tundergarth, I drew the assurance that I felt and understood the spirit of Scotland and the Scottish folk in no common measure, and that that made it possible that I would in due course become a great national poet of Scotland. My mother's people lie in the queer old churchyard of Crowdieknowe in the parish of Middlebie.

There was certainly nothing 'lowering', in Lawrence's sense of the word, in Border life when I was a boy. Langholm was full of genial ruffians like the employer to whom, communist though I am, I look back with the utmost relish, who, after carefully instructing a workman whom he was sending up Westerkirk way as to what he was to do, ended: 'and just call in when you come back and I'll gie you the sack!' Border life was raw, vigorous, rich, bawdy, and the true test of my own work is the measure in which it has recaptured something of that unquenchable humour, biting satire, profound wisdom cloaked in bantering gaiety, and the wealth of mad humour, with not a trace of whimsy, in the general leaping, light-hearted, reckless assault upon the conventions of dull respectability.

My first introduction to my native land was when my mother wrapped me well in a Shetland shawl and took me to the door to see – but, alas, my infant eyesight could not carry so far, nor if it could have seen would my infant brain have understood – the most unusual sight of the Esk frozen over so hard that carts and horses could go upon it for twenty miles as upon a road and the whole adult population were out skating upon it all day, and by the light of great bonfires at night. That, I think, has not happened since – nor anything approaching it.

These were indeed the champagne days – these long enchanted days on the Esk, the Wauchope and the Ewes – and the thought of them today remains as intoxicating as they must have been in actual fact all those years ago. I have been 'mad about Scotland' ever since.

There were scores of animals and birds I knew far better than I now know the domestic cat, which is the only specimen of the 'lower animals' of which I see much. My eyes may, perhaps, still seek out and recognize and appreciate a dozen or so wild flowers in the course of a year, but my memory recalls – with a freshness and a fullness of detail with which such living specimens cannot vie at all – hundreds I have not seen for over thirty years. My poetry is full of these memories: of a clump of mimulus 'shining like a dog's eyes with all the world a bone'; of the quick changes in the Esk that in a little stretch would far outrun all the divers thoughts of man since time began; of the way in which, as boys, with bits of looking-glass, we used to make the sun jump round about us. Above all, when I think of my boyhood, my chief impression is of the amazing wealth of colour. A love of colour has been one of the most salient characteristics of Scots poetry down to the best work of our contemporary poets, and I have celebrated it again and again in my own work.

Many great baskets of blaeberries I gathered on the hills round Langholm. Then there were the little hard black cranberries, and – less easy to gather since they grow in swampy places – the speckled craneberries, but above all, in the Langfall and other woods in the extensive policies of the Duke of Buccleuch, there were great stretches of wild raspberry, the fruit of which the public were allowed to pick, and many a splendid 'boiling of jam' I gathered there – gathering more than the raw material of jam, too.

I would come cycling back into Langholm down the Wauchope road with a pillowslipful of crab-apples (as at other times a basket of plovers' eggs) on my carrier; and again there was the Scrog Nut wood, shaking its bunches of nuts like clenched fists in the windy sunlight. I have nowhere seen loveliness so intense and so diverse crowded into so small a place. Langholm presents the manifold and multiform grandeur and delight of Scotland in miniature – as if quickened and thrown into high relief by the proximity of England.

There is a place at Langholm called the Curly Snake where a winding path coils up through a copse till it reaches the level whence, after passing through a field or two, it runs into the splendid woods of the Langfall. It has always haunted my imagination and has probably constituted itself as the ground-plan of my mind, just as the place called the Nook of the Night Paths in Gribo-Shov, the great forest north of Hillerod, haunted Kierkegaard's.

My boyhood was an incredibly happy one. Langholm was indeed – and presumably still is – a wonderful place to be a boy in. Scotland is not generally regarded as a land flowing with milk and honey. Nevertheless, it can do so more frequently than is commonly understood. It certainly did so in my boyhood – with a bountifulness so inexhaustible that it has supplied all my subsequent poetry with a tremendous wealth of sensuous satisfaction, a teeming gratitude of reminiscence. I still have an immense reservoir to draw upon. My earliest impressions are of an almost tropical luxuriance of nature – of great forests, of honey-scented heather hills, and moorlands infinitely rich in little-appreciated beauties of flowering, of animal and insect life, of subtle relationships of water and light, and of a multitude of rivers, each with its distinct music.

31 Metaphysics and Poetry

The poet and critic Walter Perrie conducted this interview on 29 September 1974 and subsequently published a shorter version of it in pamphlet form under the above title (Hamilton: Lothlorien, 1975). This is the fuller version as published in Alan Bold's anthology *The Thistle Rises* (1984).

WP: What would you like to begin with, literature or philosophy?

CMG: Whichever you like. I don't draw any line between them.

WP: I think of your general philosophical position as monist and vitalist. Can you generalize the relation between your poetry and your philosophical ideas?

CMG: That's an impossible question because there's no such thing as poetry. There are many different kinds of poetry. In respect of one kind one might emphasize the monism but in others take a different angle of approach. I refuse to be screwed down to one particular philosophical position.

WP: So the emphasis varies to fit the poem.

CMG: Yes. But the variation of course arises from my own personality. I refuse to be labelled as one thing or another. As you know, I'm a member of the Communist Party and an important thing for me about the British Communist Party was that when the executive sent me a congratulatory message on my eightieth birthday, it read: 'Mr Grieve has not always agreed with us, nor we with him. Nor would we wish it otherwise', and that's very important from my point of view. It was a very honest declaration.

WP: Do you regard reality as a fundamentally spiritual entity, or are you at heart an empiricist?

CMG: I see it as a spiritual thing, in so far as reality is conceivable by the human mind. It's possible, of course, to think or to imagine that only a very small portion of reality is accessible to the human mind: which is why I am a materialist and an atheist.

An interesting point was raised recently about my philosophical position. I find a lot of people who think they are Christians very anxious to call me a Christian poet, perhaps because I use a certain number of references to Christian dogma, because I may show a compassionate spirit in certain connections. Professor MacKinnon, who holds the chair of Divinity at Cambridge, recently published a little book summarizing what he had said in the Gifford Lectures at the University of Edinburgh. He called it *The Problem of Metaphysics*. In it he devotes an entire chapter to one of my poems, and he points out the assurance of atheism which permeates that particular poem, and deprecates the tendency of many Christian apologists to say – 'He really is a Christian poet without knowing it.' He points out that the poem with which he deals confutes that idea entirely. One must remember that both theism and atheism are ontologically based. If you're an assured atheist, there's no reason on earth why you should not create great poetry. As a matter of fact, study of literary history shows that far more of what we call the body of great poetry in Europe has been written by materialists than by believers, and that what is called religious poetry in any of the European literatures is derived largely from non-Christian and, indeed, anti-Christian sources. Not only that, but in British poetry, English poetry if you care to call it, whenever in recent times there's been a recession to Christian belief, the poets who have experienced that recession have lost their creative power: Wordsworth, Auden and so on. Others again, like Yeats, had to flee from it into esoteric religious substitutes – I think that's inevitable.

WP: Do you think then that all good poets are essentially pagans?
CMG: Yes, of course they are.
WP: Difficult to see in a case like Dante's.

CMG: Yes, I agree about that – and there are exceptions in Eastern literature – but then we're talking about Buddhism rather than Christianity.

WP: You perhaps know the essay by John Crowe Ransome on the ontological status of poetry. Is your poetry somehow dependent on the sort of ontology which you specify?

CMG: I should say that it's entirely dependent on the ontology which the poet adopts or expresses. That's one reason why poetry is one of the rarest things in the world. There are all kinds of versifiers but extremely few poets – and it's also one of the reasons why I'm opposed to a great deal of contemporary versifying. Although there is currently an upsurge of popular poetry, it's not poetry. It's not poetry at all. It's anti-poetry, characterized by one or two main qualities or characteristics: emotion without intellect, fancy without imagination, and a tendency to bring the whole thing down to the level of entertainment. I am opposed to all these tendencies.

WP: What role does contradiction play in your thought? It is often said that you present frequent contradictions.

CMG: Like Whitman I would say 'I contradict myself? Very well, I contradict myself.' The variety and the enormity of the world and the infinite possibilities of the human mind are such that contradictions are inevitable for anyone who has a certain depth of intellectual perception. Only shallow minds fancy that they are being consistent. And they can only be consistent within a very narrow ambit. As soon as they endeavour to take in the whole, what Rolfe called the desire and pursuit of the whole, they are lost, completely lost, unless they have learned to juggle with contradictions. Lord Raleigh said that the ability to believe two mutually contradictory things at the same time was one of the infallible tests of a good mind in the modern world.

WP: That, of course is very much a neo-Hegelian view. Have you been influenced directly by the neo-Hegelians? I am thinking of Bradley and Bosanquet.

CMG: Oh, I read them, long ago – before I became a convinced Marxist. They are a very fertile influence, a wonderful breeding ground for poets – unlike those who are opposed to them.

WP: Would you agree that there is a chasm today between sensibility and sensuality so that we no longer have any genuinely sensual poetry – such as the sonnets of Michelangelo, or Yeats's last poems? All that we have is a poetry of the senses.

CMG: Inevitably, the kind of poetry I'm interested in has tended, in the last half-century, to become more and more highly intellectual – more mathematical. I find the same tendency in ultra-modern music and I think the two things are marching together. But it brings me back again to the rarity of poetry. The great majority of people who write verse haven't got to that stage at all. They are full of sensuality – which isn't a bad thing – but it cannot be associated with any sensibility they have without a loss. If they could conjoin the two, or penetrate the one with the other, without losing power, then it would be a very good thing. But they can't do that and there is that lack, as you say, of genuine sensuality in modern poetry. Even those poets to whom I attach most importance in the modern world show that. There's no English poetry of course, we're ruling that out completely – it doesn't exist.

WP: I take it that you regard communism as essentially a spiritual force rather than in materialist terms?

CMG: Yes, I do.

WP: Given the nature and the trends which are evident in the contemporary world, do you see spiritual forces developing coherently in that world? When society is going through a period of great fragmentation, do you see communism as a spiritual force and the practice of poetry developing along fruitful lines?

CMG: It may take time. We are living at a very critical period in world history. But it was, I think, an American who said that the main task confronting the poet today is a great task of assimilation. I agree with that. If poetry is to reassert itself as the Queen of the Arts then what Ezra Pound called 'poppycock', that's to say that store of outworn theories and superstitions, must be swept clean away. Very few poets are attempting to do that. They're still thirled to the 'poetic' which is the worst enemy of poetry. I'm brought back to that by thinking of perhaps the greatest technical change I've seen in poetry. Heine wrote a couple of volumes of song lyrics which were enormously popular – and still are. And then, at a given juncture, he said, 'I'm not going to write any more of that kind of damned thing!' and he spent the remaining years of his life trying to break up the tonality of the lyric and introduce into his work elements up to then considered non-poetical. He succeeded, but his later poetry has, of course, never been popular – and never will be. Pasternak was in the same position. He said, 'The lyric is hopeless in the modern world.' And I've done the same thing, followed the same example. I still adhere to that. One of the reasons is that the lyric, by its very nature, cannot reflect the complexities of modern life. But, apart from that, it necessarily ignores something even more important, and that is the enormous new perspective of the sciences. That can't be encapsulated in a short lyric. It's because of that enormous variety (which ought to be the pre-occupation of poetry and so seldom is) that most modern poetry is trivial and worthless.

WP: You would agree then that an important poem is necessarily a long poem?

CMG: I think so. The epic is the only form which can discharge the duties of the poet in the modern world; not lyric, not any subordinate forms. That's why at the Foyle luncheon which was given when Larkin's Oxford anthology came out I made a speech asking why he had left out the greatest poet living in the British Isles – David Jones. He didn't reply. He couldn't reply. It would have confuted the whole basis of his anthology.

WP: What political trends do you see developing in, say, the coming century?

CMG: The greatest force in the modern world is communism. That doesn't necessarily mean that we'll see an extension to other countries of the kind of social system we have today in Russia or in Yugoslavia. But I think they will approximate more and more fully to the idea of a communist state.

WP: And in Britain, will this so-called social democracy ever approximate to communism?

CMG: I think it will, yes. More and more I think the working class are finding out, as the present crisis in this country shows, that right throughout history social democracy has ended up by betraying the workers and the only way to avoid that betrayal is by going further left – to communism.

WP: You regard communism as the philosophy of the future. Does that philosophy leave room for the arts?

CMG: In this country we have a long tradition of popular education and as a result people are less and less well educated. In Russia, despite certain features of the communist regime which I deplore, there has been an enormous advance in educational facilities. They had to face a huge illiteracy problem, and that has been almost entirely eradicated. They are far ahead of us in certain directions, although we must remember the historical background. They were far behind us in certain respects so they had, more or less, to concentrate on scientific development and on large-scale industrialisation; and that has inhibited a corresponding development in aesthetics. But that is temporary. After all, although a great deal of fuss is made in this country about people like Solzhenitsyn, and about Pasternak before that, a tremendous amount of good work had been done in poetry and in other departments of literature of which most people in the West know little or nothing. Solzhenitsyn is a menace. The West has bolstered him up as a great crusader against communist tyranny, for freedom for the artist and all that sort of thing. But he's not an artist at all – he's a reporter – and his reportage is very poor stuff at that. I know half a dozen American writers who for sheer reporting, documentation, are far ahead of him. The *Observer*, for instance, likened him to Tolstoy. He's not fit to brush Tolstoy's shoes.

WP: If we are working towards the emergence of a more egalitarian world, what sort of ideal of man is going to emerge? Will it, for example, be along the lines of *uomo universale* of the renaissance – or might it be some sort of Goethean ideal of the integrated man?

CMG: Most people know nothing, and the educational system equips them only to do a job, not to live, not to become human beings. The fragmentation that is going on whereby specialists in one science are unintelligible to specialists in another has got to end – in the interests of all the sciences. It's that bringing together of these disparate elements again that seems to me to be essential – and it will happen, it's bound to. Not as a result of anyone making a political programme of it but because it's inherent in the nature of things. Otherwise, people are not going to survive.

WP: And you see such a general synthesis coming about in the near future?

CMG: Yes. Yeats, who had a very untrained mind, attempted it in his own way. His ideal was the man who was at home in all the sciences. Wordsworth said it before him, but others have gone a great deal further than that. Somehow or other we've got to get rid of the fact that there's a tremendous amount of indifference on the part of the great majority of people in western, so-called civilized countries: indifference to everything outwith the ambit of their own personal lives. We have to couple that with the fact that it's in the so-called civilized countries that we are seeing this recrudescence of barbarism: torture, massacre and so on. It will happen in this country too. We're going to have an enormous backlash of fascism.

WP: Which literary influences have you consciously

	rejected?
CMG:	I suppose it was inevitable that I should be influenced by most of the English lyric poets, because it was on English lyric poetry that we were fed at school. It wasn't until I turned to the great Scots poets of the fifteenth and sixteenth centuries that I began to see that I had no affiliations whatsoever with English poetry – and rejected it. In my early development I was influenced by the *Arbeiter* poets of Germany, Richard Dehmel and others, but I think that the greatest influence on my ideas about poetry, if not reflected in my actual poetry, was Paul Valéry and the Italians who followed in his wake: Montale and Ungaretti and Quasimodo. I knew both Montale and Quasimodo myself – I've been very lucky that way. It cuts both ways of course. I also knew Yeats and Eliot so there are flaws in my luck. Yeats was very nice to me but I soon got what I regarded as his measure. He was a monologuist and didn't like other people to speak when he was speaking or to introduce new subject matter but on this occasion he wanted to know about Douglas' Social Credit. I hadn't said but a few things to him about it when I discovered that he knew nothing about how the present banking system worked and therefore couldn't possibly understand how the other would work. I told him so. We parted amicably.
WP:	You have said that there is no English poetry. Why not?
CMG:	The whole framework of English society has been against it. Their schooling system kills the imagination – their whole system is opposed to the emergence of aesthetic values. They claim that there is a great tradition of English poetry. Where did it come from? Very little of it was English in an exact sense. In modern times you have two Americans, an Irishman and a Welshman. There are none at the moment. Auden was a complete wash-out. The last thing he said to me was – in a very husky voice – 'Grieve, there's no future in communism.' And I said – 'I

don't think there's any future in anything else.'

WP: Do you think there is a connection between the fact that so much fine poetry is now coming out of Central Europe and their, in one sense, more naked experience of the last war?

CMG: I couldn't say about that. I think one of the reasons for it is that they always had to fight for their languages and for the maintenance of their native traditions.

WP: Nationalism in Scotland is currently giving something of a boost to the arts in some respects. Do you think that will last?

CMG: Yes. I think that there is something deeper in the proliferation of nationalisms all over the world. Millions of people have come to feel isolated from their native roots and are trying to reroot themselves in some indigenous tradition, reviving their native languages and so on. That will continue and it is an insistence on maintaining the variety of life. On that level the main objection to capitalism is that it kills. Centralism always comes from the demands of orthodox finance. And if you're standing at an assembly belt doing the same repetitive job day in, day out, six days a week, then of course it will kill everything else stone dead. It dehumanizes the workers – which is one of its attractions from the capitalist point of view.

WP: Is it not the case that any industrialized society – communist or capitalist – involves this sort of dehumanization to some extent?

CMG: Oh, so long as you have an industrialized society there will be distasteful jobs which someone has to do, but on the other hand, the perpetuation of that sort of society has been largely due to the fact that capitalism puts into cold storage all sorts of labour-saving, production-increasing devices. There is no reason on earth why at the present time anyone should have to work more than four hours a week. There could be abundant leisure but then all the force of society, the media and so on, prevent people from knowing what in the hell they could do with their spare time. You have to fight all the popular things: the press, radio, television and organized commercial sport.

WP: You have a low opinion of contemporary Scottish literature.

CMG: It's largely a subdivision of English literature. There hasn't been any recurrence to any great extent on the part of Scottish writers to the staples of the independent Scottish tradition. Until that happens I can't see much creative development in Scottish literature. An American professor who runs the *Studies in Scottish Literature* – Professor Roy, he was working in the Mitchell Library in Glasgow – wrote to me and said: we're going to give a double number to contemporary Scottish literature. He wanted a long essay from me, up to about 10,000 words, and was inviting two others to do likewise. Who do you think they were? Eric Linklater and Naomi Mitchison! I wrote back and declined. So far as I was concerned they had nothing to do with contemporary Scottish literature and I wouldn't be associated with them.

WP: In the thirties and later you exercised an obvious influence over a number of writers. Among younger writers that influence is now perhaps less obvious. What effects or influence do you think that you have exercised in this area?

CMG: It's very difficult to tell. I've had this effect, that up until a few years ago there was no systematic teaching of Scottish literature in universities or in senior secondary schools and there's a good deal of it now in all these quarters. Now that's a big change, and it means that those who are students and pupils today will in ten or twenty years time show the benefit of that change. They will know the stuff. Now all these poets who followed my example, who looked up Scots words in dictionaries and so on, they've all faded out. They hadn't got it natively and that's where I had the advantage. I was born into a Scots-speaking community and my own parents and all those round about spoke Scots. But these poets hadn't that advantage and, of course, I have antagonized them – politically and otherwise. I don't think that any of them has really followed my example – certainly not technically. Their poetry has no resemblance to mine except at the mere level of vocabulary and in some uses of the language. But they don't seem to me to be using the language creatively at all. So I don't think I've had a good influence on them. But then, one doesn't expect influences to be good. Basically, I don't think I've been influenced by anybody at all. I'm a great admirer of Valéry and others but I haven't been influenced by them. I'm not writing the kind of stuff they were writing at all. At least, I don't think I am.

WP: Do you see any change coming about in the attitudes of educationalists towards the arts, towards poetry in particular?

CMG: No. There's a great deal of activity going on and a lot of facilities being offered – but this business of having poets in residence at universities and so on – it's a bad thing. There's no doubt that there is an enormous frustration of the creative impulses in the modern world. Most people think they could do it with just a little luck but it doesn't work that way at all. You can't multiply the number of poets in a country of five and a half millions overnight. It's a bloody lucky country if it's got one or two. And that's a general thing. I cannot remember offhand who said, but I agree with them, that from the beginnings of recorded human history in all centuries and in all countries, the arts, the sciences, everything that could be regarded as constituent of a civilized order was the work of an infinitesimal proportion of the population, which was a constant. And that if that constant could be eliminated from the mass of humanity, all the rest couldn't do anything to reconstitute the arts and sciences and civilization in general. I think that's true. Although it may be possible to find techniques for creating a greater

	proportion of genius to the population than has existed in human history so far.
WP:	Genetic engineering and the like?
CMG:	Yes, that kind of thing. There's a lot going on in fields such as brain physiology and so on, and that may be one of the hopes for the future. But one thing which we must do if we are to derive the advantage one would wish from that kind of thing is to draw a clear distinction between talent and genius. Talent's the enemy. The good is the enemy of the best. It's too easy. People want it on a plate. They think they have a little talent and can't for the life of them see why they aren't as good as anybody else.
WP:	Yes, that's true. Yeats was a case in point. A man who had little or no talent. Who achieved what he did by damn hard work.
CMG:	Exactly. It was Kierkegaard who said that if a man's doing something it's all right so long as he's one of a number who are doing it. But let him raise his head above the ruck and he'll be trampled to death under the feet of geese.
WP:	The supernatural, the larger than life, do you agree that it's essential for poetry?
CMG:	I think it's essential for life. Human life itself implies a belief in, a desire to participate in, the transcendental. It's inherent in us without reference to any religious belief. That is the answer to your question.
WP:	And how does that square with your materialism?
CMG:	The transcendental, if I am right, comes out of the seeds of things. It's inherent in the original substance – it's part of the materialism.

32 The Poetry of Bertolt Brecht

MacDiarmid reviewed Bertolt Brecht's *Poems 1913–1956* (London: Eyre Methuen) in the 'Books of the Day' column of the daily newspaper the *Guardian* on 6 May 1976, under the headline, 'Our Brecht'. The review was introduced as follows: 'Hugh MacDiarmid welcomes the edition which establishes Brecht "completely and conclusively, not as a dramatist, but, far more importantly, as a great poet."'

'AS the epoch raised its hand to end its life, he was just that hand.' So wrote Brecht of Karl Kraus, the relentless satirist of Austrian society.

Other such valedictory handraisers have been discerned (or thought to be discerned) by other watchers of the literary sky today – by W. B. Yeats in his controversial *Oxford Book of Modern Verse*, where he opted for 'bare-bones poetry' as Arthur Hugh Clough had done before him and as Ezra Pound did later. Then there was F. R. Leavis who in his *New Bearings in English Poetry* failed to discern the really important ones, and most recently, with an eye incapable of missing anything, Dr George Steiner, who in his massive *After Babel* says:

> The major part of Western literature, which has been for two thousand years and more so deliberately interactive, the work echoing, mirroring, alluding to, previous works in the tradition, is now passing quickly out of reach. Like far galaxies bending over the horizon of invisibility, the bulk of English peotry, from Caxton's Ovid to *Sweeney Among the Nightingales*, is now modulating from active presence into the inertness of scholarly conversation . . . the unbroken arc of English poetry, of reciprocal discourse that relates Chaucer and Spenser to Tennyson and to Eliot, is fading rapidly from the reach of natural reading. A central pulse in awareness, in the language, is becoming archival.[1]

---

[1] This quotation actually comes from Steiner's *In Bluebeard's Castle* (London: Faber and Faber, 1971), p. 78 – Ed.

Of Leavis and others who have sought to 'ring out the old and ring in the new,' Steiner says, 'The new, even at its most scandalous, has been set against an informing background and framework of tradition. Stravinsky, Picasso, Braque, Eliot, Joyce, Pound – the "makers of the new" – have been neo-classics, often as observant of canonic precedent as their seventeenth-century forbears.'[2]

Who then are really 'the new' – the writers who are 'just that hand'? They are almost certainly Kraus, Brecht, Mayakovsky, and Mao Tse-tung, and if these are not English, then English translations of Brecht's work are subject to the general verdict. It has taken a long time for Brecht to appear above the horizon. But in this book he does so completely and conclusively, not as a dramatist, but, far more importantly, a great poet. The work here has been done by John Willett and Ralph Manheim with the co-operation of Erich Fried, and upwards of thirty translators have been drawn upon. The editorial apparatus of the book leaves nothing to be desired. As is said in the introductory essay, 'Disclosure of a Poet': 'Well after his death in 1956 Brecht the poet remained like an unsuspected time-bomb ticking away beneath the engine-room of world literature. This aspect of his writing has long been concealed by the mass of his dramas, together with his theories about them, not to mention other people's theories about what those theories might mean. And yet it was the primary aspect, both in time and in terms of artistic importance.'

Both Mao Tse-tung and Brecht produced a great body of poetry over a period of forty years, often under conditions of great difficulty, in the stress of arduous careers, and in both cases the poetry was utterly unadorned, free of all poeticisms, and destitute of what Pound called 'poppycock'. In other words, it was free of all fat and flannel – *desuetised* poetry in fact, conforming to what the present reviewer sought forty years ago when he wrote: 'I insist upon a poetry of fact. What my ideal amounts to is a poetical equivalent of one of nature's miracles – the flowering of *Daphne Mezereum*. Many people can never quite get used to this sudden burgeoning of beauty

---

[2]This quotation does come from *After Babel* (London: Oxford University Press, 1975), p. 465 – Ed.

from the bare brown twigs, for it seems all against the natural run of things that this wealth of blossom should come without the formality of green-sprouting leaves.' The explanation of Brecht's and Mao's success is simply that both men were far too busy to be other than perfectly sincere and direct. They had no time for nonsense. In both cases it was true, in Rilke's words:

> Gesang wie du ihn lehrst, ist nicht Begehr,
> Nicht Werbung um ein endlich noch Erreichtes;
> Gesang ist Dasein.
>
> (Song, as you teach, is not desire,
> not striving for something eventually attained;
> song is Being)[3]

The main reason for the delay in Brecht's arrival is because the Nazis so disapproved of his writings that his first book virtually disappeared from view within six or seven years of publication, while his second and third were only published in small editions by emigré firms, and could not be brought into Germany until after 1945.

Roughly five hundred poems are included in the present volume, while as much as 64 per cent had never been published in any form, however ephemeral, before the 1960s. The notes supply a mass of valuable information much of which is difficult of access anywhere else, and the arrangement of the poems, together with the indices of the titles, complete a most important and invaluable volume. It should be read by the English reader anxious to get a thorough grip of the subject, along with Walter Benjamin's *Understanding Brecht*, and to discover that the phenomenon is not an isolated one but part of the general supplanting of the old order, recourse should be had to *The Poetry of Mao Tse-tung*, by Hua-ling Niel Engle and Paul Engle (1973).

---

[3]Rainer Maria Rilke, *Sonette an Orpheus*, I, 3 – Ed.

33 Previews

From 1976 until shortly before his death in 1978, MacDiarmid contributed a series of sixteen columns to the *Radio Times*, commenting on the programmes he hoped to watch or listen to in the week ahead. More often than not, he chose to comment on programmes he intended to avoid. This extract comes from volume 212, number 2758, the issue for 18–24 September 1976. The last sentence is a masterly piece of journalism.

IT is close on fifty years since I last contributed an article to *Radio Times*. A great deal has happened in the interval. I have always been a regular listener and viewer, especially concerned with Scottish arts and affairs. While by no means confined to these, in this column I am solely concerned with programmes made in Scotland either for local consumption or for network showing. In both of these categories I am convinced there has been a great improvement in recent years. The criterion must be that the work in question can stand beside, and can be shown to stand beside, the best of contemporary production anywhere in the world, and yet be distinctly Scottish. That is a tall order. While an increasing percentage of our programme material may show a rise out of the old provincial rut, public taste may well lag behind any such development, so the need to appeal to the largest possible listening and viewing public must hamper innovatory tendencies and perpetuate the old outworn themes and attitudes regarding what is 'really Scottish'.

Nevertheless steady progress is being made in lifting the arts in Scotland from the ruck of the average, the lukewarm, the mediocre to which almost all Scottish creative effort was confined for several centuries before the arrival of better things about half a century ago. This effort at higher standards has inevitably been exemplified only in a few pioneers, but the rest were not unaffected, and while a measure of general improvement has ensued, there is still far too heavy a hangover of the old stuff. To say this, of course, betrays an élitist attitude on my part, and I do not apologize for that.

At eighty-four, I am an old square and have little or no use for most of the things exceedingly popular with the great majority of listeners and viewers. I select what I listen to, and look at, on that principle. Unfortunately the week's programmes I have under review here show little of the general improvement in question, and certainly no outstanding example of it. So what I have said in these preliminary remarks must be accepted as a matter of faith rather than fact.

Having all these considerations in mind there will be no surprise that I should hail the repeat of the 'Scotland and the Future' (Sunday 10.30am Radio Scotland) series broadcast earlier this year. Scottish attention has been fixated far too long on the past, and anything at all looking towards the future must be welcome. Alas, there are still far too many stiff necks to resist any turning of heads in that direction. So I take as my first 'must' to listen again on Sunday to George Bruce's talk about the milieu in which the artist in Scotland has to work. Mr Bruce, who is on the point of leaving Scotland now to take up a visiting Professorship in America, has rendered great services to the BBC in Scotland and as poet-in-residence at Edinburgh and Glasgow Universities and he is a very persuasive speaker. I look forward to hearing him again, all the more so since he has so much in common with the mentality – or lack of mentality – it is so desperately necessary Scotland should outgrow, that he is sure to carry with him the understanding and approval that any more advanced and original speaker on the subject would forfeit.

> The later items in MacDiarmid's 'Preview' columns were ghost-written by his daughter-in-law, Deirdre Grieve, but since they appeared with MacDiarmid's approval and were published under his name, and since they display such a typical blend of generosity and ferocity, there is no reason why they should not be included here. This extract comes from volume 215, number 2788, the issue for 16–22 April 1977.

In the countryside where I live the dustcart is unknown. Everything that can be recycled *is* recycled. If the dogs won't eat it, it goes into the soup, and if the soup can't use it, it goes to make compost. Old newspapers are made into bonfires by my wife, often before I have finished with them, and the ash goes with the compost back into the ground. All this bounty is returned to us in the form of home-grown new potatoes, broad beans, lettuces and rhubarb. Old items of furniture can always be mended and used by someone somewhere. And the remaining tins and bottles that defy recycling add up to a very modest heap.

So it is with the wonder of an alien that I shall watch 'Unwanted' (Sunday 10.15 BBC1), the story of what goes into a city dustcart when it might very well be of use to someone else. Dustmen talk of the valuable things they find in other people's rubbish that they know could find a thankful recipient somewhere. Parallels are also drawn with various human situations – children and old people in homes, down-and-outs and unwanted pets. I fear this programme will be too facile and tear-jerking for my taste. But the same applies to people as to things . . . in the countryside or a small community the problem scarcely exists. There's a place for everybody and everything.

This is from the final column MacDiarmid published in the *Radio Times*, in volume 220, number 2859, in the issue for 26 August–1 September 1978. He died on 9 September 1978.

Embarked on my eighty-seventh year, I should not be surprised that the months flip over like weeks and the years like seasons. But I find it very hard to believe that a whole year has passed since I last allowed my blood to boil over on the subject of the Edinburgh Tattoo. Yet here it is again, 'The Edinburgh Military Tattoo of 1978' (Monday 11.10 BBC1), as relentless as Christmas and twice as garish. The year has done nothing to soften my feelings. I still consider the event an annual atrocity perpetrated by an army of occupation on a city of sheep. Tasteless sheep. Would the Athenians allow majorettes to prance about the Parthenon? Only the Athens of the North could condone such vulgarity.

But I suppose a rock which has weathered assault and

battery, the droppings of many billy goats and ponies, the daily explosion of the one o'clock gun and the nightly fall-out of crisps and peanuts will come through yet again. If anyone can make sense and sanity of it, it is that excellent actor and poetry reader, my good friend Tom Fleming, who bravely takes on the commentary for the televized performance.

Much though I love my country I always wonder what brings people from other equally passion-inspiring countries to settle here. Can a Jamaican really be happier in Birmingham?

A six-part radio series, 'New Britons' (Tuesday 10.5 am Radio 4), takes individual immigrants and traces their stories and, in the case of Omero Ginestri at least, the reason sounds simple enough. Love. For the love of a Scots-Italian girl he came here in 1948, jobless, speaking no English. He learnt his English from the *Daily Express*, and now makes and sells ice-cream in Stonehouse, Lanarkshire. A happy ending. But, impaling the sevenpence cornet with the Cadbury's Flake, does he never dream of Tuscany under the stars?

As to those of us born and brought up in Scotland, the relationship is harder and more painful to fathom. In the last programme of one of these analytical series to which we are prone – 'Checkpoint' (Thursday 11.10 BBC1) – Joan Bakewell looks at the parallel between the upsurge of Scottish Nationalism and of Scottish culture, and seeks the views of a number of writers, musicians and artists, myself among them. I find it very difficult to answer questions about Scottish Nationalism, as I was one of the founder members of the present party. But I now believe we will never regain our rightful independence without a revolution – a psychological revolution that will set us on the road to establishing a completely separate identity from that of England.

Index

Abercrombie, Lascelles, 216
Acland, Valentine, 204
AE, see Russell, George
Aeschylus, 261
Agate, James, 43
Alasdair MacMhaighstir Alasdair, 69, 77
Alberti, Rafael, 189
Aldington, Richard, 267
Angus, Marion, x
Annenkov, Pavel, 30
Antonovich, 29
Aretino, Pietro, 261
Ariosto, Ludovico, 261
Arnold, Matthew, xx, 16, 22, 129, 157, 255, 256
Arundel, Honor, 244
Ascham, Roger, 136
Auden, W. H., 126, 131, 217, 275, 281

Bach, J. S., 70
Bacon, Francis, 136
Bahr, Herman, 43
Bakewell, Joan, 292
Bannister, Winifred, 176
Baudelaire, Charles, 188, 237
Beddoes, Thomas Lovell, 132
Beethoven, Ludwig van, xxi
Bell, J. J., 13
Belloc, Hilaire, 37
Benjamin, Walter, xv, 288
Berry, William, 137
Bewley, Marius, 227
Bialik, Chaim, 226
Bjørnson, Bjørnstjerne, 128
Black, Robert McKelvie, xiii
Blackmur, R. P., 234
Blake, George, x, 13
Blake, William, 65, 129, 195, 237
Bold, Alan, xxii, 44, 81, 99, 111, 274
Bosanquet, Bernard, 276
Bosanquet, Theodora, 88
Boston, Thomas, 16
Bottomley, Gordon, 66
Bowra, Maurice, 187, 189

Bradley, F. H., 276
Brandane, John, 13
Branford, Frederick, 69
Braque, Georges, 287
Braun, Otto, 42
Brecht, Bertolt, xiv, 286–8
Bridges, Robert, 132, 134
Bridie, James, x, 174, 191
Brocket, Lord, 179–83 *passim*
Brooke, Stopford, 5
Brown, George Douglas, 57, 196
Brown, Oliver, 170, 184
Bruant, Aristide, 66
Bruce, George, 290
Bruce, Robert, 184
Buchan, Elspeth, 137
Buchan, John (John Tweedsmuir), 75, 157, 158
Buchanan, George, 13, 133
Burns, Robert, xv, 3, 9, 21, 22, 25, 62, 73, 99–105, 121, 140, 145, 169, 195, 202, 220, 221
Burns, Thomas, 170
Buthlay, Kenneth, xiii, 44, 61, 81, 85, 99, 111, 137, 191
Byron, George Gordon, Lord, 129, 145, 256

Calderon de la Barca, Pedro, 261
Calverton, V. F., 67
Cameron, James, 244
Cameron, Norman, 169
Campbell, J. L., 78
Carco, Francis, 66
Carleton Green, Sir Hugh, 249
Carlyle, Thomas, xx, 195, 245
Carroll, Lewis, 66
Carroll, Paul Vincent, 170, 174
Carswell, Catherine, x
Carswell, Donald, 72
Catullus, 261
Caxton, William, 286
Cervantes, Miguel de, 261
Chaucer, Geoffrey, 68, 286
Chernyshevsky, Nikolai, 29, 30, 31
Chesterton, G. K., 28

Chevalier, Maurice, xxi
Chopin, Frederic, 207
Cicero, 157
Clark, Alex, 245
Clough, Arthur Hugh, 286
Collins, H. P., 63, 65, 255
Comfort, Alec, 216
Connolly, Cyril, 169
Cooke, Alistair, 191
Corbière, Tristan, 188
Corkery, Daniel, 71, 77, 79
Corrie, Joe, 57
Coulton, G. G., 131
Cowley, Abraham, 138
Craig, Cairns, xix
Craig, David, 235–38 *passim*
Crawford, Joan, 152
Cunard, Nancy, 204
Cunninghame Graham, R. B., xii, 4, 44, 56

Daiches, David, 190, 220, 231
Daniel, Samuel, 71
Dante Alighieri, 78, 79, 225, 275
Davidson, John, 4, 69
Davie, George Elder, xviii, xix, xx
Daviot, Gordon, 174
Day Lewis, C., 126, 216, 217
de Blacam, Aodh, 78
de Chardin, Teilhard, 257
de la Mare, Walter, 267
de Nerval, Gérard, 224
de Quincey, Thomas, x
de Selincourt, Basil, 66, 130, 131
De Valera, Eamon, 54
Debussy, Claude, 207
Dehmel, Richard, 281
Democritus, 177
Desjardins, 211
Deutsch, Babette, 216
Dill, Samuel, 26
Disraeli, Benjamin, 154
Dobrolubov, Nikolai, 29, 30, 31
Donaldson, Arthur, 158, 239
Donaldson, William, xv
Dostoevsky, Fyodor, 16, 22, 27, 53
Doughty, Charles Montagu, xiv, 64, 125–36
Douglas, Alfred, Lord, 4
Douglas, Gavin, xv

Douglas, Major C. H., xi, xxiv, 57, 90, 91, 115–24, 263, 264, 265, 266, 281
Douglas, Norman, 3
Douglas-Home, Sir Alec, xiv 239–53
Drinan, Adam, (Joseph Gordon MacLeod), 169
Druzhinin, Alexander, 30
Dunbar, William, xv, 51, 62, 73, 75
Duse, Eleonora, 43

Eliot, T. S., xi, xiii, xv, 61, 76, 131, 135, 222, 224, 225, 254, 256, 257, 259, 260, 267, 286, 287
Elliot, G. R., 64, 65
Elstob, Elizabeth, 68, 128
Eluard, Paul, 187, 188, 190
Emerson, R. W., 195, 214
Empson, William, 235
Engels, Friedrich, 201, 212, 213
Engle, Hua-ling Niel, 288
Engle, Paul, 288
Epictetus, 17
Erskine of Marr, Hon. Ruaraidh, 232
Ervine, St John, 62, 66
Euripides, 79
Evans, B. Ifor, 131

Fairley, Barker, 125, 127, 132, 135, 136
Fergus Mor mac Erc, 184
Ferguson, Sir Samuel, 53, 78
Fergusson, J. D., xxii
Fergusson, Robert, xv
Fishta, Gjerj, 231
Fitzgerald, Edward, 261
Fitzgerald, F. Scott, 198
Flaubert, Gustave, 207
Fleming, Dr Hay, 3, 4
Fleming, Tom, 292
Fletcher of Saltoun, Andrew, 155
Fletcher, Sir Walter, 119
Flower, Robin, 78
Ford, Ford Madox, 206
Fowler, Dr Ward, 26
Fraser, G. S., 169
Fraser, Norrie, 202
Fraser, Sir Robert, 249, 250

Index

Fried, Erich, 287
Fyffe, Will, 196

Gallacher, William, 243
Galloway, Alex, 169
Garnett, Edward, 130
Gawsworth, John, 69
Geddes, Sir Patrick, 6, 209, 210, 219, 232
George, Lloyd, 106
Gibb, E. J. W., 232
Gibbon, Lewis Grassic (James Leslie Mitchell), x, xvi, xviii, 115, 216
Ginestri, Omero, 292
Gladstone, William Ewart, 123
Glen, Duncan, xiii, 39, 201
Goethe, Johann Wolfgang von, 43, 223, 224, 261, 280
Gogol, Nikolai, 114
Golffing, Francis, 221
Gollancz, Victor, 216
Gosse, Edmund, 30
Graham, Charles, 239
Graham, Duncan (the 'Skellat Bellman'), 73, 142
Graham, Elizabeth (poet's mother), 270
Graham, W. S., 169
Grant, Neil, 13
Graves, Robert, 64, 65, 70, 125, 131, 267
Gray, Cecil, 43
Grayson, Victor, 203
Gregory, Horace, 204
Graig, Dr J. Y. T., 66
Grierson, H. J. C., 68, 71
Grierson, John, 152
Grieve, Deirdre (poet's daughter-in-law), 290
Grieve, John (poet's grandfather), 27
Grigson, Geoffrey, 131
Gunn, Neil, x, xii, xxiii, 61
Gurdjieff, G. I., 222

Haldane, J. B. S., xix
Haliburton, Hugh, 75
Hamilton, Ian Robertson, 184
Hamilton, W. H., 18
Hannah, John, 169

Harben, Henry, 203
Hardie, Keir, 203
Hardy, Thomas, 16, 20, 65, 130, 206
Harrison, Frederic, 25
Hartshorn, Vernon, 203
Hauptmann, Gerhard, 221
Hay, George Campbell, xix, 49, 151, 169
Hegel, Georg Willhelm Friedrich, 276
Heine, Heinrich, 255, 261, 278
Henderson, Hamish, 179
Hendry, J. F., 169
Henryson, Robert, xv, 68
Herman, Josef, 204
Hicks, Granville, 215
Hikmet, Nazim, 187, 188, 190, 260
Hindemith, Paul, 230
Hird, Denis, 203–4
Hitler, Adolf, 209
Hobbes, Thomas, 64
Hodges, Frank, 203
Hofmannsthal, Hugo von, 221, 222
Hogg, James, 73
Holloway, John, 228
Home, William Douglas, 174
Homer, 64, 261
Honeyman, T. J., xxii
Hopkins, Gerard Manley, 132, 133, 134
Housman, A. E., 267
Howells, William Dean, 211
Hugo, Victor, 225
Hume, David, 232, 233
Humphreys, Emrys, 222, 267
Hunter, John, 232
Hyde, Douglas, 63, 127

Ibsen, Henrik, 66
Irwin, Margaret, 154
Isaakyan, Avetik, 231

Jackson, Kenneth, 228
Jacob, Violet, 11, 75
James, D. G., 258
Jamieson, John, 20
Janacek, Leo, xxi
Johnson, Dr Samuel, 72
Johnstone, William, xxii, 170
Jones, David, 237, 278

Index

Jordan, Robert Furneaux, 207
Joyce, James, xiv, xx, xxiii, 20, 61, 66, 130, 195, 196, 220–38 *passim*, 287

Kant, Immanuel, 259
Keats, John, 258
Keith, Hon. H. S., 249, 250, 251, 252
Kennedy-Fraser, Marjorie, 57
Ker, W. P., 50
Kerrigan, Catherine, 125
Keyserling, Count Herman, 42, 66
Kierkegaard, Søren, 273, 285
Kilbrandon, Lord, 249
Kipling, Rudyard, 267
Koch, Vivienne, 217
Korzybski, Count Alfred, xviii
Koussevitzki, Serge, 21
Kraus, Karl, xiv, 286, 287
Kruchonyk, 66

Laforgue, Jules, 188
Lang, Andrew, 3
Larkin, Philip, 278
Lauder, Harry, 12, 13, 14
Lautrec, Toulouse, 195
Lawrence, D. H., xi, 22, 207, 208, 271
Lecouvreur, Adrienne, 262
Leavis, F. R., 216, 286
Lehmann, John, 169, 217
Lenin, Vladimir Ilyich, xvii, 130, 154, 212
Leopardi, Giacomo, 207
Lermontov, Mikhail, 32
Lessing, Gotthold Ephraim, 261
Lewis, Wyndham, 229
Lindsay (Lyndsay), Sir David, xiii, xv, 13, 173, 174–5
Linklater, Eric, x, xxiii, 283
Littlewood, Joan, 173
Lom, Iain, 69
Lope de Vega, 261
Lugovski, Vladimir, 260
Lully, Jean Baptiste, 262
Lyndsay, Sir David, *see* Lindsay
Lysohorsky, Andra, 231

M'Gillivray, Dr Angus, 52

Mac Colla, Fionn (T. D. MacDonald), x, xxiii, 78
MacAlpin, Kenneth, 184
Macartney, Lowden, 144
MacCaig, Norman, 169
MacColl, Ewan, 173–8 *passim*
MacCormick, John, 54, 118, 184
MacDonald, Ramsay, 115, 119, 129, 214
Macgillivray, Pittendrigh, xvi, 49
MacGregor, Rob Roy, 72
Machiavelli, 261
MacIntosh, Dr John, 3
MacIntyre, Duncan Ban, 69
MacKechnie, John, 78
Mackenzie, Stuart Q.C., A. J., 249, 250, 251, 252, 253
Mackenzie, Compton, xi, xvii, 54, 56, 209, 221, 222
Mackinnon, D. M., 275
MacLaren, Moray, 187–90 *passim*
Maclean, John, 129, 154, 155, 216
MacLean, Sorley (Somhairle Mac Gill'Eathain), xix, 49, 151, 163–8
MacLellan, Robert, 170, 174
MacLellan, William, xiii, 173, 187, 220
MacLeod, Norman, 204
MacPhee, Alexander (Sandy), 182–3
Macpherson, Father Colin, 179, 180
Macpherson, Mary (Mary of the Songs), 77
Magnus, Dr Laurie, 66, 68
Mahler, Gustav, xxi
Mallarmé, Stéphane, 169
Malraux, André, 229
Manheim, Ralph, 287
Mann, Thomas, 221
Mann, Tom, 203
Mao Tse-tung, xiv, 287, 288
Marcus Aurelius, 227
Marshak, Samuel, 209
Martin, David, 216
Martin, Troy Kennedy, 173
Marx, Karl, 27, 201, 207, 212, 213
Matthiessen, F. O., 228
Maurois, André, 154
Mayakovsky, Vladimir, xiv, 216, 260, 287

McCance, William, xxii
McCarey, Peter, xvi
McCrie, Lilias, 116
McEwan, Alexander, 118
McGill, Jack, 239
McGlynn, Patrick, 78
McGonagall, William, 137–50
Megroz, R. L., 132
Mehring, Franz, 213
Melville, Robert, 170
Meredith, George, 22, 130
Merriman, Brian, 70
Michelangelo, 277
Migdale, Lord, 249, 251
Millar, J. H., 69, 173
Miller, Karl, 268
Milton, John, 64, 78
Mirski, D. S., 126
Mitchison, Naomi, x, 283
Molière, 68, 262
Monboddo, Lord, 137
Monro, Harold Edward, 267
Montale, Eugenio, 187, 188, 190, 281
Montrose, Duke of, 56, 58, 118
Moore, Marianne, 231
Moore, Nicholas, 169
Morgan, Edwin, xv
Morris, Margaret, xxii
Morris, William, 134, 207
Mortimer, Raymond, 210
Mozart, W. A., xxi, 230
Muir, Edwin, x, xvi, xvii, xviii, xix, 39, 69, 71, 151, 159
Muir, Willa, xvii
Munson, Graham, 121
Murray, Alexander, 232
Murray, Charles, 11, 75, 249
Mussolini, Benito, 34, 36

Napoleon, 5
Nash, Beau, 72
Neill, A. S., xvii
Neruda, Pablo, 260
Nietzsche, Friedrich, 28, 207

O'Casey, Sean, 175, 204, 257
O'Conaire, Padraic, 66
O'Rathaille, Aodhagan, 77
Ogilvie, George, ix

Ollivant, Alfred, 131
Orage, A. R., ix, xi, 16, 17, 39, 115, 159, 217, 254
Orr, John, 159
Osborn, E. B., 30
Ovid, 286
Oxenhorn, Harvey, xx

Palgrave, Francis Turner, xviii, 125, 258
Pascal, Blaise, 225
Pasternak, Boris, 189, 279
Patchen, Kenneth, 204
Patmore, Coventry, 130
Perrie, Walter, 274–85
Petrarch, (Francisco Petrarco), 261
Picasso, Pablo, 287
Pindar, 261
Pisarev, Dmitri, 29, 30, 31
Plato, 227
Plekhanov, G. V., 151
Politian (Angelo Poliziano), 261
Pope, Alexander, 237
Pound, Ezra, xii, xiv, 34, 130, 188, 189, 220, 222, 232, 237, 254–67, 278, 286, 287
Power, William, xiii, xvii, 149, 159
Price, Richard, xxiii
Proust, Marcel, 22, 189
Pushkin, Alexander, 29

Quasimodo, Salvatore, 281

Rachmaninoff, Sergei, 21
Raleigh, Lord, 276
Ransom, John Crowe, 235, 276
Read, Herbert, 67, 75
Reid, Robert, 162
Remisov, Alexei, 66
Richards, I. A., 16, 190, 231
Richthofer, Laura, 255
Rilke, Rainer Maria, 88, 188, 288
Rimbaud, Arthur, xi, 41, 169, 175, 188
Rimsky Korsakov, Nicholas, 21
Roberton, Sir Hugh, 13, 57, 214
Robertson Nicoll, Sir William, 4
Robeson, Paul, xxi
Roy, G. Ross, 283
Rukeyser, Muriel, 204

Ruskin, John, xx, 207
Russell, George (A. E.), 63, 267

Sanazar (Jacopo Sannazaro), 68
Santayana, George, 5
Sappho, 261
Sassoon, Siegfried, 267
Saurat, Denis, xi, 39, 53
Saussure, Ferdinand de, 16
Scarfe, Francis, 169
Schiller, Friedrich, 261
Schoenberg, Arnold, xxi, 230
Schubert, Franz, 230
Scott, Francis George, xxi, xxii, 78, 160
Scott, J. D., 196
Scott, Sir Walter, xv, xvi, 70, 145, 191
Scott-Moncrieff, C. K., 189
Seneca, 80
Shakespeare, William, 5, 64, 78, 79, 140, 143, 189, 222, 225, 237
Sharp, William (Fiona Macleod), 5, 6
Shaw, George Bernard, 175
Shelley, Percy Bysshe, 129, 256, 261
Shepherd, Nan, x, 218
Shestov, Leo, 4
Sidney, Sir Philip, 68
Sieveright, Sir James, 3
Simonov, Konstantin, 209
Simpson, Professor, J. Y., 31
Sinclair, Donald, 74
Singer, John, 218
Sitwell, Edith, 267
Sitwell, Sacheverell, 267
Sitwell, Sir Osbert, 267
Skelton, John, 125, 131
Slater, Montagu, 131
Smith, Professor G. Gregory, 13, 16, 18, 19, 70
Smith, Sydney Goodsir, 169, 196
Solovyov, Vladimir, 31
Solzhenitsyn, Alexander, 279
Sophocles, 261
Sorabji, K. S., xi, xxi
Soutar, William, x
Southworth, James G., 219
Speirs, John, 159
Spence, Lewis, 54, 55, 56

Spender, Stephen, 216, 217
Spengler, Oswald, 16, 26, 27, 28, 31, 66
Spenser, Edmund, 68, 134, 286
Spinoza, 227
Squire, Sir John, 62, 128
Stalin, Josef, xx
Stein, Gertrude, xi
Steiner, George, 286, 287
Stephens, James, 78, 267
Stevens, Wallace, xi, 232
Stevenson, Robert Louis, 3, 196
Stewart, Dugald, 162
Stock, Noel, 254
Stravinsky, Igor, xxi, 287
Strindberg, August, 66
Stuart, Prince Charles Edward, 72
Surkov, Alexei, 209
Swinburne, A. C., 261
Symon, Mary, 11
Synge, J. M., 22, 63

Tasso, 261
Tate, Allen, 235
Tchaikovski, Peter Ilich, 21
Telford, Thomas, xxi, 270
Tennyson, Alfred, Lord, 62, 125, 138, 262, 286
Theocritus, 68
Thomas, Dylan, 169
Tolstoy, Leo, 27, 280
Tonge, John, xxii
Tourneur, Cyril, 77
Treneer, Anne, 125, 127, 133, 136
Trotsky, Leon, 201
Turgenev, Ivan, 29
Twain, Mark, 145
Tychina, Pavlo, 209

Ungaretti, Giuseppe, 281
Untermeyer, Louis, 68
Urquhart, David, 135
Urquhart, Sir Thomas, 137

Valéry, Paul, xi, 39, 88, 281
Verlaine, Paul, 261
Victoria, Queen, 143, 147
Villa-Lobos, Hector, xxi
Virgil, 68
Voltaire, 261

Wagner, Richard, 126, 127, 129, 207
Walden, Herewath, 41
Wallace, William, 184
Wallas, Graham, 25
Walsh, Dr Walter, 21
Walter von der Vogelweide, 217
Ward, A. C., 67
Warner, Sylvia Townsend, 204
Watson, James Carmichael, 168
Watson, Sir William, 63
Wells, H. G., 25
Wheelwright, John, 235
Whitman, Walt, 65, 276
Whyte, James H., xiii, 54
Wilder, Thornton, 223–6

Willett, John, 287
Williams, William Carlos, 206
Wilson, Edmond, 213
Wilson, Harold, 241
Woodburn, Arthur, 180
Wordsworth, William, 63, 65, 129, 138, 256, 258, 275

Yeats, W. B., 54, 58, 63, 70, 195, 217, 267, 275, 277, 280, 281, 285, 286
Young, Douglas, 169

Zhdanov, A. A., xxi

THE GREATER MACDIARMID

Six recordings on cassette by Hugh MacDiarmid

In these poetry readings, commentaries, lectures and conversations – all drawn from recordings made by MacDiarmid during his last nineteen years – he ranges across the full span of the verse, early to late. Nearly all published in full for the first time, the recordings constitute a remarkable document in the understanding of his achievement as poet and as leader of Scotland's literary renaissance.

I and II (Double cassette)   1959
A Drunk Man Looks at the Thistle

III   10 June 1960: Reading with commentary:
The Watergaw · The Sauchs in the Reuch Heuch Hauch · Moonstruck · The Eemis Stane · The Innumerable Christ · On A Raised Beach · Stony Limits · In the Caledonian Forest (excerpt) · Vestigia Nulla Retrorsum · Overinzievar · In the Hedge-Back · Country Life · O Jesu Parvule · Farmer's Death · A Moment in Eternity · Aodhagán Ó Rathaille Sang This Song · Harry Semen · Hymn to Sophia · Cattle Show · The Frightened Bride · Cophetua · The Man in The Moon · The Huntress and Her Dogs · Red E'en.

IV   1962, 1963: Readings with commentary:
The Eemis Stane · Farewell to Dostoevski · O Wha's the Bride · Empty Vessel · The Love-Sick Lass · Crowdieknowe · Island Funeral · Excerpt from *The Kind of Poetry I Want* · Moonstruck · Ye Kenna Wha I Am · The Bonnie Broukit Bairn · Focherty · Man and the Infinite · In Memoriam Dylan Thomas · I Heard Christ Sing · The Salmon Leap · An Apprentice Angel · Skald's Death · Lo, A Child is Born · A Golden Wine in the Gaidhealtachd (excerpt) · North of the Tweed · At Darknin' Hings Abune the Howff.

V   1967: Reading and Lecture.   1968: Reading
The Bonnie Broukit Bairn · The Watergaw · The Sauchs in the Reuch Heuch Hauch · Crowdieknowe · The Eemis Stane · Wheesht, Wheesht · Milk-Wort and Bog-Cotton · O Wha's the Bride · Water-Music (excerpt) · Men Canna Look on Nakit Licht · Reflections in A Slum · I Have Been Frequently Astonished · Excerpt from *The Kind of Poetry I Want* · Edinburgh ('The capital of Scotland') · In the Fall · Scotland Small? · Poetry and Science · A Golden Wine in the Gaidhealtachd · The Glass of Pure Water · Old Wife in High Spirits · Crystals Like Blood · Direadh III · The Parrot Cry.

VI   1969: Readings, Lecture, and Conversation with George Bruce.
Reading and conversation with Norman MacCaig.
The North Face of Liatach · Whuchulls (excerpt) · Drums in the Walligate · At My Father's Grave · Crowdieknowe · The Eemis Stane · Poetry and Science (excerpt) · Milk-Wort and Bog-Cotton · At My Father's Grave · Crowdieknowe · Scotland Small? · Reflections in A Slum · Old Wife in High Spirits · Me · Of John Davidson · Focherty · The Eemis Stane · O Wha's Been Here Before Me, Lass? · The Glass of Pure Water (excerpt) · Water Music (excerpt) · Empty Vessel · A Vision of Myself.

Except for the double-cassette recording of *A Drunk Man Looks at the Thistle*, all cassettes may be purchased singly. For catalogue and prices write to Richard Swigg, Department of English, Keele University, Keele, Staffordshire ST5 5BG, UK. Tel: (0782) 621111. FAX: (0782) 713468.